Untapped

Untapped

Exploring the Cultural Dimensions of Craft Beer

Edited by Nathaniel G. Chapman, J. Slade Lellock, and Cameron D. Lippard

WEST VIRGINIA UNIVERSITY PRESS

MORGANTOWN 2017

ISBN:

cloth   978-1-943665-67-9
pb   978-1-943665-68-6
epub   978-1-943665-69-3
pdf   978-1-943665-70-9

Library of Congress Cataloging-in-Publication Data
is available from the Library of Congress

Cover design by Than Saffel
Cover image Than Saffel

CONTENTS

PHOTOGRAPHS, MAPS, TABLES, AND FIGURES

FOREWORD

IAN MALCOLM TAPLIN

The ubiquity of beer is really quite amazing, and I'm not talking about just the recent growth of craft brewers that is the subject of this book, but also about the fact that historically it has been a beverage of choice by many societies. Humans, it seems, have spent an inordinate amount of time exploring the mysteries of fermentation. Realizing at an early date that those crops in the fields could be put to a use other than satisfying hunger, human experimentation resulted in a liquid product that proved less nutritious but in many respects far more enjoyable. The resilience shown by humans in their attempts to transform vegetables, fruits, and crops into alcohol is truly remarkable, even if one discounts problems with potable water that plagued most societies prior to the twentieth century. Prodigious amounts of alcohol were made and consumed in the United States in the nineteenth century—a testament to ingenuity and perhaps a persistent need to dull the senses after a day of hard physical labor. Germany's ancient beer laws are evidence of both regulatory parameters and an institutional endorsement of the product's centrality to German life and culture. Similarly, the English pub, especially in its Arcadian village setting, is not merely a place that dispenses ale but also a core feature of rural social life—a meeting place that predates the notion of democratic assemblies as a setting for vigorous discussions. In the village in southern England where I grew up, people repaired to the local tavern after church on Sunday, where they debated the sermon with the rector over a pint. Here, alcohol fueled theological debates rather than stymieing them! Visit a pub in central London at 6:00 P.M. toward the end of the working week and you will witness an almost tribal affirmation of beer's role in easing the transition from work to play for the city's professionals in their pinstriped suits and smart dresses.

Despite the salience of beer in many cultures, alcohol consumption also has its darker side. For those of a fundamentalist religious bent it was, and often still is, the epitome of evil; the devil incarnate in a beverage that dulled the senses and diminished responsibility. For many of the women who were instrumental in the Anti-Saloon League in the United States, it was a beverage that separated their husband from their paychecks and left many a family further impoverished.

Similar sentiments (and behavior) were found in industrial cities throughout northern Europe as workers sought daily refuge from their labor. Even today there is widely held belief that young men in most societies apparently have difficulty taming their boisterous senses, and beer has often been the lubricant that facilitates the inevitable misbehavior. Look no further than the ongoing debate about alcohol-fueled incidents of rape on college campuses to appreciate that beer and young people can be a toxic combination. And so the list of detractors continues.

Moral opprobrium, delinquency, and criminal acts notwithstanding, there are many who affirm beer's centrality. Benjamin Franklin's (apocryphal?) quote that "Beer is proof that God loves us and wants us to be happy" clearly legitimized the beverage for many. It was an important cargo for the passengers on the *Mayflower*, who in 1620 set sail with a hold full of small (low alcohol) beer and sought land sooner than they might have liked because their food and beer supplies were exhausted. The Dutch settlers in New Netherland contained prominent families whose fortunes had been made in commercial brewing. German settlers to the upper Midwest took their brewing traditions with them and essentially established the style of beer that would become commonplace in the United States. Several continents away, English merchants developed a beer (India Pale Ale—the forerunner of current IPA) that would travel long distances and remain reasonably fresh in the hot humid conditions of the South Asia. If we fast-forward to the twenty-first century we find beer to be the third most popular beverage in the United States (after water and soft drinks) and a quarter trillion–dollar industry. Emerging countries such as China have massive brewing industries, slaking the thirst of the countless millions in their rush to modernity and a consumer culture built around alcoholic beverages. So despite the detractors, beer occupies a central position in many cultures.

While beer's current acknowledged role in society lacks much of the earlier controversy, understanding its historical roots as well as recent trends merits further study. We are familiar from stories in the press about the growing concentration among the major global brewers. Currently underway is AB-InBev's $108 billion offer for SAB Miller PLC, which if successful will result in a global mega brand. However, this follows a century of mergers and acquisitions in the West, where first local, then regional, and finally national brands were acquired and consolidation took place with relentless efficiency. By the 1970s and 1980s, however, small breweries were reemerging, emphasizing better ingredients, finely crafted quality, and limited production. It was a new style of beer that attempted to reinterpret old ways of making beer and differentiate itself from the increasingly homogenized product associated with the mega brewers that dominated the supermarket shelves and bars. Academic studies were soon to realize that these two sets of players occupied different niches and therefore competition between the two remained limited (Carroll and Swaminathan 2000). In recent years though, as the bigger brands became even larger, the smaller ones became more numerous and the craft beer revolution became headlines.

As with any entrepreneurial endeavor, the supply of a new product requires a demand to sustain it. Thus, understanding the broader cultural consumer environment that surrounds the fascination with craft beer merits investigation. With more than four thousand breweries in the United States today and new ones opening every week, who exactly is drinking all of this beer? The Real Ale Movement (CAMRA) in England has an almost apostle-like zeal among its adherents, and no good pub is without such a product. Will this save the traditional pub? Are other significant trends in consumer behavior exemplified by craft brewing?

While craft beer prices soared, supply of and demand for the product seemed to increase. Almost inevitably, the major companies started acquiring craft brewers but retained the name and local identity to retain authenticity. This is not atypical for an industry that responds to the growth of successful niche players, so there is nothing surprising about corporate behavior here. On the other hand, many young, bearded males continue to see beer as an avocation rather than a means of inebriation. Curiously, young women do not possess the same enthusiasm for making the product, unlike wine, which has attracted this demographic to the ranks of winemakers. Will this change? Finally, are we seeing a continued diversity of product—one that represents a certain local capability and style? Or are we beginning to see what many argue is an inevitable homogeneity in products as tastes become standardized? Will IPAs become the new brewing norm?

All of these and many other intriguing issues are dissected and analyzed in this fascinating and timely book. As sociologists examine these trends, they bring insights that journalistic interpretations often gloss over. They provide nuanced answers to far-ranging questions of how a seemingly commonplace product such as beer can have such a fascinating and esoteric heritage. In doing so, they tell a story of a product that has essentially been reinvented for the current day and age by invoking practices and ingredients of old. In a postmodern industrial age, it seems we relish our premodern artisanal practices. Craft brewing is just one example of such a trend—albeit one that provides a multiplicity of pleasures and sensory (re)awakenings.

REFERENCE

Carroll, Glenn, and Anand Swaminathan. 2000. "Why the Microbrewery Movement? Organizational Dynamics of Resource Partitioning in the US Brewing Industry." *American Journal of Sociology* 106 (3): 715–762.

Exploring the Cultural Dimensions of Craft Beer

Introduction and Overview

NATHANIEL G. CHAPMAN, J. SLADE LELLOCK,
AND CAMERON D. LIPPARD

Over the past 30 years, the production and consumption of craft beer has boomed in the United States and Western Europe. Much of the economic growth in U.S. breweries is attributed to the sharp increase in and popularity of craft beer breweries. In the United States between 2007 and 2012, there was a 118% increase in established breweries—from around 398 to 869 breweries (U.S. Census 2014). By 2015, over 4,000 breweries existed in the United States, which is the largest number of breweries in this country since 1873, at which time there were around 2,000 breweries (Brewer's Association 2015). The profits from sales of kegs, cans, and bottles of craft beer have increased concomitantly, leading to an industry worth over $100 billion as of 2013 (Brewers Association 2013b). In addition, the number of individuals employed by breweries increased by 17.2%, and about 81% of those new employees worked in smaller breweries, which hired 19 employees or fewer (U.S. Census 2014). The increases of established breweries, employment opportunities, and profits have also outpaced those in the wine and spirits industries across most of the United States (U.S. Census 2014).

The Brewer's Association (2013c) bases their definition of craft breweries on three criteria. The brewery should be small (produce less than 6 million barrels of beer a year). It should be independent (not owned by an alcoholic beverage corporation). And the beers should come from traditional to innovative brewing ingredients. These criteria led to the inclusion of many microbreweries, brewpubs, and regional breweries, accounting for 98% of the breweries but only $14.3 billion of the $100 billion beer market.

A notable trend in the growth of craft breweries and the brewing industry in general is the movement into new regions across the United States. At the beginning of the craft beer revival in the United States in the 1990s, breweries were more highly concentrated along the West Coast and particularly in the state of Washington. However, since the early 2000s, the growth of new microbreweries and brewpubs in the South, North, and Midwest has outpaced the initial growth in the West. For instance, although the Brewer's Association consistently ranks California, Washington, and Colorado as the top three states in the number of breweries, Michigan, New York, Pennsylvania, Texas, North Carolina, and Illinois were in the top ten as of 2015 (see table i.1). As of 2001, most of these states, excluding the top three, had fewer than ten craft beer breweries. In fact, states like North Carolina now have 161 breweries, adding $1.2 billion to the state's economy.

Western European countries have also seen a boom in craft beer production and consumption. For example, in 2016 Cabras and Bamforth reported that the number of breweries in Great Britain was the highest in 1900, but by 1980, it had dropped to only 142. However, by 2015, the number of breweries increased to over 1400 in Great Britain; the majority were microbreweries. As in the United States, the rise in breweries happened largely because of three things: the public's dissatisfaction with the variety of beers and clear marketing campaigns for traditional ales as an alternative to mass-produced beer (Cabras and Bamforth 2016; see also, Smith Maguire et al., chapter 1 in this volume). Beginning in the 1990s, Great Britain also saw more individuals, such as retirees and beer-lovers, shifting into careers in brewing, which surged the industry forward once more. In addition, political moves in legislation such as the Beer Orders in 1989 required larger brewers in the United Kingdom to either sell or relinquish a large number of their brand-owned pubs, allowing these pubs to sell other beers, particularly craft beers (Preece 2016).

By the turn of the twenty-first century, the United Kingdom saw significant increases in the number of microbreweries; at least 100 new breweries were started in 2014 and another 150 in 2015 (Brewers Association 2015). In addition, the United Kingdom saw a 4.2% increase in beer sales, equaling about $5.3 billion. Even SABMiller agreed to acquire Meantime to compete against the growth of craft beers in the United Kingdom (Boyle and Buckley 2015). Boyle and Buckley (2015) suggest that in 2015 Great Britain had more breweries per person than anywhere in the world; about forty new microbreweries ring the city of London, which was a thirteenfold increase from the previous decade.

Table i.1. Craft Beer Sales and Production Statistics by State, 2015

Rank	State	Number of Craft Breweries	Economic Impact (millions)	Barrels of Craft Beer Produced	Breweries per Capita (per 100,000 adults 21 or over)
1	California	518	$6,890	3.8 million	1.9
2	Washington	305	$1,650	426,000	5.9
3	Colorado	284	$2,720	1.8 million	7.3
4	Oregon	228	$1,830	1.1 million	7.7
5	New York	208	$2,290	1.1 million	1.4
6	Michigan	205	$1,850	770,000	2.9
7	Texas	189	$3,770	1.1 million	1
8	Pennsylvania	178	$4,490	4.1 million	1.9
9	North Carolina	161	$1,200	676,000	2.2
10	Illinois	157	$2,270	595,000	1.7

Source: Brewer's Association, "State Craft Beer Sales & Production Statistics, 2015." Accessed September 8, 2016, http://www.brewersassociation.org/statistics/by-state.

Although not as robust as in the United Kingdom, other examples of the expansion of craft beer across Western Europe include the rise of specialty beers and microbreweries in "beer-drinking" countries such as the Republic of Ireland, Denmark, and Germany. For example, Guinness, Ireland's largest and global beer company, released two beers in 2014 to compete with the craft beer market: a Dublin Porter and a West Indies Porter that stayed with the tradition of dark and heavy beers (Kedmey 2014). This company has also created beers that are hoppier and lighter, including a Guinness Blonde Ale, to compete in American markets.

In Denmark, where Carlsberg has been the beer of choice for decades, the twenty-first century has seen the opening of 200 microbreweries; there are now 700 different kinds of beers in the area (Stächelin 2014). While these microbreweries still have only less than 5% of the market share in Denmark, these beers are selling better in other European countries. In Germany, the 1516 *Reinheitsgebot,* or German Beer Purity Laws, that required beer in Germany be made with only three ingredients—water, barley, and hops—has restricted brewers from making distinctive beers with different flavors and ingredients. In the 1990s, German brewers realized that they could not compete with world market demands for craft beer and have started smaller operations to brew new beers outside of the laws. In addition, American craft brewers like Stone Brewing have set up shop in Germany to bring pale ales and coffee stouts to the German market (Stächelin 2014). However, it should be noted that Germany continues to be highly traditional in their brewing processes, with continual emphasis on regionally crafted beers from large breweries.

The Evolution of Craft Beer: Locally and Globally

The United States

Brewing in the United States and around the world is not a new phenomenon. U.S. immigrants brought their brewing techniques to their new communities, opening breweries to produce beers that matched their tastes (Ogle 2006). At its peak, the pre-Prohibition U.S. brewing industry was comprised of over 1,700 individual breweries (Brewer's Association 2015). Each brewery offered its own unique recipe for traditional styles that reflected the beer that was common to the brewer's place of origin (Ogle 2006). However, as the end of the nineteenth century approached, the number of breweries began to decline (Brewer's Association 2015). Some of this decline was due to market and business practices of individual brewers, as well as to the growing resentment of immigrant groups. In addition, the temperance movement sought to bring an end to the "plagues" of alcoholism and drunkenness (Ogle 2006). These movements would eventually become codified into the Eighteenth Amendment, which brought about Prohibition.

Prohibition was a dark period for American brewing. For 13 years the U.S. brewing industry was at a standstill. Some of the breweries sold their buildings to other industries, while others simply went bankrupt. However, a handful were more fortunate. Larger breweries (Pabst, Anheuser-Busch, and Schlitz, to name a few) were able to stave off the drastic economic and social effects of Prohibition through acquisitions of and mergers with smaller firms (Tremblay and Tremblay 2009). Upon the repeal of Prohibition in 1933, those lucky few breweries opened their doors to almost no competition. The effects of Prohibition on the brewing industry cannot be understated: it completely devastated any form of competition among breweries and allowed for the monopolization of American brewing by what was referred to as "the Big Three" (Anheuser-Busch, Coors, and Miller). However, with the recent beverage companies' merger of Anheuser-Busch InBev and SABMiller in 2015, all three are included in the same beverage conglomerate, making up over 80% of all beer sales in the United States (Brewer's Association 2015).

In the wake of Prohibition and the closing of hundreds of breweries, the Big Three took American beer down a road from which it has yet to return. During the 1950s, a time of wealth, prosperity, and postwar celebration, much technological advancement affected the households of everyday Americans in consequential ways. Two of the more notable inventions were the domestic refrigerator and the television set. The impact of these inventions on the brewing industry and the life of the typical American is twofold. If every home had a refrigerator, there was no need to go to the local bar and have a few beers with some friends. In addition, the TV eliminated the need for Americans to leave their homes for entertainment. Now after a family meal, most likely spent in front of the television where watchers were beginning to be bombarded with advertisements, adults could sit in the comfort of their homes and drink an ice cold beer. This kept Americans out of the bars and provided an opportunity for the Big Three to capitalize on the domestic beer market.

During the 1960s, Fritz Maytag purchased a fledgling brewery called the Anchor Steam Brewing Company. His motivation was simple: he liked the "steam" beer that they produced and he had just inherited a large sum of money from the family fortune. Over the next decade, Maytag and the Anchor Steam Brewing Company would struggle to turn a profit (Acitelli 2013). They could not, and to some degree did not want to, implement new brewing technologies such as advanced transnational refrigeration, aluminum cans, advanced bottling techniques and equipment, and a new three-tier distribution system (Ogle 2006). Maytag felt that his beer was special. He produced Anchor Steam beer and distributed kegs within the San Francisco area. One result of this was that it began to create a taste for local and regional products. Maytag would be heralded as a pioneer by localists and brewers alike (Hindy 2014). Also, although he did not know it, Maytag was laying down the foundation of a brewing revival that would rise from the underground homebrew clubs, such as the Maltose Falcons, and eventually reach Jimmy Carter in the White House. In 1978, President Carter passed a law legalizing homebrewing. What followed next was nothing short of revolutionary.

Prior to the passage of the Home Brew Act in 1978, craft beer was produced illegally in the home. After Jimmy Carter signed the Home Brew Act, craft breweries began to spring up in southern California as well as in some major cities in other Western states. As word of Maytag's model reached the East Coast, and homebrewers from all over the United States came out of their basements, a cultural movement began to gain momentum. Craft brewing was making a name for itself, in much the same way as the immigrant brewers of the nineteenth century had. Craft brewers returned to the Old World traditions and began producing styles of beer that were bold, contrasting starkly against the pale, light pilsners that the Big Three were producing. Suddenly, Americans had a choice of beers to consume. Choice, independence, and freedom were flavors Americans had savored in the past, and they wanted more.

After the passage of the Home Brew Act in 1978, the craft beer movement never looked back. In 1966, there stood only one craft brewery; today there are more than 3,400, a number that seems to grow by the day (Brewer's Association 2015). As of 2012, the number of breweries in the United States has exceeded the numbers from the nineteenth century, quite a remarkable feat for just a 35-year time frame.

In addition to craft brewing, homebrewing also took off like never before. Throughout antiquity, homebrewing existed to provide the individual in ancient Rome, China, and Europe a steady source of beer outside of the pub, a cleaner water source, and merchant capitalist opportunities (German Beer Institute 2006). However, today it represents a middle-class hobby for about 1.2 million homebrewers in the United States and another 5 million to 6 million worldwide (Brewers Association 2013a). In the United States, the average homebrewer is around 40 years old, married, college-educated, and has an income of $75,000 or more (Brewers Association 2013a). This hobby has led to a separate but growing market of brew shops locally and online that provide fresh ingredients and brewing equipment.

Relatively new pioneers in craft brewing or microbrewing set the stage for the craft beer movement to come. Throughout the 1980s and 1990s, more and more craft breweries opened and a craft beer culture began to emerge in the United States. This culture, which started out in underground homebrew clubs, such as the Maltose Falcons, was manifested in the form of national homebrewer's organizations, beer festivals, and international craft beer competitions (Acitelli 2013; Ogle 2006). Today, craft beer is becoming increasingly popular and has begun to chip away at the market share of the larger corporations. In the United Kingdom and Western Europe, brewing's historical roots started those same traditions in the United States.

Thus, popular accounts of the rise of craft beer and its attendant culture (particularly in the U.S. context) have focused on the pioneering success of pivotal brewers such as Fritz Maytag, Jim Koch (Boston Beer Company, producer of Sam Adams), Ken Grossman (Sierra Nevada Brewing Company), and Jack McAuliffe (New Albion Brewing Company) (Acitelli 2013; Hindy 2014; Ogle 2006). These accounts suggest that craft beer emerged from the efforts of a few homebrewers-turned-entrepreneurs as a response to the homogenized American adjunct lagers that dominated the brewing industry after the repeal of

Prohibition. Economic accounts have focused on the structure of the brewing industry and how high industry concentration and the dominance of a few firms created an unmet need, which craft beer was able to fulfill (Edgar 1991; Tremblay 1987; Tremblay and Tremblay 2009). Other explanations have focused on the structure of organizations within the brewing industry and have suggested that larger firms are less well equipped than smaller microbreweries to handle changes in consumer tastes (Carroll and Swaminathan 2000; Crane 1997; Greer 1998). These studies have not provided a sociological perspective on the craft beer phenomenon. They have focused on only one aspect of the production of craft beer in the United States. A more holistic and nuanced understanding of this phenomenon is needed.

Outside the United States

Outside the United States, such as in the United Kingdom and Germany, beer brewing activities date from before the Roman Empire. Several chronicles reported the presence of well-established activities in various parts of the island, with Roman legions purchasing *cerevisa*—the Roman name for beer—from native populations during the occupation. Similarly, forms of public house retailing of beer in the United Kingdom can be traced back to at least Roman times (Preece 2016). In the Middle Ages, across what would become Belgium, Germany, and parts of France, beer brewing was carried out mostly in monasteries and abbeys, with ales used to feed and restore pilgrims and, at a later stage, as a source of financial income.

By the dawn of the twentieth century, Western Europe saw a clear shift to industrialization and mass production to sell products on a global scale. Industrialization was made possible by technological innovations and developments such as the introduction of refrigeration, the development of pasteurization, and the use of mechanics and steam. Brands like Guinness, Grolsch, and Weihenstephan were shipped around the world by the 1920s. Also, the development of large-scale transportation infrastructure and improved packaging enriched the quantity and quality of beer distribution, increasing the global presence of beers from around the world (Cabras and Bamforth 2016; see also, Smith Maguire et al., chapter 1 in this volume).

While two world wars would stifle beer production and consumption in Europe, brewing would rebound in the 1960s and 1970s. For example, the U.K. market saw a new boom and a rise of six major corporate players: Bass, Allied, Guinness, Scottish & Newcastle, Courage, and Whitbread. These companies, frequently referred to as the "Big Six," accounted for about 80% of total production in 1970 (Preece 2016). The Big Six initially focused their strategies on brewing activities and pub premises, but later tried to diversify and expand their interests in different markets, needing to grow in size and capacity to create the base for significant financial operations. Expanding into the leisure market allowed the Big Six to further increase their control on total volumes of beer sold, since about 80% of the beer drunk in the United Kingdom was sold in pubs and other licensed premises (Preece 2016). Many pubs were directly controlled by brewers via the tie system—that is, pubs were either managed on behalf of the breweries or rented to tenants forced by contract to buy supplies from their company landlords. Of approximately 72,400 pubs open in the country in 1974, about 38,300 (53%) were owned by or rented to the Big Six (Preece 2016).

However, a change in consumer tastes occurred in the 1960s: up until then the bulk of British beer comprised low-end alcohol-by-volume (ABV) cask-conditioned ales, with a very limited consumption of lagers that accounted for a small fraction of beers sold in the country (Smit 2014). With concentrations and mergers occurring in the industry at a global level, and the advent of marketing strategies associated with mass-media advertising, the consumption of lager passed from 450,000 to nearly 4 million hectoliters between 1960 and the late 1970s, reflecting a 20% increase in imports of beer in the United Kingdom in the same period (Cabras and Bamforth 2016).

Even more interesting is the pursuit of knowledge in brewing beer. While the homebrewer was always present, the craftsman, artisan, or academic of beer brewing has recently become important in shaping craft beer culture. The sustained growth of the brewing and subsidiary industries have spurred academia to examine the merit of offering college-level programs targeted at preparing students for careers in brewing science, as well as the wine and spirits industries. As of 2014, more than 20 universities and community colleges offered a program focusing on fermentation and/or brewing sciences or had programs in active development (Lippard and Cohen 2015). These programs have offered a variety of academic degrees, including undergraduate and graduate certificates (in person and online), as well as associate's, bachelor's, master's, and doctoral degrees. However, all but two of these programs are in their infancy of developing curriculum and attracting majors for academic training in brewing. Prior to this there were only two universities that offered an academic degree catering to employment in the brewing industry: the University of California, Davis and Oregon State University.

This recent and rapid development of a relatively high number of academic programs across the United States on the back of the growth in the number of small breweries has led to concern from many in the industry and academic cohorts. Some have speculated that these programs exist to placate professors' growing interests in fermentation sciences outside of their original specialties, to provide an outlet for excusing alcohol consumption, and to allow for specialization without real industry experience (Gordon 2013). However, others point out that the consumer demand for craft beers and the many people attempting to brew their own has led to a call for a specialized academic niche for students entering college or for those who want to better understand the science of brewing (Gordon 2013; Tickell 2012). As noted by Gordon (2013, 1), "The level of difficulty as well as the skills required to make beer have led to schools' developing some interesting degree programs. While it may sound like a joke, it's not." Or, as Tickell (2012, 1) quoted one of the recent fermentation sciences program director's stating, "Without an in-depth knowledge of the processes [of brewing], you're kind of at the whim of trial and error, which can be quite a long process." Tickell (2012) also quoted other professors in these programs pointing out that their programs taught students more than just how to brew but also how to work in various food industries that require fermentation, such as cheese production.

The history of this industry has not necessarily been about more college education but rather about apprenticeships and hands-on training. As suggested by the Brewer's Association (2013a), while there are a number of professional brewing schools even outside of college curriculums (e.g., Siebel Institute of Technology and World Brewing Academy), many brewers and brewmasters in the United States have learned and cultivated their skills on the job. Outside of the United States, many have attended professional and university-affiliated brewing programs to be certified as a brewmaster (e.g., VLB Berlin, International Center for Brewing and Distilling, The Scandinavian School of Brewing). However, this formulation and official certification as a brewmaster has not been popular to date. In fact, the Brewer's Association (2013a) suggests that most craft breweries rely on a brewmaster who has been traditionally an entrepreneur and homebrewer before entering into larger production. In short, there is no formal education or certifications necessary to be call one's self a brewmaster or to work within the industry within the United States.

For example, Lippard and Cohen (2015) found that 50 identified North Carolina microbrewery brewmasters did not have a specific education in brewing. Of brewmasters surveyed, 95% had some college or professional degree. Only about 5% had a professional degree (MBA, PhD) but most had a four-year college degree. Of those individuals, only three brewmasters had a college degree that was related to fermentation sciences, which included chemistry and bioengineering. The diversity of degrees was vast, and included nursing, graphic design, culinary arts, anthropology, sociology, and interior design. More important, only two brewmasters had acquired official certification and recognition for being a brewmaster based on international brewing standards. Thus, being a brewmaster for most was an honorary title bestowed by themselves with no official certification.

There was also a wide range of training and experience levels across these 50 brewmasters. For example, 75% suggested that they had no formal training in brewing before entering the industry and the other 15% had brewing certificates earned before and after starting as a craft brewmaster. However, over 90% had at least done homebrewing before starting up a brewery. As stated by one brewmaster, "My trajectory into my current position was really about friends urging me to make my beer. I had brewed for like three years and I was serving my beers [at] every party I went to . . . people loved it and my friend, who is the owner, said, 'I got the money and you've got the beer.' That's when we opened our brewery" (Lippard and Cohen 2015, 10). This type of story was common (65%) among brewmasters—they homebrewed for an average of six years and then had friends or individuals who supported them financially in branching out as a craft brewer.

Based on this social history of brewing and craft beer, one can now find oneself standing in the beer aisle at a local grocery store with several choices available. In fact, one could be standing on the brink of a beer destiny full of exotic and foreign choices. One choice is to go with what you know, which may be the ice-cold harshness of "American" beer, which has come to represent in the twenty-first century the repression of individual expression locally and globally. This beer, which sits distinctively apart from all the "craft beers," also champions conformity, loyalty, patriotism, and a measure of "the regular guy's" beer. At the other end of this spectrum is the seemingly endless array of regional and local craft beers that represent ingenuity, craftsmanship, appreciation, and choice. What do you do? This question is not so easily answered, but it is one worthy of sociological inquiry. If we look at history, it is easy to see the cultural significance of beer. It is a cultural product born of necessity and refined through the melding of mastery and skill with cultural taste and preference. To put it simply, beer is sociologically important. The legacy of the craft beer movement needs to be understood sociologically.

What Is Sociological about Beer?

The resurgence and growth of the craft beer industry in the United States and Europe represents a finite moment in our history, one that can be better understood through deconstructing and analyzing the current cultural, economic, and political trends in craft beer through a sociological lens. To provide a sociological perspective on a given phenomenon is to systematically examine it through various theoretical lenses and methodological approaches with the goal of understanding how human social relationships are implicated in that phenomenon. In this book, we focus on three sociological perspectives to examine the craft beer industry.

First, we examine the structural forces that impact individuals across Western society, which seem to push and pull people to want and to drink craft beer. As suggested above, we certainly see that there is a connection between the history of beer and the history of choice. Based on the historical trajectories of beer production, it is clear that individual choices of beer were broadened or narrowed based on the economics and politics surrounding the production of beer. One could argue that beer and its production simply changed because of economic factors surrounding the costs of production, distribution, and demand. However, this would be too simplistic and teleological, since it does not explain why beer drinkers across the United States and Europe have called for more craft beers—more expensive and less available—despite the overwhelming availability and distribution of "big beer" brands around the world. In short, why would we see a cultural resurgence in wanting to make and drink craft beer when all economic signs suggest it is more expensive to make and drink? Thus, while in this book we certainly recognize the economic impacts of the craft beer movement, we want to better understand the impacts of history, social structures, and culture on this trend.

Second, using a sociological lens requires us to view craft beer as a pursuit and expansion of cultural knowledge. In the twenty-first century, people interested in craft beer have begun to reach back to other times and cultures to find better ways to live, from more sustainable practices of agriculture that reduce environmental impacts and increase health, even to ways of producing a beer that is more flavorful and fuels the local economy with jobs and profits. Sociology requires us to deconstruct the historical knowledge of brewing and then discuss how today's knowledge of brewing has possibly changed to meet cultural and economic demands. We want to understand whether the knowledge of brewing is about reinvigorating old traditions or about creating new ways to address an age-old process. We also have to ask whether this uptick in craft beer consumption has led to a call for new knowledge and skills on how to brew based on the experiences of today's consumers and brewers.

Finally, sociology demands that we understand social context and that place, space, and identity formation matters. Although history tells us similar stories about the rise of craft beer in the United States and Western Europe, there are clear nuances as to how the beer is made, what tastes people want, and who drinks it. As we have already seen, beer production and consumption from place to place can be shaped by different cultural views and attitudes. Many of the chapters in this volume begin to illuminate the myriad ways that craft beer is used by individuals and groups in diverse locations. Clearly, the types of beer and methods of brewing have common ancestors, but we see that when brewed in small towns or large cities where beer was not a commodity or common-place, it takes on a distinctive flair and represents the uniqueness of space and place. We also have to note that beer consumption, whether a mainstream Bud Light or a craft Hop Devil IPA, sets consumers apart in socially stratified situa-tions. In other words, beer can highlight issues of identity and power in terms of the ways craft beer is used to challenge or reinscribe distinctions based on social class, race, and gender. Thus, questions of "taste" for certain types of beer should be raised throughout the relatively short history of the craft beer movement in the twentieth and twenty-first centuries. For example, the recent increase in popularity of supremely hopped India pale ales (IPAs), barrel-aged beers, and sour beers suggests that certain sets of tastes are valued differently in varying historical and social contexts. What makes these beverages so spe-cial? How and why have they transformed from a vital necessity to a commod-ity that fetches prices in the thousands of dollars? Has beer itself changed, or just the way we view beer? All of these questions deserve to be examined. It is the goal of this volume not only to introduce these questions, but also to gener-ate conversations.

Overall, sociology and its accompanying perspectives may be perfect for de-constructing and explaining this trend of craft beer brewing because it provides a framework to understand the craft beer revolution more holistically. Using both microlevel and macrolevel analysis, this volume seeks to illuminate both the contexts of production and the contexts of consumption of craft beer. In order to more fully analyze the complex arrangements surrounding the craft beer industry and culture, a sociological approach is needed.

Organization of the Book

This volume is organized into three thematic sections—Part I: Global Political Economy; Part II: Space and Place; and Part III: Intersecting Identities. In them, we explore various macrolevel and microlevel discussions to better understand and frame this growing trend for beer outside the typical iterations of "big beer." Social scientists have long been sensitive to the myriad ways that social structures shape cultural trends, economies, and the everyday experiences of individuals in society. More important, we take the position that the beer culture of today, in which many are impressing the notion of getting back to the "roots" of beer making and consuming, is often a rehashing of a global history of beer brewing. Moreover, we see cultures and communities embracing this move back to craft beer because they have the economic means, it is a popular consumerist trend, and it meshes well with the recent push for a sustainable and local economy.

In Part I: Global Political Economy, we first examine the various ways in which American and European societies culturally embrace or challenge the recent craft beer culture. Authors of the chapters in this part of the book had to look to the past and compare it with the present beer culture in order to better digest trends in the acquisition of knowledge on brewing. This section also discusses the types of economies created in this revitalized beer culture. In chapter 1, Jennifer Smith Maguire, Jessica Bain, Andrea Davies, and Maria Touri analyze how craft brewers use storytelling devices in order to position themselves in and communicate to the craft beer market in the United Kingdom. Ignazio Cabras, in chapter 2, investigates the role that craft beer is playing in the revitalization of cities and local economies in the British context. In chapter 3, Michael A. Elliott examines the rationalization, scientific standardization, and technical expertise involved in craft beer production through a Weberian lens by tracing its roots back to the Middle Ages. J. Nikol Beckham provides an analysis of work, labor, and leisure within the context of the craft beer revolution in the United States in chapter 4.

The authors of the chapters in Part II: Space and Place ask how public space and place are brought to bear on discussions of craft beer. Certainly, the global traditions in brewing are different, but the question still remains: How does a "big beer" consumer culture in the United States or Europe change in a few decades to almost reflect old European—specifically German—traditions of local or regional craft beer? In their case study of Jacksonville, Florida, in chapter 5, Krista E. Paulsen and Hayley E. Tuller provide a detailed account of the role of craft beer in the construction of socially meaningful places. They conclude that craft beer can create, remake, and promote authentic local identities for neighborhoods and even, perhaps, entire cities. In chapter 6, Ellis Jones and Daina Cheyenne Harvey focus on the craft beer movement in New England and analyze how it is being framed by brewers and brewery owners in terms of ethicality. In chapter 7, Thomas Thurnell-Read analyzes the spatial and social atmosphere of the Great British Beer Festival. Given craft beer's enormous potential for local economic revitalization, in chapter 8 Jesus Barajas, Geoff

Boeing, and Julie Wartell explore both the geospatial distribution of craft breweries across the United States and also the characteristics of neighborhoods in which craft breweries operate. In chapter 9, Tünde Cserpes and Paul-Brian McInerney provide a sociological account of the craft beer industry by analyzing the spatial dynamics and organizational identities among craft brews.

Finally, in Part III: Intersecting Identities, authors examine how craft beer filters through the various social strata of consumption. More specifically, authors explore how race, social class, and gender interact to shape craft beer consumption practices in the United States. In chapter 10, Andre Maciel considers the relationship between taste refinement and American middle-class masculinity. Maciel illuminates the ways that craft beer aficionados must carefully negotiate socioeconomic, moral, and cultural boundaries that are often at odds with ideals of American masculinity. Helana Darwin analyzes the prevalence and consequences of gender stereotypes as they relate to craft beer consumption in chapter 11. In chapter 12, Erik Withers explores the racial dynamics involved in upholding inequalities within the craft beer culture.

REFERENCES

Acitelli, Tom. 2013. *The Audacity of Hops: The History of America's Craft Beer Revolution.* Chicago: Chicago Review Press.

Boyle, M., and T. Buckley. 2015, May 15. "SABMiller Agrees to Acquire Meantime to Add U.K. Craft Beers." *Bloomberg Business.* http://www.bloomberg.com/news/articles /2015-05-15/sabmiller-agrees-to-acquire-meantime-to-add-u-k-craft-beers.

Brewers Association of America. 2013a. "Craft Brewer Defined." Accessed February 4, 2015, https://www.brewersassociation.org/statistics/craft-brewer-defined.

———. 2013b. "National Beer Sales & Production Data." Accessed February 2, 2015, https://www.brewersassociation.org/statistics/national-beer-sales-production-data.

———. 2013c. "Number of Breweries." Accessed February 2, 2015, https://www .brewersassociation.org/statistics/number-of-breweries.

———. 2015. "Number of Breweries." Boulder, CO: The Brewer's Association. Accessed January 25, 2016, https://www.brewersassociation.org/statistics/number-of-breweries.

Cabras, I., and C. Bamforth. 2016. "From Reviving Tradition to Fostering Innovation and Changing Marketing: The Evolution of Micro-brewing in the UK and US, 1980–2012." *Business History* 58 (5): 625–646.

Carroll, Glenn, and Anand Swaminathan. 2000. "Why the Microbrewery Movement? Organizational Dynamics of Resource Partitioning in the US Brewing Industry." *American Journal of Sociology* 106 (3): 715–762.

Crane, D. 1997. "Globalization, Organization Size, and Innovation in the French Luxury Fashion Industry: Production of Culture Theory Revised." *Poetics* 24: 393–414.

Edgar, David. 1991. "A Growth Industry." *All About Beer* 12 (5): 22.

German Beer Institute. 2006. "The German Beer Portal for North America." Accessed April 14, 2015, http://www.germanbeerinstitute.com/history.html.

Gordon, Samantha. 2013. "Students Can Earn Science Degrees in Making Beer and Wine." *US News and World Report*. Accessed January 30, 2015, http://www.usnewsuniversitydirectory .com/articles/students-can-earn-science-degrees-in-making-beer-a_13276.aspx#.Vhvo PMtVhHy.

Greer, Douglas F. 1998. "Beer: Causes of Structural Change." In *Industry Studies*, edited by L. Deutsch, 28–64. Armonk, NY: Sharpe.

Hindy, Steve. 2014. *The Craft Beer Revolution: How a Band of Microbrewers Is Transforming the World's Favorite Drink*. New York: Palgrave MacMillan.

Kedmey, Dan. 2014, September 3. "Guinness Launching 2 New Beers to Crack into Craft Beer Market." *Time*. http://time.com/3265098/guinness-craft-beer.

Lippard, Cameron, and Seth Cohen. 2015. "More than Just Beer: The Pedagogy of Fermentation Sciences." Unpublished paper. Appalachian State University.

Ogle, Maureen. 2006. *Ambitious Brew: The Story of American Beer*. New York: Harcourt.

Preece, D. 2016. "Turbulence in UK Public House Retailing: Ramifications and Responses." In *Brewing, Beer and Pubs: A Global Perspective*, edited by I. Cabras, D. Higgins, and D. Preece (forthcoming). London: Palgrave Macmillan. Preece, D., G. Steven, and V. Steven. 1999. *Work, Change and Competition: Managing for Bass*. London: Routledge.

Smit, B. 2014. *The Heineken Story: The Remarkably Refreshing Tale of the Beer that Conquered the World*. London: Profile Books.

Stächelin, Daniel. 2014, October 20. "Crafting a Revolution: The Rise of Craft Brewing in Europe. *Cafebabel*. http://www.cafebabel.co.uk/lifestyle/article/crafting-a-revolution-the -rise-of-craft-brewing-in-europe.html.

Tickell, Sofia C. 2012, October 8. "You Could Major in Beer (but Really)." *USA Today*. http://college.usatoday.com/2012/10/08/you-could-major-in-beer-but-really.

Tremblay, Carol Horton, and Victor J. Tremblay. 1988. "The Determinants of Horizontal Acquisitions: Evidence From the US Brewing Industry." *Journal of Industrial Economics* 37 (1): 21–45.

———. 2009. *The US Brewing Industry: Data and Economic Analysis*. Cambridge, MA: MIT Press.

Tremblay, Victor J. 1987. "Scale Economies, Technological Change, and Firm Cost Asymmetries in the US Brewing Industry." *Quarterly Review of Economics and Business* 27 (2): 71–86.

U.S. Census. 2014. "US Breweries Are Booming According to Census Bureau." Accessed February 2, 2015, http://www.census.gov/newsroom/press-releases/2014/cb14-127/htm.

PART I

Global Political Economy

CHAPTER 1

Storytelling and Market Formation

An Exploration of Craft Brewers in the United Kingdom

JENNIFER SMITH MAGUIRE, JESSICA BAIN, ANDREA DAVIES,
AND MARIA TOURI

Introduction

This chapter examines the creation of a British craft beer market from the point of view of producers. The story of craft beer in Britain is one of revival. The organized, small-scale production of beer in Britain extends back centuries, but by the end of the First World War, brewery numbers had begun to stagnate (Cabras and Bamforth 2016). An intensive period of consolidation in the middle of the twentieth century led to an overall decline in breweries and a concentration of ownership and production (Boak and Bailey 2014, 2). Cabras and Bamforth (2016, 629) note that from a peak of 6,447 breweries in Britain in 1900, by 1980 the number had dropped to only 142. Yet, in 2015, the number of breweries in Britain is said to top 1,400 again for the first time since the early twentieth century (Boak and Bailey 2014; Brown 2015). According to Naylor (2015), production output by members of the U.K. Society of Independent Brewers (SIBA) rose by almost 16% in 2014, while market research company Mintel estimates that 20% of the British public have drunk craft beer in the past six months (Brown 2015). Cabras and Bamforth (2016, 7–9) attribute this rise of microbreweries in Britain to three "waves," beginning with the creation of CAMRA (Campaign for Real Ale) in the late 1970s, moving to the introduction of legislation in the 1990s that removed barriers to the market for smaller breweries, and most recently to substantially decreased production and technological costs.

A similar revival of craft brewing has been noted in the United States, and this has received scholarly interest (Carroll and Swaminathan 2000; Flack 1997; Murray and O'Neill 2012). Yet the U.K. context is perhaps more complex and contentious than its American counterpart. In the United States, the definition of a craft brewer, "small, independent and traditional," is policed by the Brewers Association, whereas the United Kingdom "has no comparable definition" (Brown 2015, 34). Terminology and labeling with regard to British brewing is highly contested, with the product variously known as microbrews, craft beers, "real" ale, cask beer, new wave beer, "small scale," and independent; the terms are often used interchangeably in popular and scholarly accounts. "Craft accounts for 2 percent, 10 percent or maybe 20 percent of the market, depending on who you ask, and how they define it" (Brown 2015, 34). For CAMRA, real ale is a specific product: "brewed using traditional ingredients and left to mature in the cask (container) from which it is served in the pub through a process called secondary fermentation." Microbrew, too, can be attributed to a specific amount of beer output; in Britain the term *microbrew* is most routinely applied to denote the product of breweries with an output of 5,000 hectoliters, which under the Progressive Beer Duty Act entitles them to a reduction in duties (Cabras and Bamforth 2016, 625). *Craft beer* is a more ambiguous term, but its use often refers to a binary; that is, a "craft brewer" is not a "big brewery." In this context craft beer defines itself against the big business that has dominated the British beer market for so long (Brown 2015). Yet, this arguably leaves the term open to misuse and misappropriation. For Thurnell-Read (2014, 47), a more critical conception of *craft* in the context of microbrewing relates to the use of the term by brewers to articulate an identity, both for their product and for the embodied practice of brewing.

In this context of confused and competing terminology, and increased competition in the market by an ever-growing number of breweries, this chapter asks: How do small regional breweries in Britain position themselves? And how do they use storytelling devices to communicate themselves to the market? Our focus is on the perspectives and narratives of craft brewers; in this, we take up the call to look "inside" the construction of markets (Zwick and Cayla 2011) and focus on the understudied dimension of producer subjectivities and material practices (Paxson 2010; Smith Maguire 2013). We draw from an ongoing exploratory research project involving a small sample of microbrewers in the East Midlands, United Kingdom. Our concern is not with parsing the contested definitions of craft brewing or microbrewing; rather, we explore how these and other terms and definitions of the market operate in the narratives of the brewers.

The chapter proceeds with a discussion of how existing literature informs our research with regard to understanding microbrewing as a craft market and the role of storytelling as a market device. We then discuss the design of the research on which the chapter is based and provide an overview of the project's respondents. We follow with an analysis of the data, and we give particular attention to the character and implications of storytelling in relation to the brewers themselves, to their customers, and to their peers in the market.

Literature Review

Research on craft brewing has typically been consumer-oriented, or focused on the marketing strategies of craft, micro or boutique brewery products (see, for example, Carroll and Swaminathan 2000; Flack 1997; Holden 2011; Land and Taylor 2014; Spracklen et al. 2013; Wesson and De Figueiredo 2001). Thurnell-Read's study (2014) is unusual for its explicit producer-oriented perspective. Focusing on the occupational identities of British microbrewers, his respondents' narratives reveal how tangible, affective, and embodied dimensions of the work make it meaningful, thereby blurring product and producer. It is to this largely neglected question of producer orientations and experiences—within the relatively understudied domain of craft beer—that this chapter is addressed. Three interrelated themes frame our research: the defining characteristics of craft work; the importance of identity to craft products; and the role of storytelling in craft markets.

First, we draw on a range of literature to understand craft work. The skill of a specialist is a necessary but not sufficient component of craft work, which is identifiable through two interrelated, subjective dimensions: quality and passion. For example, Banks (2010, 307) defines craft as "a form of skilled labor that is quality-driven, materially specific and motivated by internal, as well as external rewards." In craft, a concern with quality is a personal concern; this is a form of embodied, affective labor marked by an intensely personal identification with and through work (Thurnell-Read 2014). That passionate identification affords particular benefits for producers, which are generally understood as a response to or at least dependent on the deficiencies and disadvantages of the hegemonic relations of production typical of late capitalism (see, for example, Sennett 2008). The discussion of craft is linked to a notion of a "new spirit of capitalism," which is both ennobling (creating the conditions for Hesmondhalgh and Baker's [2011] notion of good work) and potentially exploitative in that it "guarantees workers' commitment without recourse to compulsion, by making everyone's work meaningful" (Boltanski and Chiapello 2005, 76; see also, Gregg 2011). We are thus concerned with the theoretically rich question of how producer subjectivities are bound up in craft production (and how that does or does not differ from producer subjectivities in mass production—although that falls beyond the scope of the present research).

This brings us to the second theme: the importance of identity to understanding craft products. Here, we find two approaches in the literature—consumer-oriented and producer-oriented—with the latter being the road less traveled. On the one hand, consumer-oriented perspectives on markets highlight that consumers are motivated to purchase products in part because of their perceptions of, and feelings of identification with, a particular organization and their espoused values (see, for example, Bhattacharya and Sen 2003). Such issues are especially relevant to studying craft producers in any cultural field because the small scale of production and independent ownership (Pozner et al. 2014, 11) blur the lines between a particular producer and the organization. The salience of producers' identities and stories may diminish (i.e., the gap between an individual producer and an organization may grow) over time with growth in scale, as Pozner et al. (2014) find with U.S. craft brewing: past a certain point, product stories become decoupled from producer stories, and it is consumer identities that increasingly drive the definition of the market. This is a view of market construction that affords much of the power, however socially constrained, to consumers:

> Certainly, it is the consumer who appraises a producer's status and authenticity, themselves both social constructs, and who reinforces his own identity by consuming the products of the particular firms he has selected. Yet, the consumer is not fully agentic in this process; he is enveloped in multiple communities and social contexts that work to shape his tastes. (Pozner et al. 2014, 9)

On the other hand, producer-oriented approaches examine the impact of producers' identities and subjective experiences on the process of production (Thurnell-Read 2014) and on the product itself. For example, Hesmondhalgh and Baker (2011) argue for the potential of a causal link between the experience of "good" cultural work (associated with autonomy, interest, sociality, self-esteem, and so forth) and the creation of superior quality cultural products that contribute to the common good. Similarly, work on cultural intermediaries and other market actors underlines how the self-investment of personal dispositions, tastes, and affect in work practices and identities is crucial to the construction of markets and formation of value (Smith Maguire and Matthews 2014; Zwick and Cayla 2011).

By differentiating between these two research approaches, we do not suggest that producers and consumers necessarily have divergent values: opposition to mass-scale products, and more generally a notion of authenticity, is shared by producers, intermediaries, and consumers in the case of craft or artisanal goods (DeSoucey 2010; Sikavica and Pozner 2013; Smith Maguire 2013). Moreover, research highlights the blurring and bridging of consumption and production; markets are co-created, with producers, intermediaries, and consumers having a hand in constructing and reproducing market norms, practices, boundaries, and definitions (Slater 2002). Rather, our goal in disentangling the two approaches is to highlight what goes missing when the producers' identities and experiences are present in research only through the eyes of consumers. To return to the findings of Pozner et al. (2014), we would suggest that such a view of market construction risks conflating outcomes with process. To put it another way: if two market-construction processes reach the same end, it nevertheless remains that a grasp on how ends are reached is required to understand—and potentially intervene in—how markets (present and potential future markets) are made. This hidden potential schism between consumer and producer orientations is underlined by Paxson's research with artisanal cheese makers, for whom it may not matter what consumers think:

> It remains to be seen how successful cheesemakers will be in conveying their understanding of the value of what they are doing to consumers. Indeed, it may not matter. So long as cheese sells at a price that fairly compensates artisan labor, whether on taste alone or with appreciation for its instrumental values, producers' goals for the practice of their everyday lives may be furthered. For this reason, consumer perception is not essential to my analysis. (Paxson 2010, 446)

Even for larger-scale producers, it may be the case that producer identities and stories remain a primary focus in defining how (when, where, by whom, and why) an organization operates, irrespective of whether or not consumers "see" or understand that. Hence, our focus is on the microbrewers alone.

Third and finally, our particular theoretical interest lies with the role of storytelling in the creation of markets and market relations. Our research is informed by performativity-oriented theories of how the practices of actor-entities perform, shape, and reshape markets (Callon 1998; Geiger et al. 2012; Kjellberg and Helgesson 2007). We also build on narrative approaches to the construction of identities, institutions, markets, and cultures (Boje 2008; Davies 2011; Langellier and Peterson 2011; Squire 2013). This leads us to narrow our focus empirically to producers' narratives, to explore how the beer market and the "even newer spirit of capitalism" (Land and Taylor 2014) are performed and shaped through the stories producers tell. Furthermore, this literature—and what we perceive as its dearth of engagement with the very notions of passion and affect that are central to the preceding two themes—pushes us to narrow our focus to the role of stories as market devices. Devices "act or they make others act" (Muniesa et al. 2007, 2). We thus ask: What does storytelling-as-device do? What does it make possible (enable), but also what does it push microbrewers to do (constrain)? In what ways do those stories contribute to the manifestation of product properties, market definitions, understandings of consumers, and the relations of consumption anticipated for the product?

Thus, by selectively focusing on producers' perspectives, we attempt to re-capture the work that stories do "behind the scenes" in positioning products via the motivations and mentalities of producers themselves. Such work is lost from critical view when the focus is trained (as it more often is) on the market as confronted—as a fait accompli—by consumers. Yet, as suggested by the exist-ing literature, it is precisely this performative work of producers that animates the new spirit of capitalism and legitimates craft products by embedding them in personal narratives of quality and passion.

Methods

In-depth interviews are used as techniques to help us as researchers to under-stand the experience and meanings of our research participants. In this study we use narrative theory (Langellier and Peterson 2011; Mishler 1995; Squire 2013) to frame our interviews and analysis, that is, narrative is used ontologi-cally as well as analytically (Shankar et al. 2001). Narrative theory was cho-sen because it recognizes the intentionality of communication, stories and myth-making (Samuel and Thompson 1990). The experiences told to us by our participant breweries are not treated as fact or as evidence of events that have occurred. Rather, narrative theory suggests that stories are ways in which people make sense of their lives. As such, our participants' accounts—their stories—provide us with insight into their motivations and the ways in which they interpret events and the world around them. Narrative theory emphasizes meaning-in-action instead of facts (Georgakopolou 2006). In our study, we con-sider intentionality at two levels: first, intentionality is recognized in that the descriptions of craft brewing and the market are understood as ideas, events, and emotions that are remembered. Laid down in memory, these frame brew-ers' current practices and future intentions, and we carefully acknowledge that the findings we present here do not necessarily match the real-life experience(s) of brewers (Davies 2011; Moisander et al. 2009). Second, we are sensitive to the narratives brewers can share and choose to share with the researchers, and we see the interview data as narrative acts (Samuel and Thompson 1990). Our research sought to capture the narratives of brewers so as to understand producer subjectivity and their view of the craft beer market.

The findings presented in this chapter are based on interviews with microbreweries from the East Midlands, United Kingdom.[1] The population of breweries in the region was first mapped onto a typology developed from our analysis of website and promotional material. Dimensions that framed the typology were size (smaller to larger), positioning (traditional heritage/local image to a lifestyle branding), and geographic location (across the region and proximity to large urban centers). Based on this mapping, breweries were selected purposively to maximize variability in the experiences and histories of the breweries. From an initial sample of six breweries, we completed data collection with five.[2] Table 1.1 provides an overview of the sample and demonstrates the diversity of brewers present in our research.

Interviews were conducted with one key representative from each brewery. All participants were knowledgeable and involved with the market-facing activities of the company. All described themselves as microbrewers (when *craft beer* was mentioned in interviews, this had more of an association with the United States). Two participants (Windmill and Hillside[3]) described themselves as predominantly involved with marketing and sales and, although their role was less involved with the hands-on brewing, they often participated, helping the brewer. Two participants were chiefly responsible for brewing but also had a leading role in the decisions about market-facing activities (Bootmaker and Gismonda). One participant (Church Spire) was remote from the day-to-day brewing, describing himself as a "cuckoo brewer" who sent the recipe to be brewed in another county but sold the beer as a local beer; his was a principally marketing role. The breweries were all fairly well established, trading for 15 years or longer. There were no new brewery start-ups included in the sample. All the participants were male, except for the brewer at Gismonda.

Two researchers co-interviewed each participant; the interviews lasted between 1 hour 45 minutes and 2 hours 20 minutes. The interviews were participant-led to enable participants' narratives and stories to unfold. A semi-structured approach was taken, to ensure consistency in the scope of the interviews, while retaining the flexibility to follow participants in the issues and experiences they chose to discuss. Topic areas in the interview guide included descriptions of the following: the brewery today and its history; the beer(s), including the brand and any branding activities; the role of the interviewee in the company; the brewery's routes to market and how they managed relationships with intermediaries and retailers; end consumers and the level of contact

Table 1.1. Breweries and Participants in Our Study

Brewery	Established	Scale of Production	No. of Employees	Cask, Bottle, or Both	Participant Role in Brewery	Participant Gender	Participant Experience (years in industry)/ Formal Qualifications Relevant to Food/drink
Windmill	1994	5,000 hectoliters per year	8	Both	Marketing & sales	Male	11 years with Windmill; in brewing since graduated with Physics degree
Hillside	2000	45 barrels per week	5	Bottle	Marketing & sales	Male	15 years in brewing, previously a pub landlord
Bootmaker	1984	320 nines per week	2.5	Barrel to pubs, bottles to shops	Brewing & sales/marketing	Male	Whole life, grew up in the industry
Church Spire	1997	25,000 bottles and 15,000 casks per year	2	Bottle	Marketing & sales	Male	18 years, previous experience in food and drink fast-moving consumer goods (FMCG) marketing/ management
Gismonda	1997	50 barrels per week	3	Cask	Brewing & sales/marketing	Female	Whole of professional career, worked at larger brewery before setting up own business, BSc in Biochemistry, Masters in Brewing

with end customers; ingredients and procurement arrangements; and a description of the craft beer market and their main competitors and any collaborators. Interviews were recorded and later transcribed verbatim. A thematic data analysis approach was adopted, in which from initial close readings of the transcripts by each researcher, themes were shared, discussed, modified, and reframed (Spiggle 1994). The first stages of analysis were paper-based, but during subsequent coding and refinement NVivo software was used.

Findings

A full account of our findings is beyond the scope of this chapter. Rather, we focus on three themes that emerged from the data analysis that relate to storytelling as a device for market formation: stories that the brewers told about themselves (their occupational and organizational identities), about their customers, and about their market peers.

Stories about Themselves

For all five breweries, size appears to be a defining element of their identity and philosophy, since it determines not just their yearly turnover, but also the uniqueness of the product and the personality of the company. In contrast, growing in size was associated with personality loss, as "it all becomes a machine . . . you've got to get bigger vehicles, more employees, health and safety suddenly becomes three times as important" (Windmill).

This uniqueness and personality appears to be directly linked to the passion and enthusiasm that characterizes these brewers, and this sets them apart from the big nationals. For example:

> I really enjoy it, brewing days are just great. There's a nice view, you sit outside, have a bit of lunch. Some days are full on and on a brew day when you're doing two brews, there's a certain time you can't be disturbed because one brew's going in, one's coming out, you've got to be 100 percent focused. (Bootmaker)

> [Getting into brewing] really was a serendipitous move, it has been really good in the industry and you realize how friendly it is. If I'd gone into food science or something like that I'd probably be in a lab testing out the crispness of a wafer which wouldn't have been so much fun. (Gismonda)

The passion and genuine interest in the brewing process is a vital source of energy, motivation, and commitment for the brewers. For example, this was true for Church Spire, even if he considered the brewery a "hobby" that was enabled by his other, unrelated, and more profitable businesses:

> I'll be honest and say I'm still having a lot of fun with it and it pays for the holidays but I'm not fully convinced I'm at a point yet where I have a viable business. Fifteen years down the line, I still haven't got a viable business but I'm still having fun. (Church Spire)

On the other hand, it is this passion that can become an asset, bringing the brewers closer to the customers and helping to strengthen personal relationships:

> We don't employ anyone that's not interested in beer . . . unless they're really interested in the product, it's very difficult to get excited and sell it. If you can show that passion of interest to people, they're more likely to buy it. (Windmill)

For our participants, an integral part of their personality and philosophy as genuine microbrewers is the guarantee for the highest quality of the product as well as their commitment to getting it right every time. Using the purest of ingredients, such as malted barley, and avoiding any artificial elements is a rule of thumb, while the soil and locality of the ingredients are also believed to contribute to the good taste of the beer. Yet, it is the consistency of this quality that proves most challenging, and achieving it is seen to be what sets a successfully brewery apart, and for which those microbrewers appear particularly proud:

> It has to taste exactly the same all the time. It's a very critical bit of it. Lots of people can set up a little brewery and make a good beer. To go on and make it again and again and exactly the same is very, very difficult. (Hillside)

> Consistency is the key to everything. The most successful food industry in the world is McDonald's and nobody would ever say it's good because it clearly isn't, but it's always consistent. . . . We always follow the recipe, we always put it in the same sized container. (Windmill)

Stories about Their Customers

Consistency appears to be key not only in terms of quality and the science that goes into the beer itself, but also in building and maintaining close relationships with the customers, including pub landlords as a well as end consumers:

> We always send the same drayman to the same pub so that he gets to know the landlord and the landlord gets to know him. . . . We always try and make sure we've got the same drivers going to the same pubs, and it's all about consistency. (Windmill)

On the one hand, the personal relations that brewers maintain with their customers appear as a taken-for-granted extension of their own personal attachment to and passion about brewing. It is this passion that makes them keen to engage with people and educate them about the culture of brewing and drinking beer. More importantly, it is this passion that turns them into more than just another salesperson:

> I love serving the beer and being part of it. . . . I like talking to people and listening and figuring out what's what. (Bootmaker)

> I'm not a sales type of person and initially I thought, "How on earth am I going to sell anything?" And a friend of mine said, "If you can talk to people, you can sell"; and that's all it comes down to at the end of the day. . . . The important thing is to go out and meet the customers. They're really pleased to see you and when you do phone them up they are, "How you doing?" (Gismonda)

At the same time, they all recognized the marketing advantage and customer loyalty they can gain from interacting and connecting with their customers, either through festivals and tasting events or through more indirect communications channels, such as websites and social media. More interaction is likely to generate more interest from the side of the consumers, who are then more likely to return. Similarly, our brewers made a point of keeping the customer aware of that they are being looked after:

> The most important thing, and particularly on our website, is to respond to their review because then they know you're looking and they know you're interested and they know you care. (Windmill)

> People always want to know what's going on at the brewery. It's PR, meeting the customers. You get people in the market, going around the market who are landlords or drink at a regular pub or that sort of thing. "Yes, I'll tell my landlord about this." (Hillside)

Promoting local tastes and flavors is also core to their marketing practices, in line with local food movements and recent trends and attempts to reconnect producers with consumers. Small-scale breweries seem to fit nicely into the category of local food, where people know where the beer comes from and can also see where and how it is being made:

> Well, we have some little toppers that go on top and say, "Brewed within 30 miles" or "Brewed in [East Midlands]" just to try to get local people to promote it, like local food or something. We try to promote the local drink angle which I think is winning a bit more these days. (Gismonda)

> There are lots of pubs that promote drinking local, local produce, fresh produce.... They say this is local, it's come from within 25 miles. People are getting into the ethos of it and there are pubs where the bar staff is educated and does talk to you about it. (Bootmaker)

The history or the myths hidden behind each brewery are also valuable sources of stories for brewers to share with their customers, often adding a fairy-tale dimension to the brand:

> If you read the label for [Dragon's Breath], it says it's rumored that St. George stopped in [the village] on his way to slay the dragon. We know that's not true but it's one of those things that can enter into folklore in a very small area. (Church Spire)

Interestingly, however, and despite their emphasis on interaction and relationships, most brewers seemed to know little about their target customers' preferences and tastes, focusing instead on having a selection of beers that appealed to everyone. All brewers identified their customer base in vague terms, for example as primarily male and over 35 years of age, although there was some appreciation of new trends, particular young, urban "hipster" interest in craft beer:

> Our consumer base is very broad. I have no figures to back it up but I think ... it's probably skewed to the over thirty-fives.... We make sure we have something for everybody. I do a number of [tasting] events mostly for my customers ... and also take notes during the day. I'll reflect at the end of the day and see what went well. Generally everything goes well. (Church Spire)

> What we want to be doing is selling beer that's around about the 4 percent mark, that people will go and have three or four pints a night because we want to be selling quantities of it, the landlord wants to be selling quantities, he wants to be turning over. (Hillside)

For some brewers, more emphasis appeared to be placed on the task of educating rather than listening to the consumer, which appears to sprout from their conviction that there is a general lack of knowledge regarding what good beer really is:

> A lot of people that drink in that pub [gestures to the independently run pub adjoining the property of the brewery] drink lager and they think what's made over here is hobbyist and they don't know what they're doing and they drink lager or they drink Bass or Pedigree. (Bootmaker)

To a certain extent, the emphasis on this rather one-way customer education stems from the limited resources and time these microbreweries can devote to conducting systematic market research. As a survival strategy, it is the stories about themselves and the industry that gain more weight, enabling them to cope with the challenges of the market and with the competition. Such stories tend to center on specific ideas and myths of the market that many of them share.

Stories about Their Peers

What was notable—surprising, even, given the dynamic and increasingly competitive nature of the market—was the palpable sense of collegiality that emerged from the interviews. All five brewers acknowledged the friendliness and collaboration that characterize the relations among them. The majority of breweries work closely together and alongside each other, exchanging recipes and swapping or supplying ingredients.

Trade forums have offered a useful platform for them to discuss the various problems they encounter and to identify solutions. To a large extent, and as most of them recognized, the whole setup of the industry and the uniqueness of each brewery, in terms of their ingredients and brewing process, leave little room or desire for competition:

> If we taste somebody's beer and think it's really good and ring them up and they'll tell you what recipe is in it, simply because every brewery has a unique flavour as to how it's brewed. If I got the recipe for Greene King IPA, exactly the recipe, and tried to brew it here, it would taste different.

It's because everybody's got their own hand on it's slightly different. (Hillside)

More crucially, though, collaboration also serves an additional purpose: survival against the national brands, especially since pubs do not tend to keep a brewer's beer on a permanent basis. In this case, collaboration ensures that a rotation system remains in place, with every brewery selling to pubs at least once every three weeks:

> The more you go out and you compete with other people, you're just eating your own pie, as it were. . . . If you lose that, everybody loses because what you don't want is the big national brands to come in and stick their beer on the bar permanently. (Windmill)

It is through this collaborative approach that part of the brewers' identity is also formed, as they gain credibility and stand against not just the big nationals but also those competitors that, in their eyes, lack credibility. These would include amateur brewers that lack passion and knowledge, trendy, hip brands as well as clubs and organizations that undermine the value of good microbeer and the work and science that goes into it:

> I don't agree with most of the organizations that are trying to promote the product. CAMRA have a good ethos and a good idea but they're all about discounts, how to save their members money, not how to look after the publicans or promote the breweries. Awareness is good, make them aware of beer but if you're passionate about something you're prepared to pay for it. Why is it because you belong to a club should you get discounts and those pubs that give discounts should get preference in a beer magazine and advertising because they're giving a discount? (Bootmaker)

In conjunction with stories about themselves and their consumers, the brewers' stories about the market, their peers, and their competitors enabled them to maintain a quite collegial brewing community and make sense of their place within it, positioning themselves as distinct from not only the large-scale brewers but also the newer (perhaps poorer-quality) microbrewers.

Discussion and Conclusion

We return to our research question and ask: When exploring the perspective of the producer, what do stories and storytelling do? One part of a response to this question, based on our research, falls in line with the typical consumer-oriented approaches to studying markets and stories. That is, each of the breweries has a brand "story." Those stories are always about more than the beer in the glass. All of the brewers had stories linked to local characters, heritage, and landscape, as well as their own biographies and tastes. These stories are used to mark the difference between big breweries and microbreweries, and they add distinctive value to the beers. They are embedded in packaging and promotional media such as websites, and they populate the interpersonal marketing that the respondents carry out in their interactions in pubs, at the brewery, at beer tastings and festivals, and so forth. In this regard, our producer-oriented approach confirms the general thrust of the discussion of stories in relation to content marketing (see, for example, Pulizzi 2012).

However, our focus on producers raises other dimensions of the role of stories in markets, which are veiled or forgotten when the focus is on the representation and reception of brand stories. Stories—not only their content, but also their telling—have material implications; stories translate into action. Storytelling is widely recognized as a means of preserving culture and common characteristics, passing them down through generations and across organizations (see, for example, Boje 2008; Davies and Fitchett 2015), but there has been less attention on the role of stories and storytelling in markets. Our findings suggest that storytelling is the way in which our participants structured their experiences and histories to make sense of them and to communicate them to the consumer, the pubs, and other channel intermediaries. It is through the performance of stories (in designing labels, at beer tastings, in interviews with social scientists) that our respondents actively define their products' properties and imagined conditions of use, their terms of competition and success, and their modus operandi. We can see this in the data with regard to the stories that the respondents tell about themselves, their consumers, and their peers. In conclusion, we revisit these findings in terms of drawing out three implications of storytelling as a market device.

First, we can see how multiple stories work in concert to construct markets through notions of product properties, imagined conditions of use, and terms of competition (Slater 2002). Respondents' narratives about their motivations and goals actively accomplish the product properties of passion and quality that are central to notions of craft (Banks 2010). Such narratives are a private and public performance of passion, turning what is, ultimately, an intangible property into something that can be circulated and evaluated. In addition, respondents' stories about their motivations, mode of production and products position the breweries within a crowded market, both in opposition to recent competition (from less-experienced, often seen to be "trendy" new craft producers with arguably lesser-quality products), and in distinction to the uniformity and scope of the major national brewers. This oppositional positioning within a partitioned market (Sikavica and Pozner 2013) is reinforced through the articulation of a "we image" (Elias 1991) for a cooperative community that supports the breweries materially (e.g., swapping; sourcing ingredients; apprenticeships for new entrants) and socially (e.g., social networks and moral support). This cooperative dynamic shapes in part which (local) markets our brewers enter and how. The stories they tell, then, are devices to support them—both individually and collectively in how to operate, and in guiding decisions on what they do.

Second, beyond serving as supporting devices, our data suggest how stories are operational devices: they translate into action. Each brewery's brand story—steeped in local referents—was also part of a rationale for identifying geographic parameters of a potential market, keeping a range of beers suitable to local tastes, and selectively rotating some of the beers for seasonal availability. Moreover, narratives about the perceived desire (on the part of end consumers and publicans) for novelty were used by brewers to manage their product portfolios and had implications for product development and promotional strategies. This was all the more interesting given that, while all of our brewers were able to tell us stories about their customers, none had any data or market research to support these. Instead, their assumed knowledge of what consumers want stem from stories they tell themselves as well as those they pick up when engaged in direct selling and during the interpersonal communication that occurs alongside these practices. (And, most likely, they also stem from their own tastes; four of the five embodied their own, imagined market of 35-plus-year-old males.) Thus, the assumptions about what consumers want "fits" with their definitions of their product qualities, and the stories function to perpetuate those assumptions. This ultimately gives rise to the fait accompli confronted and decoded by consumers. However, if storytelling reproduces experiences and intentions, we also need to recognize that it constrains activities and practices, silencing some narratives to privilege the communication of others. Here, performativity is starkly brought to our attention, to recognize that performing stories formats and shapes the phenomena performed in ways that enable and constrain particular modes of engagement: stories serve as a point of attachment for consumers, but reflect assumptions about the marketplace (often cast in terms of the 35-plus-year-old male) that may prevent others from being included in the market.

Finally, our data suggest the role of storytelling as a coping device, well suited to the particular tension within the new spirit of capitalism (Boltanski and Chiapello 2005) between craft and commerce. Not only do respondents' narratives about their motivations and goals construct value through rendering passion tangible; they also elide some of the contradictions surrounding the experience of passionate work. In particular, this relates to an orientation to and blending of work and life. The Church Spire respondent was perhaps most explicit in his view of microbrewing as something other than work, but this was also noted by the other respondents, including those with professional brewing qualifications. In this, microbrewing appears to be akin to serious leisure (Stebbins 2007), undertaken with the commitment and rational discipline of work, but associated with self-actualization and pleasure rather than a profit motive. The other four respondents were explicit in their pragmatic need to make a living from brewing. Nevertheless, and counter to the discourse of art/craft for its own sake that frames craft and commerce as mutually exclusive, we found across all five respondents that success is measured in personal satisfaction with the work and the quality of the product, as well as in career-like terms with regard to milestones passed, awards won, profits, and so forth. We might also mention that among the findings not included in this chapter were the respondents' descriptions of "hobbyists," who take up brewing as a lifestyle choice (e.g., using redundancy money or early retirement to set up brewing operations). The respondents' accounts of these individuals were often about failure—past anecdotes or future predictions of how such an approach to brewing was ill fated because of a failure to understand and operate within the realities of the marketplace. This suggests how the "new" spirit of capitalism can be markedly conservative—an optimistic utopianism that works within the status quo, rather than a full-scale retreat or radical alternative to the established way of doing things.

Indeed, it is in the stories about personal biographies and motivations that we most clearly see the implications of stories (which go missing when the focus is on the consumer): stories about passionate production reconcile the inevitable instrumental practicalities and logics that attend any entrepreneurial venture with the need for personal passion as a guarantor of craft products. Through stories and storytelling, the brewers animate their products and reconcile through narrative what is, ultimately, irreconcilable in practice. Thus, we suggest that storytelling is a coping device well suited to the new spirit of capitalism. As a market device, it offers the discursive flexibility to espouse a nostalgic utopianism for a "return to something 'primordial' . . . and basic in human nature, . . . to something that had been lost in the progress of modernity" (Land and Taylor 2014, 211), while at the same time accommodating and incorporating both the existing structures and logics of hegemonic capitalism and embracing new technologies and being forward-looking. Stories of passionate self-investment in the enterprise (echoed through storytelling as marketing practice and supported through shared stories of cooperation) operates as an alibi for concerns with the maximization of profit and a prophylactic against the modern disease of rationalization and accumulation without enjoyment.

NOTES

1. The research was funded by the European Regional Development Fund (ERDF) Innovation Partnership Scheme and was carried out in accordance with University of Leicester ethical procedures.

2. One brewery withdrew from the study because of the pressures of managing a smaller enterprise, which underlined a challenge throughout the recruitment process.

3. Respondents have been anonymized with pseudonyms.

REFERENCES

Banks, Mark. 2010. "Craft Labour and Creative Industries." *International Journal of Cultural Policy* 16 (3): 305–321.

Bhattacharya, C. B., and Sankar Sen. 2003. "Consumer-Company Identification: A Framework for Understanding Consumers' Relationships with Companies." *Journal of Marketing* 67 (2): 76–88.

Boak, Jessica, and Ray Bailey. 2014. *Brew Britannia: The Strange Rebirth of British Beer.* London: Aurum.

Boje, David M. 2008. *Storytelling Organizations.* London: Sage.

Boltanski, Luc, and Eve Chiapello. 2005. *The New Spirit of Capitalism.* London: Verso.

Brown, Pete. 2015, March 21. "Trouble Brewing: How Craft Beer Fomented a Battle for the Soul of Booze." *The Guardian.* https://www.theguardian.com/lifeandstyle/2015/mar/21/trouble-brewing-how-craft-beer-fomented-a-battle-for-the-soul-of-booze.

Cabras, Ignazio, and Charles Bamforth. 2016. "From Reviving Tradition to Fostering Innovation and Changing Marketing: The Evolution of Micro-brewing in the UK and US, 1980–2012." *Business History* 58 (5): 625–646.

Callon, Michael. 2009. "Introduction." In *The Laws of Market,* edited by M. Callon, 1–57. Oxford: Wiley-Blackwell.

Carroll, Glenn R., and Anand Swaminathan. 2000. "Why the Microbrewery Movement? Organizational Dynamics of Resource Partitioning in the US Brewing Industry." *American Journal of Sociology* 106 (3): 715–762.

Davies, Andrea. 2011. "Voices Passed." *Journal of Historical Research in Marketing* 3: 469–485.

Davies, Andrea, and James A. Fitchett. 2015. "In the Family Way: Bringing a Mother-Daughter (Matrilineal) Perspective to Retail Innovation and Consumer Culture." *Environment and Planning A* 47 (3): 727–743.

DeSoucey, Michaela. 2010. "Gastronationalism: Food Traditions and Authenticity Politics in the European Union." *American Sociological Review* 75 (3): 432–455.

Elias, Norbert. 1991. *The Society of Individuals*. Oxford: Basil Blackwell.

Flack, Wes. 1997. "American Microbreweries and Neo-Localism: 'Ale-ing' for a Sense of Place." *Journal of Cultural Geography* 16 (2): 37–53.

Geiger, Susi, Hans Kjellberg, and Robert Spencer. 2012. "Shaping Exchanges, Building Markets." *Consumption Markets and Culture* 15 (2): 133–147.

Georgakopolou, Alexandra. 2006. "Thinking Big with Small Stories in Narrative and Identity Analysis." *Narrative Inquiry* 16: 122–130.

Gregg, Melissa. 2011. *Work's Intimacy*. Cambridge: Polity.

Hesmondhalgh, David, and Sarah Baker. 2011. *Creative Labour: Media Work in Three Cultural Industries*. London: Routledge.

Holden, Stephen S. 2011. "Three Cheers for New Beers: Marketing Insights from the Birth of Boutique Brewing in Australia." Paper presented at the Australian & New Zealand Marketing Academy Conference ANZMAC 2011, Perth, Western Australia. Accessed June 15, 2015, http://epublications.bond.edu.au/business_pubs/423.

Kjellberg, Hans, and Claes-Fredrik Helgesson. 2007. "On the Nature of Markets and Their Practices." *Marketing Theory* 7 (2): 137–172.

Land, Chris, and Scott Taylor. 2014. "The Good Old Days Yet to Come: Postalgic Times for the New Spirit of Capitalism." *Management & Organizational History* 9 (2): 202–219.

Langellier, Kristin, and Eric E. Peterson. 2011. *Storytelling in Daily Life: Performing Narrative*. Philadelphia: Temple University Press.

Mishler, Elliot. 1995. "Models of Narrative Analysis: A Typology." *Journal of Narrative and Life History* 5 (2): 87–123.

Moisander Johanna, Anu Valtonen, and Heidi Hirsto. 2009. "Personal Interviews in Cultural Consumer Research—Post Structuralist Challenges." *Consumption, Culture and Markets* 12: 329–348.

Muniesa, Fabian, Yuval Millo, and Michael Callon. 2007. "An Introduction to Market Devices." In *Market Devices*, edited by M. Callon, 1–12. Oxford: Blackwell.

Murray, Douglas, and Martin O'Neill. 2012. "Craft Beer: Penetrating a Niche Market." *British Food Journal* 114 (7): 899–909.

Naylor, Tony. 2014, August 13. "The Craft Beer Revolution: How Hops Got Hip." *The Guardian*. http://www.theguardian.com/lifeandstyle/2014/aug/13/craft-beer-revolution-hops-brewers-flavours.

Paxson, Heather. 2010. "Locating Value in Artisan Cheese: Reverse Engineering Terroir for New-World Landscapes." *American Anthropologist* 112 (3): 444–457.

Pozner, Jo-Ellen, Michaela DeSoucey, and Katarina Sikavica. October 2014. "Bottle Revolution: Constructing Consumer and Producer Identities in the Craft Beer Industry." IRLE

Working Paper No. 118-14. Accessed June 15, 2015, http://irle.berkeley.edu/workingpapers/118-14.pdf.

Pulizzi, Joe. 2012. "The Rise of Storytelling as the New Marketing." *Publishing Research Quarterly* 28: 116–123.

Samuel, Raphael, and Paul Thompson. 1990. *The Myths We Live By.* London: Routledge.

Sennet, Richard. 2008. *The Craftsman.* London: Allen Lane.

Shankar, Avi, Richard Elliott, and Christina Goulding. 2001. "Understanding Consumption: Contributions from a Narrative Perspective." *Journal of Marketing Management* 17: 429–453.

Sikavica, Katarina, and Jo-Ellen Pozner. 2013. "Paradise Sold: Standards, Social Movement Identification and Competition in Identity-Partitioned Markets." *Organization Studies* 34 (5–6): 623–651.

Slater, Don. 2002. "Capturing Markets from the Economists." In *Cultural Economy: Cultural Analysis and Commercial Life*, edited by P. du Gay and M. Pryke, 59–77. London: Sage.

Smith Maguire, Jennifer. 2013. "Provenance as a Filtering and Framing Device in the Qualification of Wine." *Consumption, Markets and Culture* 16 (4): 368–391.

Smith Maguire, Jennifer, and Julian Matthews. 2014. *The Cultural Intermediaries Reader.* London: Sage.

Spiggle, Susan. 1994. "Analysis and Interpretation of Qualitative Data in Consumer Research." *Journal of Consumer Research* 21 (3): 491–503.

Spracklen, Karl, Jon Laurencic, and Alex Kenyon. 2013. "'Mine's a Pint of Bitter': Performativity, Gender, Class and Representations of Authenticity in Real-Ale Tourism." *Tourist Studies* 13 (3): 304–321.

Squire, Corinne. 2013. "Experience-Centred and Culturally Oriented Approaches to Narrative." In *Doing Narrative Research*, edited by M. Andrews, C. Squire, and M. Tamboukou, 47–71. Thousand Oaks, CA: Sage.

Stebbins, Robert A. 2007. *Serious Leisure: A Perspective for Our Time.* New Brunswick, NJ: Aldine Transaction.

Thurnell-Read, Thomas. 2014. "Craft, Tangibility and Affect at Work in the Microbrewery." *Emotion, Space, and Society* 13: 46–54.

Wesson, Tom, and Joao Neiva De Figueiredo. 2001. "The Importance of Focus to Market Entrants: A Study of Microbrewery Performance." *Journal of Business Venturing* 16 (4): 377–403.

Zwick, Detlev, and Julien Cayla. 2011. "Inside Marketing: Practices, Ideologies, Devices." In *Inside Marketing: Practices, Ideologies, Devices*, edited by D. Zwick and J. Cayla, 3–22. Oxford: Oxford University Press.

CHAPTER 2

A Pint of Success

How Beer Is Revitalizing Cities and Local Economies in the United Kingdom

IGNAZIO CABRAS

Introduction

In the United Kingdom, the numbers of breweries have increased significantly since the 1980s, with many small and micro businesses successfully able to diversify their offers and to expand their operations well beyond their local areas. While the implications for the industry derived from this growth have been investigated by a number of studies (Carroll and Swaminathan 1991; Swaminathan 1998; Tremblay and Tremblay 2005), more recent research has focused on the impact of new beers and brewing on local economies and on the development of business strategies targeting a growing demand for diversified artisan beers (Cabras and Bamforth 2015; Danson et al. 2015; Moore et al. 2016).

This chapter contributes to these studies by investigating how the revival of microbrewing has influenced, and is currently influencing, the beer scene in the United Kingdom. I use primary and secondary information, collected between 2009 and 2015 and related to British breweries and pubs, to explore and examine how patterns and growth and decline of these two types of businesses have affected and still affect local economies and communities. In addition, I use in-depth interviews with brewers, representatives from industry organizations, beer festival organizers, and publicans to analyze and further evaluate the social and economic effects associated with changes in the brewing industry.

The Rise of Microbreweries and the Decline of Pubs

In 1980, the number of breweries in the United Kingdom was about 142. As shown in figure 2.1, by 2015 the number had increased to 1,424 (British Beer and Pub Association 2015; Campaign for Real Ale 2015), registering an astonishing 10-fold growth within this period. The rise of these businesses can be described in three consecutive, interrelated waves (Cabras and Bamforth 2015).

The first wave, arriving between the late 1970s and mid-1980s, was mainly due to a general dissatisfaction with the decline in the variety of beers available to customers. This situation led to the creation of the Campaign for Real Ale (CAMRA), a movement of beer lovers who lobbied for the revival of real ale— cask-conditioned ales brewed by traditional methods. CAMRA's relentless activities and campaigns increased awareness about traditional ales and helped to create a potential customer base for new breweries that represented an alternative to mass producers (Mason and McNally 1997). Moreover, CAMRA changed the image of real-ale drinkers, frequently pictured as "bearded besandalled and with a generous girth born of sampling a 'tad' too much ale" (extracted from the Carlsberg-Tetley 1994 Report and quoted in Mason and McNally 1997, 408), by promoting them as customers keen to preserve beer traditions and values. The many opportunities related to an increasing demand for real ales attracted a variety of entrepreneurs, many with some previous experience in the brewing industry, to enter the market (Mason and McNally 1997).

The second wave, which arrived in the early 1990s, was mainly characterized by the entrance to the industry of new founders with little or no previous connection with breweries or brewing, such as retirees or beer lovers in search of a career change (Knowles and Egan 2002). Two factors characterize this period: the rapid increase in the number of new businesses brought the development of specialized real-ale producers, which enabled many new breweries to start with more efficient and more cost-effective brewing equipment; and the introduction of the Beer Orders of 1989, which forced the larger brewers to either sell or free a large number of their pubs from being tied to them (Preece et al. 1999). The latter enabled the formation of large retailing companies or pubcos purchasing the majority of pubs and selecting a very limited range of breweries as their suppliers, creating fewer opportunities for new breweries to expand their supply network (Pratten 2007; Preece 2016).

The third and most recent wave arrived early in the 2000s, which saw a further and sharper increase in the number of microbreweries, sustained by cheaper and easier-to-install equipment (Mason and McNally 1997; Wyld et al.

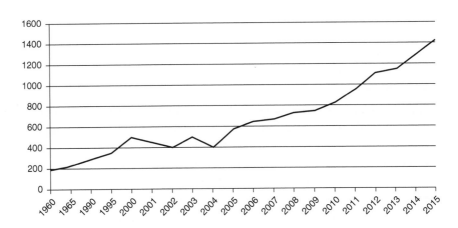

Figure 2.1. Number of U.K. Breweries, 1980–2015. Source: BBPA 2015; CAMRA 2015.

2010) and by the introduction of Progressive Beer Duty (PBD) to support smaller brewers, granting these businesses a lower tax levy than large brewers. The PBD boosted the growth of microbrewing throughout the country, shaping the size of new businesses, which tended to keep their production volumes low in order to take advantage of the tax break. Moreover, the most recent financial crisis hit large pubcos severely, forcing them to put large parts of their estates on the market and creating more opportunities for small breweries to acquire their own pubs (Preece 2016; Preece et al. 1999).

In contrast with the tremendous growth registered by microbreweries, the number of pubs in the United Kingdom declined significantly since the 1980s, decreasing from about 64,000 to less than 49,500 during the period 1990–2012 (British Beer and Pub Association 2013). This decline can be explained by a variety of causes and factors that affected the sector in the recent past and still affect British pubs today.

One of the main causes lies in the changes that occurred in the sector since the 1960s, which saw the progressive separation of pubs from breweries that traditionally owned them. In particular, the Beer Orders forced breweries to sell pubs at very attractive prices, and this led to the rise and enlargement of corporate pubcos dedicated to retail. From the early 1990s, these companies dominated the sector. Figures related to lease and tenancy holders exploded, bringing the vast majority of pubs under direct control of large national brewers and corporate pub chains (Pratten and Lovatt 2002). Conversely, the number of free houses (privately owned or family-managed pubs) decreased. "Tied pubs"—those that are tied to buy their beverages and other supplies from specific retailers, most frequently the pubco owning or leasing their premises—soon became the majority in the market, with pubcos controlling approximately 55% of all pubs in 2011.

The financial crisis brought heavy financial losses for some of the largest pubcos, which catalyzed significant disinvestment, ownership changes and several pub closures. In 2015, two- fifths of British pubs were owned by pubcos, two-fifths were free houses, and the rest were owned by breweries. Despite this rebalance in the market and the introduction of self-regulatory bodies to monitor the industry, some sources (Cabras 2011; Institute for Public Policy Research 2012) still indicate that tenants are struggling financially, with many generating a profit below minimum wage (All Party Parliamentary Save the Pub Group 2014).

Changes in the ownership structure also brought about changes in the marketing strategies pursued by pubs with regard to customers. Many pubs ceased their traditional beer-oriented vocation and started to develop into different types of businesses (e.g., gastropubs or European-style cafes, or the so-called theme pubs), which combine drink-retailing with a specific environmental setting (i.e., sophisticated premises, 1980s designed style etc.) (Lincoln 2006; Pratten 2003). Other examples include sports bars, which target customers by showing a wide range of sporting events (Pratten 2003).

A significant decrease in prices for food and alcoholic beverages from off-licenses and supermarkets has also had an impact on customers' choices and on the attractiveness of pub nights. More affordable prices provided by the off-license trade give incentives for people to drink at home rather than in public places (Pratten 2004). In addition, the growth of home entertainment has also contributed to making pub nights less attractive. Devices such as high-definition TVs and home-theatre sound systems have become progressively more affordable in the past 20 years, and the commercialization of video-game consoles that enable players to play in groups of two or more has provided significant opportunities for in-house gatherings. As a consequence, the average number of nights out among households has been progressively reduced and mainly pushed to the weekend (Cabras et al. 2012).

Methods and Data

In order to investigate the impact of microbreweries and pubs on British communities and societies, I present and investigate secondary data collected from several sources, including CAMRA, the Society of Independent Brewers (SIBA), and the Neighbourhood Statistics of the Office for National Statistics (ONS). In addition, I present information gathered from interviews I conducted with representatives of the brewing industry and of business organizations operating within the beer and pub sector and with residents from a number of local communities. The information was collected on various occasions as part of different research projects led by me between 2010 and 2015.

The analysis developed in this section has three main objectives: to evaluate the impact of small and medium businesses operating in the brewing sector within local supply chains; to investigate relationships among brewers and local organizations with regard to initiatives aimed at promoting beer; and to verify the potential of microbreweries with regard to preventing the decline of pubs, together with their essential functions in terms of facilitating social aggregation and engagement within local communities. The evidence gathered from interviews is not intended as a representative sample. Rather, the material is used to provide greater depth concerning several points related to the investigation of microbreweries within local supply chains

This section presents information extracted from the British Beer report prepared by me for SIBA (Small Independent Breweries Association 2015). Established in 1980 to represent the interests of the growing number of independent breweries in the United Kingdom, SIBA represents more than 825 craft and microbrewers—about 57% of all British breweries.

Data analyzed were gathered by means of a questionnaire survey, which comprised six sections aimed at gathering information such as members' locations, the quantity and types of beers brewed, their annual turnover and average prices to on-trade and off-trade customers, the level of employment generated, and members' plans for future expansion and development. The survey was officially launched online in November 2014, and data collection ended in January 2015. At the end of this exercise, 270 responses were selected for the analysis, accounting for 83.5% of the total responses received and for 34.3% of total memberships, meaning that about one out of three SIBA members took part in the survey.

According to responses, levels of beer production amounted to a cumulative total of 1.07 million hectoliters (about 0.91 million U.S. barrels). This equates to roughly 226 million pints produced by respondents and translates to approximately 665 million pints brewed by SIBA members. More than two-thirds of production was cask (68%), followed by bottled/canned beers (27%), and kegs (5%). However, in 2014, bottled beers represented a relatively small part of the overall production: nearly half of the respondents indicated that 10% or less of their productions were of bottled beers; almost one out of five breweries indicated no bottled-beer production at all, while less than 5% of surveyed breweries reported that bottled beers accounted for the majority of their brewed output.

More than 90% of surveyed members indicated that they regularly produced golden bitter/ale beers, followed by traditional bitter ales, stout/porters, and strong bitter India pale ales (more than two out of three members indicated that they brew these styles on regular basis). Conversely, only a handful of breweries said that they regularly brewed gluten-free and low-alcohol beer. Beer portfolios were also interesting: more than two-thirds of respondents indicated having more than four different brands regularly brewed at their premises, with a quarter indicating having at least seven different brands in regular production. Engagement with seasonal or one-off beers is also significant: almost all surveyed brewers brewed seasonal products in 2014, with only 23 breweries (about 8%) brewing no seasonal beers.

The small nature of breweries in relation to business activities is confirmed by the relatively low levels of annual turnover indicated by respondents. The majority of responses obtained are comprised in the income range of £50,000 to £250,000, but one of four breweries indicated an annual turnover for 2014 that was below £50,000 (about $70,000 U.S.) and only 10% of respondents reported an annual turnover above £1 million (about $1.4 million U.S.). In terms of employment, the total workforce captured by the survey comprised 1,549 staff employed, of which 1,125 were full-time. Three of four employees were men. About 43% of part-time employees worked between 10 and 20 hours per week, with another 26% working more than 20 hours. Figure 2.2 classifies employees by age ranges and residency: half of the employees surveyed were between 35 and 54 years old average; about one of three employees were younger than 34. Interestingly, the number of employees grouped in the oldest range (55 years or older) outnumbered those grouped among the youngest category (16–24 years old). The majority of workers lived in the same town or village as the brewery, with about two out of three employees living within five miles.

These data confirm the importance of breweries in terms of impact on local employment. In addition, the vast majority of breweries surveyed indicated their intention to expand their staff in the next twelve months, with three of four breweries planning to recruit two or more new employees. Overall, estimates for the next 12 months seem very positive: three out of four respondents expected an increase in annual turnover in 2015, with nearly one out of five forecasting growth above 25%.

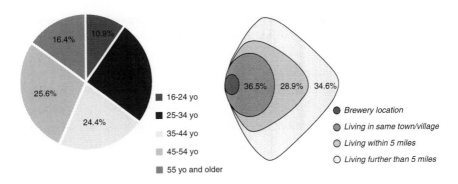

16.4% 10.9%
25.6%
24.4%

■ 16-24 yo
■ 25-34 yo
☐ 35-44 yo
▨ 45-54 yo
■ 55 yo and older

36.5% 28.9% 34.6%

● Brewery location
◉ Living in same town/village
◎ Living within 5 miles
○ Living further than 5 miles

Figure 2.2. Employment in Surveyed Breweries. Source: SIBA 2015 Annual Report.

Competitive Collaborations among Brewers and the Rise of Beer Festivals

The growth of microbreweries has undoubtedly increased the interest in beer and real ales in the United Kingdom. The microbrewing movement has seen a spike in the number of new businesses at almost the same time, often located just a few miles from each other, creating an interesting entrepreneurial environment in the industry. In addition, the support given by the intensive campaigns promoted by CAMRA has contributed significantly to the development and consolidation of the demand for British beers throughout the years. There are two interesting aspects to consider in this particular context: the way almost all small and microbrewers in United Kingdom tend to operate; and the increasing number of events, namely beer festivals, organized throughout the country.

I investigate these two aspects by using extracts from interviews that I and my research team conducted on a sample comprising eight small independent breweries and four representatives from industry organizations between 2012 and 2014 and from interviews conducted with the organizers of three major beer festivals organized in England in 2015. These interviews aimed to identify processes related to local economic development, to capture brewers' attitude toward competitors and major beer events, and to further explore issues affecting the industry.

> I wouldn't say I had any official training but I've been taught a thing or two by others in the business who have kindly given me there time. [A local

brewer] has helped me a lot and that was purely because I asked him something once and he came down and we have been best mates and worked closely together ever since.

Regarding training a lot of it is more from your own experiences. A lot of it is written down, but we get a lot of help from the people who provide the raw materials. They know a lot about hops for example a lot about malt and they can be asked. As well as that there a lot of people in the vicinity who have got a vast amount of experience of microbrewing that is, not the nationals, who you can ask.

The previous owners gave us some training and showed us how they did things. We helped them to brew a number of times. Meanwhile I did a lot of reading about brewing and I also took a university course. This reinforced my confidence about lots of things, it confirmed I was doing some of them right and that I had to improve in others that were not quite right.

These statements corroborate evidence provided by other studies (Cabras and Bamforth 2015; Cabras et al. 2012; Danson et al. 2015) about the presence of a sort of "collaborative competition" in the British microbrewing market. Rather than preserving their secret ingredients and techniques, microbrewers tend to create collaborative relationships with other breweries mostly located close by. These collaborations relate not only to technical aspects of the brewing process, but also embrace other aspects of the business. For instance, breweries periodically exchange beers with one another, enabling brewers to experiment and learn as well as exchange information and opportunities available in the on-trade market. The importance of this swap system is confirmed by brewers interviewed:

If [like us] you have a broad range of beers then you automatically tied up pubs with those beers, as they will want to have the same beers that compete in fares and markets. This is a virtuous circle as we can swap casks with other breweries and makes our associated pubs aware of their selections, and the same happen with our beers.

We ask [a brewery located in the same area] to swap their casks with ours so that they can be sold to their pub . . . if some customers will try it and they will think it is bad then [the brewery] will come back to us with feedback. This is very precious information that will be help us to develop.

We rely on other breweries to help us to provide that variety for the customers, so we absolutely need them to be there.

In addition, the collaborative–competitive environment in the sector appears to stimulate creativity and innovation in the sector. The relatively high number of regular and seasonal beers included in an average brewery portfolio, as demonstrated by the results provided in the previous section, may be justified by the vibrant and dynamic exchanges among businesses operating at a local level, added to the momentum gathered by the microbrewing movement overall. This situation seems to provide an incentive to brewers to experiment and try something new:

> Yeah we are not a mainstream brewer, we don't do boring straight down the line beers. . . . All the beers we do are fairly specialized, the stouts we do, the pales we do, all have a little something about them. We don't want to be boring and have a session bitter beer no we are not interested.
>
> We are probably in a very unique situation in which we can operate part-time, we can be recognized outside, we have different pubs to supply but at the same time we are not really paying ourselves so we can have some fun, money can be invested in new beers or for going to festivals.

Despite the increasing number of breweries, which are slowly saturating the British market, the majority of businesses approached seemed not very concerned about increasing competition. Instead, the brewers appeared very keen to develop new beers by introducing new ingredients or by bringing old recipes back from the past. Some examples are the Wallop, rested in aged bourbon or whisky casks, and Bad Kitty, a flourished vanilla porter, both brewed by Brasscastle Brewery in Malton (North Yorkshire). Another example is the resurgence of barley wines, of which the No. 9 produced by Coniston Brewery (Cumbria) is probably the most well known. In addition, strawberry, raspberry, and even cherry beers have become so popular that they are now the fastest-growing area of the U.K. beer market (Smithers 2012).

The broad range of variation and styles with regard to beer and ales has widened consumers' choice in Britain. Since the microbrewing movement gathered momentum, brewers tend to use public events such as beer festivals to showcase their beers, rather than for networking purposes. The number of these events in the United Kingdom has increased significantly since the early 2000s. By examining several sources available in the public domain and mainly provided by CAMRA, I estimated that in 2014 between 800 and 1,100 beer festivals were organized across the country. The figure comprises events supported by CAMRA as well as events organized independently, although the former represents the majority.

Beer festivals are usually set up and organized by local CAMRA branches, a total of 215 spread across the country (CAMRA 2016), with all the work done on voluntary basis. Frequently, beer festivals are associated with beer contests, mostly organized by SIBA, in which brewers have the opportunity to present their beers and compete to win titles at regional and subregional levels. The evolution of these events has been exponential with regard to both numbers of beers showcased and sold and level of attendance.

I examined this dramatic development by exploring the cases of festivals in Nottingham, Norwich, and York, interviewing some of the main organizers of the local beer festivals. The three events passed from being small, locally oriented events to very large ones able to attract thousands of people from all parts of the country and even from overseas.

In the case of Nottingham, the first festival was organized in 1975 and hosted by the local University of Nottingham. After a few years, the festival moved to a Victorian swimming pool, which was also used as an exhibition center. The pool was drained to make way for scaffoldings for storing casks and dispensing beers. Attendance increased from hundreds to thousands and organizers had to increase their effort. As described by Steve Greamsby, who took part to the organization since the very beginning:

> We did not have a lot of beers, what we use to do was to rent a van, drive and get as many beers we could get depending on the directions we drove. It was very difficult to get beers in those days, There was not really a lot of real ales at that time and I used to fetch beers with my car. . . . Then, at the end of 1980s we could not cope with the demand, the number of beers needed to increase.

The size of the festival and selection of beers continued to grow, as did levels of attendance. This situation attracted the attention of the local council, which proposed to use Nottingham Castle premises in 2008, located in the city center, to host the event. The move created some issues because of the heritage site used and the thousands visitors who would be drinking during the entire week. However, organizers and the local city council worked closely to find targeted solutions to secure a sustainable future for the event. Figures gathered from the most recent beer festival, in 2014, indicate that more than 1,000 beers were showcased, with an estimated attendance above 25,000 during the four days scheduled.

As in Nottingham, beer festivals held at Norwich and York have evolved significantly since they were first launched in late 1970s. At Norwich, the event has always been organized at St. Andrew's & Blackfriars' Halls (now referred to as "The Halls"), close to the ancient Lincoln Cathedral. Initially, the event was held over weekends, but then the time span increased to four days. Ticket prices differ in relation to days, with Fridays and Saturdays more expensive to attend. The numbers of beers and ciders showcased are now about 200 and 40, respectively, a significant growth since the 40 beers available during the initial years. While the attendance passed from a few hundred to thousands, peaking at about 5,000 tickets sold in 2014, the premises never changed, providing a sense of tradition to the event.

At York, however, the beer festival evolved in a more significant manner. The very first events were organized in small premises, which allowed for only 300 people, forcing organizers to apply a one-in/one-out policy for health and safety reasons. In the mid-1980s, the festival moved to a number of buildings across town; while these moves increased capacity, the level of attendance tended to remain around an average of 2,000 people during the three days scheduled. The growing issues related to beer storage and distribution, together with restrictions imposed by closed premises, pushed organizers to find alternative solutions. In 2008, the local city council proposed to move the festival to a field relatively close to the famous York Racecourses, known as the Knavesmire, and the festival was rebranded as the Knavesmire Festival. Attendance passed from about 4,000 in 2008 (three-day event) to above 9,000 in 2014 (four-day event). The most recent event, held in 2015, showcased about 450 beers and over 100 ciders.

The Significance of Pubs for Local Communities

Several studies (Cabras 2011, 2016; Cabras and Bosworth 2014; Cabras and Reggiani 2010; Mount and Cabras 2015) have demonstrated the crucial role played by pubs in fostering and enhancing a sense of community and social cohesion within local areas. *Community cohesion* is defined as the relationships and activities that make residents feel a sense of belonging to a given community, while social cohesion is the level of cohesiveness among different components forming a social context (e.g., ethnic and/or religious groups, census, etc). I have also demonstrated the significance of pubs in enhancing the level of social capital at a local level, with social capital defined as the whole of networking relationships and ties and human resources endowment in a given area.

As part of my various investigations, I conducted a large number of interviews with pub owners and managers, pubgoers and residents across the United Kingdom conducted between 2009 and 2013. This section presents some of the findings gathered from these interviews, with the objective of providing an overview of the role pubs play within local communities, including initiatives taken to rescue some of them from closure and the potential of the microbrewing movement with regard to preventing the decline of pubs.

The change in the ownership structure, with the rise of pubcos, appeared to have had a significant impact with regard to the level of survivability of pubs in the market since the introduction of the Beer Orders. The difficulties related to pub rental are confirmed by a tenant interviewed by me in April 2009:

> The company lets at a very competitive price in the first year, but then everything changes in the second year. They [the pubco] increase the rent as soon as they see the profits the pub does. If you add other costs, taxes etc. you realize that running the pub is not a way to make a living and, usually, in three years you are out of business!

This situation forced many tenants and managers to attract more custom from nonlocals and passersby to be economically and financially sustainable and to widen their business purposes. This reinforces the view suggested by Lincoln (2006), who indicated that business diversification for pubs located in rural and remote areas (such as supplying food and accommodation) was a valid solution for preserving the existence of these places. However, while these strategies may increase business perspectives for pubs, they also appear to hinder the relationship between pubs' managers/owners and their villagers and local customers in a significant manner. A pub manager interviewed by me states:

> The locals feel a lot more strongly about their pub, and feel as well that they should be given special treatment because they're local . . . but it [the pub] wouldn't survive without passing trade and people travelling just to come here as well.

These words are somehow reflected in a number of comments obtained from villagers and local residents extracted from the same sample, who expressed their views with regard to some of the pubs surveyed:

> The pub has changed so many tenants that it is almost impossible make friendship or even chat with them.
>
> The pub in this village closed because nobody liked the manager, he simply didn't understand our expectations.
>
> We [the locals] are the customers here . . . this pub can survive only with our support.

In some cases, pubs were so essential for local communities that residents joined forces and created cooperatives with the objective to purchase pubs on the brink of closure. This movement started in 2003, with the creation of the Old Crown Cooperative pub in Hesket Newmarket, a tiny village in Northern England with about 300 residents. A local committee was formed for promoting the cooperative, obtaining some financial support from the public sector and raising other funds through shares, whose price was fixed at £1,500 each. None of the shareholders was allowed to buy more than one share, although groups of individuals could join together to buy one share only. Julian Ross, the main promoter of the initiative at that time, explained to me:

> We wanted to have an egalitarian structure, so nobody can own more than one share. It didn't matter how wealthy you were, or how modest your means were: everybody had the same amount of say, but some people could not afford a share so they grouped together and formed little syndicates, and now there are several groups who have got a share between them!

After purchasing the pub, cooperative shareholders opted to lease it out rather than trying to run it themselves. The lease was structured in a way as to preserve the pub according to the cooperative's intents. In particular, the contract obliges the lessee to purchase the majority of goods from local suppliers and to consult with the cooperative before making any structural change to the building. This lease model, first implemented on a three-year projection, is still in use at Hesket Newmarket and has been adopted as a sort of template for similar initiatives across the country. In 2013, there were 22 cooperative pubs in the United Kingdom (The Plunkett Foundation, 2014).

The Role of Microbreweries in Preventing the Decline of Pubs

The impressive growth in the number of registered microbreweries since the early 2000s and the implications related to signs of saturation in the domestic beer market raise important questions about how the domestic demand will be able to absorb the supply, rather than which fiscal policy best supports this growth.

As a result, an increasing number of breweries have started to purchase pubs (and/or directly operate them under lease contracts) and use them as outlets. I investigated the pattern of microbreweries' purchasing pubs while working on SIBA's 2015 annual report. The data are also explored with regard to information gathered from a, sample of eight small independent breweries and four representatives from industry organizations between 2012 and 2014, discussed in part already in this chapter.

Findings from the SIBA 2015 annual report indicate a total of 556 pubs either owned (333 freeholds) or leased/tenanted (223) operated by the 270 breweries surveyed in the study, with 24 new pubs bought or taken during 2014. Of these breweries, 46 owned at least one pub, while 24 owned more than two pubs, and 5 even owned more than ten pubs. Freehold ownership was the preferred option in terms of acquiring control of a pub, with many indicating the intention to purchase at least one pub in the next 12 months.

Brewers confirmed that dealing with pubs was an essential part of their business. Since most of their ales were supplied to and sold by pubs, breweries could not really operate without dealing with these places. According to the majority of interviewees, owning one or more pubs appeared to be the next step in the path toward development, although some responders did not contemplate this option:

> Well, now that the Beer Orders have been revolted almost entirely there is nothing to stop brewers buying pubs, building up their estates in a sort of tying model . . . beer is a perishable product too, so selling it locally, the closest possible, where it is produced, makes a lot of sense.
>
> Very early [this year] on I went into partnership with [a local pub] and more recently I have bought [another local pub]. Since taking over these pubs I'd say that business has been successful. I have had to invest some money into improving the pubs and making them more attractive to a wider audience and not just your traditional old school drinkers but yeah business has been very good despite the market.
>
> No we haven't got a pub. But we do have a function and events area in the brewery here which we do have a license for. That was within our business plan not to have a pub but to have an events area here.

I tried to understand whether breweries could actually provide a means to halt the decline of pubs by purchasing and using them as retail outlets. A number of interviewees saw this as a possible and sustainable solution, while others tended to disagree, mainly because of factors related to financial sustainability. Breweries appeared more likely to purchase pubs in cities and town centers, as these locations offer better opportunities to attract customers. Pubs operating in the countryside are less attractive for breweries because of a number of factors, which include logistical and financial aspects. Andrew Barker, speaking in relation to York Brewery (which owns three pubs in the center of York and uses them as retail points, together with the main pub and shop attached to its premises), stated:

> York is a brand itself—(the) pubs managed by York Brewery are all within the city centre as it is better for us, we don't think to expand in rural areas as it won't be sustainable to buy pubs there now. I don't think it's feasible commercially, we need to sell beer in order to survive and there are not enough people [in rural areas] for us to make a commercial return.

These views were shared by two brewery directors based in Northern England:

> Most of the breweries I know would look for urban pubs rather than rural. . . . When you work in a village you may expect any individual in the village or passing through the village to stop at your door and drink . . . more than once per week, this is simply not sustainable.
>
> The decline of pubs in rural areas is a response to social habits, people do not see value to drive to a pub to drink, same to walking to a pub to drink, other than on an occasional basis, which is not often enough to make a pub valuable.

Discussion and Conclusion

The recent resurgence of microbreweries in the United Kingdom is due to a number of economic and social factors. Since the postwar period, the British brewing industry resembled the situation of the industry at a global level, with high levels of concentration and strong entry barriers, which may suggest a low number of new entrants in the market at least in the short term (see Boone et al. 2000; Carroll 1985; Carroll and Swaminathan 2000). However, starting in the 1970s, the number of small and medium businesses entering the market progressively increased, with hundreds of micro and craft breweries occupying the niche segments left from larger breweries.

Carroll (1985) explains market concentration in mature markets usually characterized by a finite set of heterogeneous resources by identifying firms as "generalists" (firms that move toward by acquiring larger segments after having established themselves in their respective regions); and "specialists" (firms that focus on niche production and remain at the periphery of the market). While generalist firms tend to compete with each other to acquire and control larger market segments, spreading the geographic reach of their actions; specialist firms tend to narrow their targets, mostly developing at a regional scale, remaining small and adapting themselves to the amount of resources available in their respective areas of operations. Hence, when resources are sufficient to sustain a specialist segment, the market can be said to be "partitioned," in that it appears that generalist and specialist firms do not compete because they depend on different parts of the resource base (Cabras and Bamforth 2015; Carroll 1985). Carroll and Swaminathan (1992) used the American brewing industry to illustrate the resource-partitioning model, indicating as specialists those organizational forms associated with the microbrewery movement such as microbreweries, brewpubs, and contract brewers.

This example, although with some small differences, can also be applied to the British case. Higher levels of concentration in the brewing industry and low levels of product diversification may have then prepared the terrain for the rise of microbreweries. Besides, a shift in customers' choice and taste, supported by the restless campaigning promoted by CAMRA and other organizations, created the consumer base for a niche market in which specialists firms—microbreweries in this case—had enormous possibilities to expand. High-technology and cheaper equipment provided more cost-effective solutions to new entrepreneurs, aside from the introduction of government policies and regulation that supported these businesses. A favorable context and a supportive institutional environment are likely to have fostered higher organizational founding rates in a mature market such as the British brewing market. In particular, financial incentives available at national and local levels encouraged entrepreneurial activity in the industry, often with the objectives of revitalizing economies in crisis or employment in depressed areas (Bamforth and Cabras 2016).

The rise of microbreweries has had and still has important implications for the British beer and pub industry. As shown by figures presented in this chapter, the contribution provided by microbreweries and small breweries to local economies is significant in terms of employment generated, which can be translated into skills and training for younger workers, producing positive outcomes for local supply chains. The market environment created by new brewers, based on collaborative–competitive relationships, seems to provide an incubator for creativity and innovation with regard to brewing processes and receipts. Brewers are stimulated to experiment, to try new things, and the outcomes of this process benefit the final consumers, who enjoy a greater selection of beer and ales. Forms of mutual exchange and support, such as the swap system, facilitate the distribution of beers toward the off-trade and on-trade market. In particular, breweries use pubs and beer festival to supply and showcase their beers, respectively. This situation generates multiple benefits for the operators in the market and also has a number of social implications.

With regard to pubs, the recent decline experienced by these businesses has affected many communities in the country, which in many cases lost their only places for social aggregation and engagement. The decline of pubs has also resulted in the vanishing of many opportunities associated with community cohesion and economic development, since these businesses work as incubators and hubs for communal initiatives and are frequently used as showcases and selling centers for local businesses. For these reasons, more breweries in need of supplying their beers may increase the chances for these pubs to survive. In addition, evidence from this chapter demonstrates that many small breweries and microbreweries are keen to purchase pubs and to use them as their exclusive outlets. Aside from communal initiatives, such cooperatively owned pubs and microbreweries represent another viable solution to rescue pubs from unnecessary closure.

The rise in the number of beer festivals across the United Kingdom is further proof of the vibrant environment created by the microbrewing movement. Breweries are keen to engage in such events, which enable them to introduce new brands and beers to consumers, dealing with them outside conventional premises such as retail shops or pubs. Conversely, consumers are increasingly attracted to these events by the variety of beers, ales, and ciders available at affordable prices and by the opportunity to taste different styles and types of products in one place. This context shrinks the distance between brewers and consumers, facilitating the diffusion of different beers and increasing the appreciation for product variety. Beer festivals can help to foster and enhance consumers' level of knowledge with regard to the product, as well as educating consumers about the main characteristics and qualities of different beers, many of which are locally brewed (Bamforth and Cabras 2016).

In conclusion, the growth of microbreweries in the United Kingdom demonstrates how the revival and redevelopment of a traditional industry can generate multiple positive outcomes not only for the businesses operating in the industry, but also for those operating in proximity to it and for local economies and communities in general. The wider range of beers available enables consumers to develop new tastes and experience new flavors than they could just a few years ago. Beer festivals facilitate relationships and exchanges among brewers and between brewers and consumers. In this context, consumers can be educated in beer appreciation, entering into a process of sophistication in which the overall quality of beers and ales, other than variety in styles, is enhanced and exalted. In substance, a pint of success for everyone!

REFERENCES

All Party Parliamentary Save the Pub Group. 2014. *London Economics 'Research' as Fundamentally Flawed, Biased and a Suspicious Waste of £40K of Taxpayers' Money.* London: APPSTP.

Bamforth, Charles, W., and Ignazio Cabras. 2016. "Interesting Times: Changes in Brewing." In *Brewing, Beer, and Pubs: A Global Perspective*, edited by I. Cabras, D. Higgins, and D. Preece, 15–33. London: Palgrave Macmillan.

Boone, Christophe, Bröcher Vera, and Glenn R. Carroll. 2000. "Custom Service: Application and Tests of Resource-Partitioning Theory among Dutch Auditing Firms from 1896 to 1992." *Organization Studies* 21 (2): 355–381.

British Beer and Pub Association. 2013. *2013 Statistical Handbook.* London: BBPA.

———. 2015. *2015 Statistical Handbook.* London: BBPA.

Cabras, Ignazio. 2011. "Industrial and Provident Societies and Village Pubs: Exploring Community Cohesion in Rural Britain." *Environment and Planning A* 43 (10): 2435–2451.

———. 2016. "'Pillars of the Community': Pubs and Publicans in Rural Ireland." In *Brewing, Beer and Pubs: A Global Perspective*, edited by I. Cabras, D. Higgins, and D. Preece, 282–302. London: Palgrave Macmillan.

Cabras, Ignazio, and Charles W. Bamforth. 2015. "From Reviving Tradition to Fostering Innovation and Changing Marketing: The Evolution of Microbrewing in the UK and US, 1980–2012." *Business History* 58 (5): 625–646.

Cabras, Ignazio, and Gary Bosworth. 2014. "Embedded Models of Rural Entrepreneurship: The Case of Pubs in Cumbria, North West of England." *Local Economy* 29 (6/7): 598–616.

Cabras, Ignazio, Jesus Canduela, and Robert Raeside. 2012. "The Relation of Village and Rural Pubs with Community Life and People's Well-Being in Great Britain." *German Journal of Agricultural Economics* 61 (4): 265–274.

Cabras, Ignazio, and Carlo Reggiani. 2010. "Village Pubs As a Social Propellant in Rural Areas: An Econometric Study." *Journal of Environmental Planning and Management* 53 (7): 947–962.

Campaign for Real Ale (CAMRA). 2015, September 10. "Brewery Boom Hat Trick as British Brewing Grows by 10% for Third Consecutive Year." http://www.camra.org.uk/news/-/asset_publisher/1dUgQCmQMoVC/content/brewery-boom-hat-trick-as-british-brewing-grows-by-10-for-third-consecutive-year.

———. 2016. "CAMRA Near You." Accessed September 10, http://www.camra.org.uk/camra-near-you.

Carroll, Glenn R. 1985. "Concentration and Specialization: Dynamics of Niche Width in Populations of Organizations." *American Journal of Sociology* 90: 1261–1283.

Carroll, Glenn R., and Anand Swaminathan. 1992. "The Organizational Ecology of Strategic Groups in the American Brewing Industry from 1975 to 1990." *Industrial and Corporate Change* 1 (1): 65–97.

———. 2000. "Why the Microbrewery Movement? Organizational Dynamics of Resource Partitioning in the US Brewing Industry." *American Journal of Sociology* 106 (3): 715–762.

Danson, Mike, Laura Galloway, Ignazio Cabras, and Christina Beatty. 2015. "Microbrewing and Entrepreneurship: The Origins, Development, and Integration of Real Ale Breweries in the UK." *International Journal of Entrepreneurship and Innovation* 16 (2): 135–144.

Institute for Public Policy Research. 2012. "Pubs and Places: The Social Value of Community Pubs." London: IPPR.

Knowles, Tim, and David Egan. 2002. "The Changing Structure of UK Brewing and Pub Retailing." *International Journal of Contemporary Hospitality Management* 14 (2): 65–71.

Lincoln, Guy. 2006. "Diversification in Rural Pubs: A Strategy for Survival and Community Value?" *International Journal of Entrepreneurship and Small Business* 3 (3/4): 329–347.

Mason, Colin M., and K. N. McNally. 1997. "Market Change, Distribution, and New Firm Formation and Growth: The Case of Real-Ale Breweries in the United Kingdom." *Environment and Planning A* 29 (2): 405–417.

Moore, Michael, Neil Reid, and Ralph B. McLaughlin. 2016. "The Locational Determinants of Microbreweries and Brewpubs in the United States." In *Brewing, Beer and Pubs: A Global Perspective*, edited by I. Cabras, D. Higgins, and D. Preece, 182–204. London: Palgrave Macmillan.

Mount, Matthew, and Ignazio Cabras. 2015. "Community Cohesion and Village Pubs in Northern England: An Econometric Study." *Regional Studies* 50 (7): 1203–1216.

The Plunkett Foundation. 2014. *Community Shops: A Better Form of Business.* Woodstook, UK: The Plunkett Foundation.

Pratten, John Douglas. 2003. "The Changing Nature of the British Pub." *British Food Journal* 105 (4/5): 252–262.

———. 2004. "Examining the Possible Causes of Business Failure in British Public Houses." *International Journal of Contemporary Hospitality Management* 16 (4): 246–252.

———. 2007. "The Development of the Modern UK Public House—Part 1: The Traditional British Public House of the Twentieth Century." *International Journal of Contemporary Hospitality Management* 19 (4): 335–342.

Pratten, John Douglas, and Chris Lovatt. 2002. "Can the Rural Pub Survive? A Challenge for Management or a Lost Cause?" *Management Research News* 25 (1): 60–72.

Preece, David. 2016. "Turbulence in UK Public House Retailing: Ramifications and Responses." In *Brewing, Beer and Pubs: A Global Perspective*, edited by I. Cabras, D. Higgins, and D. Preece, 247–265. London: Palgrave Macmillan.

Preece, David, Gordon Steven, and Valerie Steven. 1999. *Work, Change and Competition: Managing for Bass.* London: Routledge.

Small Independent Breweries Association. 2015. "British Beer: A Report on the 2015 Members. Survey of the Society of Independent Brewers." Burton-on-Trent, UK: SIBA.

Smithers, Rebecca. 2012, July 29. "Flavoured Beers See Surge in Popularity." *The Guardian.* https://www.theguardian.com/lifeandstyle/2012/jul/29/flavoured-beers-popularity-food-pairing.

Swaminathan, Anand. 1998. "Entry into New Market Segments in Mature Industries: Endogenous and Exogenous Segmentation in the US Brewing Industry." *Strategic Management Journal* 19: 389–404.

Tremblay, Victor J., and Carol Horton Tremblay. 2005. *The US Brewing Industry: Data and Economic Analysis.* Cambridge, MA: MIT Press.

Wyld, John, Geoff Pugh, and David Tyrrall. 2010. "Evaluating the Impact of Progressive Beer Duty on Small Breweries: A Case Study of Tax Breaks to Promote SMEs." *Environment and Planning C: Government and Policy* 28 (1): 225–240.

CHAPTER 3

The Rationalization of Craft Beer from Medieval Monks to Modern Microbrewers

A Weberian Analysis

MICHAEL A. ELLIOTT

Introduction

The craft beer "revolution" is often depicted as a triumphant tale of American ingenuity and entrepreneurial success, where grassroots enthusiasts bucked the trend of bland, mass-produced beer and created a unique and authentic product and transformed modern brewing culture in the process (Hindy 2014; Rao 2009). Traditionally, beer is seen as an everyman's drink in the United States. In other words, it is an inexpensive beverage consumed by "regular" people in casual settings like the local bar, baseball games, or the backyard after mowing the lawn. Major commercial brands like Budweiser, Coors, and Miller tend to specialize in a product that suits this image and is easy on the palate—light-bodied in taste, pale in color, and sold in bulk. Wine, on the other hand, is practiced like a kind of haute couture—consumed (nay, discriminately appreciated) by more "sophisticated" people in more formal settings who have access to a wide variety of styles (some of them very rare) that can be many times more expensive than beer.

The explosion of craft beer in recent decades, however, has transformed the image of the beer drinker. For starters, craft breweries are much smaller, more numerous, and tend to appeal to localized and specialized markets (Carroll and Swaminathan 2000), compared to the handful of "commercial" breweries that produce in mass quantities for a nationwide market.[1] What is more, the craft beer industry produces a vast array of styles reflecting Old World traditions and New World innovations that, much like wine, appeal to various palates and can be appreciated in rather discriminating ways (see Bernstein 2013, Jackson 2000, Mosher 2009, Oliver 2003). As a result, craft beer is often recognized as a hip, sophisticated alternative to its mass-produced competition.

What is less recognized by the average consumer, or by scholars for that matter, is that many aspects of the production of craft beer are exceedingly sophisticated. From the recent creation of degrees in the science of brewing and the ever-expanding number of beer styles to the widespread use of specialized ingredients, quantitative metrics, and various quality control techniques, craft brewing exhibits what sociologist Max Weber would characterize as a high degree of *rationalization*. While Weber never precisely defined this term, it became a central component of his argument in *The Protestant Ethic and the Spirit of Capitalism* (1904/2009) and referred to an unusually disciplined and methodical organization of life conduct that sought to tame and redirect spontaneous human desires (the *status naturae*) based on a set of values (116–117). Here, Weber famously argued that doctrinal changes during the Protestant Reformation encouraged this kind of "rational asceticism" that, when applied to economics, set loose a new spirit of capitalism oriented toward frugality, reliable/ mass production, steady profits, and continual reinvestment (Collins 1998). Later, Weber associated rationalization with increasing formalization, standardization, systematization, calculation, and the like, which permeated Western culture and transformed key institutions such as science, law, education, and music, as well as religion and capitalism (Weber 1978; 1920/2009).

In this chapter, I explore how the production of craft beer is thoroughly rationalized and involves a surprising amount of technical expertise and scientific standardization that have become hallmarks of the industry. Borrowing Weber's insights, I argue that the widespread application of sophisticated brewing techniques is not merely about selling a commodity and making money, per se, but rather reflects an abiding desire to systematically perfect this "craft" and signal to others that one is a legitimate brewer with the necessary expertise. At the same time, I highlight how the rational organization of craft brewing can also have some irrational consequences, such as consumer confusion and intimidation, as well as disenchantment among professionalized taste testers. Finally, building on *The Protestant Ethic*, I describe how, in small but significant ways, the rationalization of modern brewing can be traced all the way back to the Middle Ages and the religious organization of monastic communities, qualifying medieval monks as the first "revolutionaries" of modern beer brewing.

The Rationalization of Craft Beer

If you look closely at the label on a bottle of craft beer, or its packaging, it contains a surprising amount of information. In general, a beer label is required by federal regulations to include only brand name, class and type designation (e.g., beer, ale, or lager), name and address of brewer or bottler, net contents (e.g., ounces), and a health warning statement about alcohol consumption.[2] However, it is not uncommon for a craft beer label to also specify how bitter the beer is (in number of international bittering units [IBUs]), how dense it is (via an original gravity [OG] value), how strong it is (as percent alcohol by volume [ABV]), how fresh it is (depending on the bottling or expiration dates), what ingredients were used (i.e., the specific kind of malt, hops, or yeast), more specific type or style designations (e.g., amber ale, brown ale, black ale, pale ale, India pale ale), and any accolades or awards that have been garnered. No doubt, a dedicated craft beer drinker is used to seeing this kind of information, but, unless you have sufficient knowledge of the brewing process itself, some of it is rather cryptic. What does an OG value indicate, for example? Why do brewers highlight the use of a Belgian-style yeast strain? What's the difference between a German pils and a Czech pilsner? One wonders whether the average craft beer consumer is expected to understand all this!

Given that big commercial brands like Budweiser, Heineken, and Corona exclude much of this information, it probably is not required to sell beer. Indeed, I argue that all this technical information is more than just a marketing scheme. If beer was merely an everyman's drink, it would be odd to target this demographic by specifying quantitative metrics, specialized ingredients, and obscure categorical styles. But, like any modern endeavor that seeks to improve and progress, the surest and most legitimate means are those that involve the application of rationalized techniques (Ellul 1980; Meyer et al. 1987); to make the best beer, you should employ systematic, formalized, and efficient methods, calculate and measure your progress, and produce a product that is consistent and predictable (Ritzer 2013). Thus, technical information on a craft beer label looks impressive because it signals to the consumer a particular kind of brewing expertise that is perceived as more authentic and sophisticated than big commercial brewing. Craft beer fans expect to see what kind of hops are used in an Imperial pale ale, for example, and how many IBUs are registered as a result. In addition, this information may also signal to fellow brewers that the requisite degree of technical sophistication has been applied to the craft. Below, I describe some of this technical information and how it represents an effort to progressively master the art of beer brewing, above and beyond purely profit-making concerns.

Interestingly, the standard numerical indicators (or metrics) on a craft beer label were not invented by craft brewers, nor were they intended for the craft beer consumer; they were designed as "quality control" measures by scientific experts in a laboratory environment. In addition, I also highlight how these metrics and other idiosyncratic information on a beer label are just the tip of the iceberg, and point to a highly rationalized industry that is thoroughly scientific and standardized.

Quality Control Metrics

If you're a craft beer fan, you probably have enjoyed (or at least tasted) a pale ale. This has become a standard style in the American craft beer repertoire. One of the defining characteristics of this style is a distinct bitterness or tanginess, derived from the copious addition of hops to the brew. If you enjoy a stronger and bitterer version, you are probably well acquainted with India pale ales (IPAs), or the even stronger and bitterer double India pale ale (DIPA). Regardless, you may have noticed that the label often includes an IBU value, which indicates the level of bitterness in your beer; the higher the number, the bitterer the beer. IBU is a universal standard for measuring bitterness in beer (see Glossary). High-IBU or "hoppy" styles of beer have become increasingly popular in the United States in recent years. Economist Bart Watson of the Brewer's Association reports that IPAs, for example, accounted for less than 8% of craft beer sales in 2008 but that rose to 27.4% by August 2015. Moreover, given that the total volume of craft beer sales has grown considerably during this period, the size of the IPA category actually grew 10 times from 2008 to 2015. "If anything, these numbers probably underestimate the effect IPAs have had on growth, since in addition to IPAs, we've seen a trend toward the IPA-ification of everything: hoppy wheats, hoppy browns, SMASH (single malt and single hop) beers, and more. American brewers seem determined to continually put hops where no hops have gone before" (Watson 2015).

The IBU was developed by brewing scientists in the 1950s and 1960s to systematically monitor bitterness levels during the brewing process and to help maintain a consistent product across beer styles. Thus, a typical American pale ale should range from 35 to 40 IBUs (Oliver 2012, 490). While it has become a "hip" reference of potency and bitterness for particular styles (especially for IPAs and DIPAs), the IBU was never intended as a guide for the general public; it is a measure of particular chemical properties produced under controlled laboratory conditions and does not accurately indicate (by itself) how bitter the beer will taste to the average consumer. "The usefulness of the IBU to the beer consumer is highly debatable. Once the beer leaves the laboratory context, many non-iso alpha acid factors, including other hop components, roast character, carbonation, water chemistry, and residual sugar, may exert such influence as to make the IBU an entirely unreliable indicator of actual perceived bitterness" (Oliver 2012, 490–491).

Perhaps the most familiar number on a beer label (craft or otherwise) refers to the alcohol content. This is typically reported as a percentage of the total volume of beer (percent ABV), although in the United States it was predominantly reported as a percentage of the total weight (percent ABW) until recently (see Glossary). The actual process of calculating the alcoholic strength of beer is quite complicated but, once again, it is done primarily for quality control purposes to ensure consistency of style, as well as to comply with federal regulations. According to the Brewers Association's *Beer Style Guidelines* (2014), an American-style barley wine ale is one of the more potent styles and should range from 8.5% to 12.2% ABV. Whereas, an American-style lager is on the lower end, and should range from 4.1% to 5.1% ABV.

An important measurement for determining the *future* alcohol content of a batch of beer is original gravity (OG), which is one of the more obscure numbers appearing on a craft beer label (see Glossary). An American-style barley wine ale, for example, should have an OG between 1.090 and 1.120, while an American-style lager should range between 1.040 and 1.048 (Brewers Association 2014). Alternatively, this value can be expressed in terms of degrees Plato and is equal to roughly one-fourth of the original gravity (Oliver 2012, 630) (see Glossary). Thus, barley wine should range between 21.6 and 28° Plato, and the lager between 10 and 11.9° Plato (Brewers Association 2014). For the brewer, measuring and maintaining a consistent original gravity or degrees Plato from batch to batch is another way to exert systematic control over the quality and consistency of the beer. How these particular metrics are useful, or even comprehensible, to the average craft beer consumer is unclear. I would argue that their inclusion on the label is not intended to be directly useful or comprehensible to the consumer. Rather, they highlight a technical sophistication that accords value and authenticity to the brewer and the product.

Progressive Experimentation

No doubt, one of the allures of craft beer is the number of different styles that are produced by this industry. Big commercial beers, especially in the United States, tend to be variations around a single style—the pale lager or pilsner. By contrast, the array of styles in a typical craft beer aisle is dizzying. The latest edition of the Brewers Association's *Beer Style Guidelines* (2014), for example, summarizes the details of 141 styles of beer. To name just a few, there are strong ales, old ales, Scotch ales, and sour ales. There are doppelbocks, eisbocks, and gose beers. The Belgians make a dubble, a tripel, and a quadrupel. There are beers with fruit, coffee, chocolate, pumpkin, or spices and some that are gluten-free. Even pilsners are known for several distinct styles.

In general, a pilsner is clear, crisp, and pale gold in color with a more pronounced hop bitterness than pale lagers. Since their introduction in the mid-nineteenth century, they have become the dominant style of beer around the world. Czech (or Bohemian) pilsners are considered the original style and were introduced in 1842 in Pilsen, Czech Republic—hence the name "pilsner." They tend to be slightly darker in color (i.e., more golden) with a distinct floral bitterness from the use of indigenous saaz hops, have malty overtones, and are well carbonated, producing a dense head of white foam. The German pilsner (or "pils" for short) is a very close relative but tends to be lighter in color (more straw-like than golden), slightly more bitter, utilizes indigenous "noble" hops (e.g., spalt, tettnang, hallertau), and has a drier, less malty character than Czech pilsners (Oliver 2012, 651–652; Papazian 2003, 143–144). Aside from the brewers themselves or consumers with a particularly fine-tuned palette, the differences between the two may be imperceptible. Nonetheless, they are recognized by craft brewers as qualitatively distinct styles and are proudly produced and labeled as such.

In the end, whether all the different craft beer styles were invented merely for marketing and profit-making purposes is highly debatable. Clearly, the top-selling commercial brands are very successful at specializing in just one style or a couple of styles. In contrast, a hallmark of the U.S. craft beer industry is a relentless experimentation with styles; American craft brewers are endlessly modifying or resurrecting old styles or inventing new styles and categorizations (Hindy 2014). To be sure, this implies a good deal of skill and creativity. But it also implies an understanding that this skill should be applied in a continuously progressive manner, developing more and varied beers that, *in toto*, are virtually impossible for the average consumer to keep up with, let alone consume. While this provides the consumer with lots of choices, it can also be a little intimidating and overwhelming for the uninitiated. A simple Internet search of "craft beer for beginners" reveals many user guides for how to dive in and navigate the increasingly complex maze of craft beer styles. Ironically, a similar search also reveals extensive commentary on the so-called beer snob that bears little resemblance to the everyman image that is traditionally associated with beer drinkers.[3]

Scientization and Professionalization

In the world of modern beer brewing, what the average consumer sees on a craft beer label is just the tip of the iceberg. Today, the production of craft beer involves a surprising amount of scientific and technical information that, in many ways, requires very specialized knowledge and training. For starters, to produce and distribute beer in relatively large quantities, a craft brewer will likely need to acquire and operate large, industrial equipment, such as mash tuns (to mix hot water with malted grain to produce beer wort), lauter tuns (to filter out the grains from the wort), kettles (to boil the beer wort with hops), heat exchangers (to cool the wort), and tanks (to ferment and store the beer), as well as bottling, labeling, and kegging equipment. Thus, some mechanical or engineering skill is rather important, in addition to the beer-making skill required to manage the ingredients and produce a good-tasting product.

Beer does not have to be a high-tech product, however. People have brewed beer for thousands of years. It requires only three basic ingredients—water, grain, and yeast (though different spices, aromatics, and sweeteners can also be added)—and some basic equipment, such as kilns, kettles, and storage vessels of differing materials.[4] But by the ninth century, monastic communities in Europe had organized this craft in a notably rational manner and produced beer in large quantities (described below). In the Late Middle Ages and the Renaissance, the center of beer production had shifted to urban centers, where brewing became increasingly commercialized and regulated (Unger 2004). By the nineteenth century, the application of science and industrial techniques began to transform beer making into a highly specialized endeavor. For example, the Research and Teaching Institute for Brewing in Berlin (VLB) was founded in 1883 to combine the resources of the brewing industry, the scientific community, and the German state to further research, teaching, and practical brewery training (Oliver 2012, 169, 817–818). Today, in cooperation with the Technical University in Berlin, VLB offers a three-year Graduate Brewmaster degree, a Bachelor and Master of Science in Brewing and Beverage Technology, and a doctorate in Engineering Sciences.[5] Similarly, the German brewery at Weihenstephan began to offer formal academic training even earlier in the nineteenth century and now offers similar degrees in brewing and beverage technology in cooperation with the School of Life Sciences at the Technical University in Munich.[6] In the United States, aspiring craft brewers can also pursue university training in the field of brewing science and technology, as well as business operations tailored to this particular industry, in an increasing number of institutions around the country.[7] Oregon State's four-year degree in fermentation science, for example, includes courses on fermentation microbiology, food chemistry, and sensory evaluation.[8]

Outside the university setting, national associations "professionalize" the work of brewers and brewing scientists in various ways, not unlike the American Sociological Association (ASA) does for the work of sociologists. The Master Brewers Association of the Americas (MBAA), for example, was founded in 1887 and describes itself as a "non-profit (501 C3) professional, scientific organization dedicated to advance, support, and encourage scientific research into brewing malt beverages and related industries and to make that research available to the public through conventions, discussion groups, journals, publications and seminars."[9] Thus, like the ASA, they have an annual conference that is preceded by a call for papers, abstract submissions, and formal registration, while the conference itself is organized into topical sessions with associated presenters. In addition to the annual conference, members can access job listings, continuing education courses, a peer-reviewed journal (the *Technical Quarterly*), and a vast library of manuals on the scientific and technical aspects of brewing.[10]

Similarly, the American Society of Brewing Chemists (ASBC) also provides scientific support to the beer industry; it was founded in 1934 "to improve and bring uniformity to the brewing industry on a technical level."[11] Thus, in addition to their own peer-reviewed journal, technical manuals, and teaching resources, the ASBC provides standardized methods of analysis to measure and evaluate specific aspects of the brewing process. For example, members can purchase their physical tests on barley, which are designed to assist brewers in "characterization and the evaluation of quality" and include scientific methods for determining variety, test weight per bushel, assortment, 1,000-kernel weight, texture of endosperm, skinned or broken kernels, weathering and kernel damage, and injury by sprout.[12]

Since the mid-twentieth century, the Brewers Association (originally the Brewers Association of the Americas) has grown to represent virtually everyone associated with the craft beer industry, from breweries themselves to wholesalers, retailers, homebrewers, and other brewing enthusiasts.[13] Functioning like a steward of the industry, they offer an array of professional services and information to protect and promote the culture of craft beer—the latest industry standards and statistics, relevant legislation and government regulation, educational resources and opportunities, tools for business operations, and information on how to form or join regional guilds. They also organize the Craft Brewers Conference and BrewExpo America every year, which claims to involve over 10,000 brewing industry professionals.[14]

Also of note is the American Homebrewers Association (AHA), which professionalizes the craft of homebrewing. Following Prohibition in 1920, homebrewing was illegal for almost 60 years before the U.S. Congress and President Carter legalized it again in the late 1970s. Since then, the AHA has become one of the leading advocates for homebrewers' rights and of noncommercial beer making. Their website, for example, provides detailed recipes and instructions for beginning, intermediate, and advanced homebrewing, information about where to find homebrew clubs and supply shops worldwide, as well as how to participate in their homebrewers conference and homebrew competitions.[15] These competitions are particularly noteworthy not only because they award exceptional skill and brewing virtuosity (*cf.* Boli 2006) but also because they involve a highly rationalized evaluation process, as discussed below. In the end, despite the incredibly technical and specialized nature of modern brewing, it has now become standardized to such a degree that virtually anyone can brew their own beer by purchasing a homebrew kit, which comes complete with all the essential instructions, ingredients, and equipment.

Beer Judge Certification

In addition to promoting homebrew competitions around the country, the AHA formally sanctions hundreds of them every year.[16] As part of this sanctioning, organizers are provided with "established competition standards and procedures," including access to judges who have been certified by the Beer Judge Certification Program (BJCP). The BJCP is a separate entity and an integral part of these sanctioned competitions. Founded in 1985, it administers a formal examination process to certify judges; it also monitors and awards advancements in rank (e.g., recognized, certified, national, master, grand master).[17] Of course, the BJCP also offers guidelines for learning how to formally evaluate beer, which is no small undertaking. In order to be certified as a beer judge according to BJCP standards, one must demonstrate an understanding of the technical aspects of how to make beer as well as of the specific characteristics associated with particular beer styles, such that one can taste the difference based on very specific descriptors. All of these details can be found in the BJCP's *Beer Style Guidelines,*[18] which is not to be confused with the Brewers Association's *Beer Style Guidelines* mentioned above. The former is meant for homebrew competitions and focuses more on evaluation criteria, while the latter is more of a comprehensive list and summary of beer styles.

The latest BJCP guide is a 79-page document that describes the general character of various beer styles and delineates four standard descriptors for each style—aroma, appearance, flavor, and mouthfeel. For example, the aroma of a Czech premium pale lager (or pilsner) is described as follows: "Medium to medium-high bready-rich malt and medium-low to medium-high spicy, floral, or herbal hop bouquet. . . . Light diacetyl, or very low fruity hop-derived esters are acceptable, but need not be present." By comparison, the aroma of a German pils is described as "medium-low to low grainy-sweet-rich malt character (often with a light honey and slightly toasted cracker quality) and distinctive flowery, spicy, or herbal hops. Clean fermentation profile. May optionally have a very light sulfury note that comes from water as much as yeast . . ." (BJCP 2015, 5, 9).[19] Clearly, this conveys a very high level of specificity about beer that, as the BJCP states, is not intended as a guide for the general public. Indeed, much of this would be nonsensical to the average consumer. But, for a beer judge engaged in a formal, rational competition, it represents standardized criteria by which to systematically (rather than subjectively) evaluate whether a homebrewed beer is true to form and has been executed skillfully.

A similar kind of technique and training is employed by craft breweries, but not to competitively judge beer. At the Deschutes Brewery in Bend, Oregon, for example, roughly 25 "beer tasters" work on the brewery's sensory analysis panel (Kehoe 2014). Essentially, their job is to regularly taste and evaluate the quality of Deschutes beer by identifying the presence of desired flavors in each style as well as less desired, or "off flavors," that may indicate a bad batch or faulty technique. While different instruments can be used for this analysis, a standard reference is the Beer Flavor Wheel (see figure 3.1). The original wheel was developed in the 1970s by representatives from the MBAA, ASBC, and the European Brewers Association and identified 44 separate beer flavors (represented in the outer ring of figure 3.1), separated into 14 classes of odor and taste (represented in the inner rings of figure 3.1) (Oliver 2012, 362–363). Today, Beer Flavor Wheels are more elaborate than ever in their use of standardized flavor terminology and are widely available as (yet another) rationalized instrument of quality control. Given the complexity of this language, it is not surprising that each participant in the Deschutes sensory analysis panel has to undergo three to nine months of training before becoming an official "beer taster" (Kehoe 2014). Once this training is complete, it would seem like the ideal nine-to-five job for someone who loves beer. But, as Weber lamented long ago, extensive rationalization can also lead to disenchantment, robbing the world of innocent wonder and mystery. Case in point, a quality assurance supervisor on the *Deschutes* panel admits, "[s]ometimes it's not always fun. . . . It can ruin drinking beer for you because you're always trying to pick out those off flavors in other beer" (Kehoe 2014).

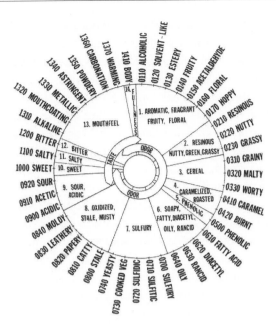

Figure 3.1. Beer Flavor Wheel. Source: http://kotmf.com/articles/flavorwheel.php.

The Original Revolutionaries

If you open a book on the popular history of beer, you are likely to see a reference to the pioneering efforts of European monks during the Middle Ages (Bostwick 2014, 52–60; Cornell 2003, 33; Glover 1997, 14–15; Jackson 2008, 260–266; Smith 2014, 14–17; Smith 1995, 19). As Bostwick (2014, 54) humorously relates:

> Benedictine monks made some damn fine beer. Tithes from farmers on church land stocked the granaries. The money [raised from] church ales . . . bought top-notch equipment such as copper kettles, large fermentation casks, and kilns to dry out malted grain for storage. . . . But most of all the beers were safe. . . . The monks kept their brew houses clean, passing laws that, to take one example, made it illegal to drink a beer in which a mouse had died.

Popular references like these have become standard lore, even though they lack scholarly rigor. Elsewhere, I have explored this phenomenon of monastic brewing in more detail (Elliott 2012) and theorized why medieval monks were proficient at making beer and what effect this may have had on modern capitalism. I employ a similar line of argument here to make a loose, yet important, connection between the practice of monastic brewing in the Middle Ages and the rationalized nature of craft brewing, described above.

Scholarly studies on brewing in the Middle Ages are rare, and systematic data from this time period are hard to come by.[20] Nonetheless, from what we know, it seems fairly clear that monasteries played a prominent role. As Unger (2004, 26) reports, the first large-scale production of beer in medieval Europe took place in the monasteries of the eighth and ninth centuries. "Large monasteries were institutions typical of the Carolingian Empire, and they were nearly always centers of brewing." Likewise, Horn and Born (1979, 261) surmise that "[b]efore the twelfth and thirteenth centuries when brewing first emerged as a commercial venture, the monastery was probably the only institution where beer was manufactured on anything like a commercial scale." Their famous study of the ideal Benedictine community in the Plan of St. Gall (discussed below) strongly suggests that monks of this era not only produced beer on a large scale but seem to have done so with considerable technique and organizational skill.

This raises an important question: why would a monk, living in a monastic enclave in the early Middle Ages, be particularly good at making beer? Once again, we can draw on Weber's sociology of religion for guidance, particularly his central mechanism in *The Protestant Ethic*—the religious activation of "ascetic rationalism." In general, the asceticism of medieval monks was less consequential in Weber's scheme, since it was confined to the monastery and directed toward otherworldly pursuits (prayer, salvation), whereas Protestant asceticism was profoundly "this-worldly" and had wide-ranging implications for social organization in the West, including the development of modern capitalism. But, Weberian scholars have recently corrected this view and explored how monastic institutions and their ascetic lifestyle had important social consequences in Western history (Adair-Toteff 2010; Collins 1986; Kaelber 1996; Snyder 2013). Collins (1986), for example, highlights the industrious activities of the Cistercians in fostering an earlier capitalist boom in Western Europe during the High Middle Ages. In his view, the Protestant ethic represented the second wave of rational capitalism initiated by, and dependent upon, the institutional structure of the Catholic Church and the economic activity of monasteries. Extending Weber in this way, we could argue that monks were good at brewing beer because they led a highly ascetic, disciplined, and methodically organized lifestyle that was very effective in its application to work of various kinds.

Until the late eleventh century, many monasteries followed the Rule of St. Benedict, a book of precepts written by Benedict of Nursia (c. 480–547) that defined, quite specifically, how monks should ideally organize their lives (2011). Contrary to Weber's original conception, the Rule promoted a "this-worldly" form of religious asceticism that paved the way for other reform movements to come, from the Cistercians to the Calvinists. Indeed, the Rule of St. Benedict was *the* foundational document of Western monasticism that encouraged monks to move away from a life dedicated solely to contemplation, prayer, and solitary devotion (the *vita contemplativa*) and to emphasize work as well (the *vita activa*) (Adair-Toteff 2010, 14). Work was highly valued in Benedict's opinion, not for personal satisfaction but for the glory of God (chapter XLVIII). Benedict's Rule also specified that monks should live together within their own communities, be self-sufficient through their own labor, and offer hospitality to travelers. This emphasis on a more active life of work and engagement connected monks to the world, rather than having them flee from it (Adair-Toteff 2010, 115–116). While it did not foster the same kind of ascetic mind-set Weber observed after the Reformation that openly pursued material success, the Benedictine reform movement was a crucial precursor by institutionalizing (through monastic communities) a daily moral drive for discipline, proficiency, and progressive enhancement in both their laboring and spiritual activities.

This emphasis on a disciplined lifestyle of communal work, self-sufficiency, and hospitality was reflected in the famous Plan of St. Gall—a blueprint for the construction of a monastery in ninth-century Switzerland. As Horn and Born (1979) and others have concluded,[21] this Plan depicted the "ideal" monastery rather than a one-off construction. In fact, there is no evidence that a monastic community with these precise specifications was ever built on the designated grounds at St. Gall. Nonetheless, the Plan of St. Gall was more than just an architectural blueprint; "the Plan might be fairly characterized as a two-dimensional meditation on the ideal early medieval monastic community, an 'objective correlative' of the Rule of St. Benedict, created at a time when monasticism was one of the dominant forms of political, economic, and cultural power in Europe" (Various 2015).

As shown in figure 3.2, the Plan of St. Gall reflected a community that was rationally planned and intended to be very orderly and self-sufficient. There are roughly 40 structures, including an elaborate church complex (#1, middle left), a garden and gardener's quarters (#20, top right), medical facilities (#15, #16, top left), a school (#12, middle left), animal shelters (#35–40, bottom right), and numerous buildings associated with the specialized economic operations of a

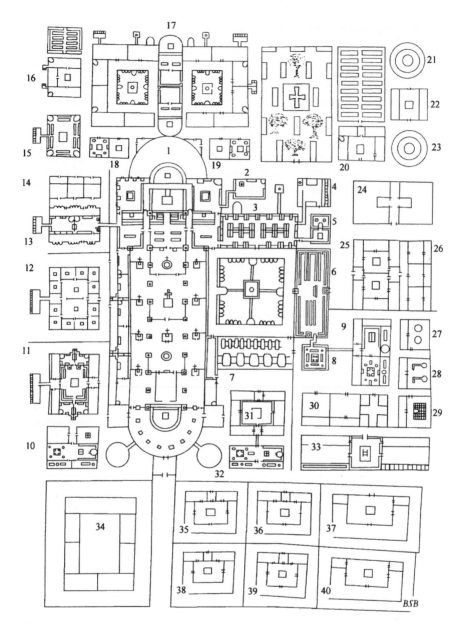

Figure 3.2. The Plan of St. Gall. Redrawn by B. S. Bowers. Numbering system from Horn and Born, 1979. Additional image editing by James Krehbiel. Used by permission.

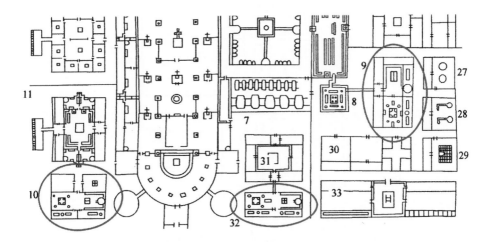

Figure 3.3. Cross Section of Brewing Complexes in the Plan of St. Gall. Redrawn by B.S. Bowers. Numbering system from Horn and Born, 1979. Additional image editing by James Krehbiel. Used by permission.

community of roughly 110 monks and between 130 and 150 servants and workers (Horn and Born 1979, vol. 1, 342).

The Plan also includes provisions for three separate brewhouses (see figure 3.3, encircled)—one to produce beer for noble guests (#10, left circle), one for pilgrims and the poor (#32, middle circle), and one for the monks themselves (#9, right circle). With three brewing facilities and demand from monks, servants, and visitors alike, it has been estimated that an average of 350 to 400 liters of beer (around 700 U.S. pints) per day would need to be produced (Price 1982, 57; Unger 2004, 29). Given that monasteries were the only institutions in Europe at this time with large quantities of surplus grain, no other social units had enough resources to produce beer in these quantities (Unger 2004, 27).

Figure 3.4 shows a close up of the monks' brewery and bakery complex and exemplifies further the rationalized layout of the Plan. Here, notice that servant bedrooms, presumably for specialists in beer and bread making (9A) are located on site, while houses for the processing and storing of grain are situated immediately around the complex—the granary for storing threshed grain (#30), the kiln for drying or roasting the grain (#29), the mortar for crushing the grain (#28) to be used for beer, and the mill for grinding the grain into flour (#27) to be used for bread. The description of this layout by Horn and Born (1979, vol. 2, 254) perfectly summarizes the systematic planning of the Benedictines:

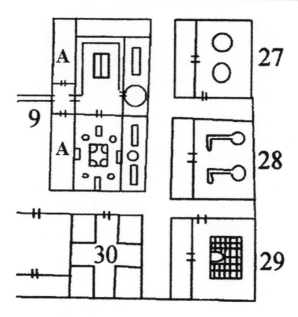

Figure 3.4. Monks' Brewery and Bakery Complex. Redrawn by B.S. Bowers. Numbering system from Horn and Born, 1979. Additional image editing by James Krehbiel. Used by permission.

The efficiency internal to the Plan of St. Gall is nowhere better demonstrated than in the relationships among the Brewers' Granary, Mortars, Mills, Drying Kiln, and Monks' Bake and Brewhouse. The traffic patterns demonstrate with what economy of movement raw material, grain—bulky and heavy even after threshing—could be moved from the Brewer's Granary to facilities where it was further refined, and finally into the Brewhouse where the end product, beer, was produced.

Though wine was generally considered the "superior" drink within the Catholic Church, there is additional evidence of monastic brewing innovations. As Price (1982) observes, the potential use of water power for the processing of grain is also suggested in the Plan of St. Gall. "Alignment of mills and mortars on the Plan indicates that given a source and the correct land gradient, water power could have driven both. . . . [I]n the fifth through eighth [centuries], water-powered mills were recorded in Frankish monastic communities. The impetus to apply water power may have spread in the West with Benedictine monastic life" (Price 1982, 57, 60). Horn and Born (1979, vol. 1, 352) also discuss improvements to the technique of storing and transporting beer via wooden casks, which were "large and ingeniously constructed" to withstand the internal pressure of fermentation as well as transportation over long distances. Monastic records in northern France indicate that hops became a regular beer additive by the early ninth century, perhaps for their preservative qualities more than for their flavor (Nelson 2005, 104–109; Unger 2004, 54). In his study of ale production and consumption in late medieval England, Slavin (2012) finds that monastic accounts clearly distinguish between different grades of ale: a first grade for monks and high-ranking guests and a second grade for servants and laborers, and (on occasion) some produced a third-grade ale that was likely the weakest version. Finally, there is evidence that monasteries engaged in the sale of surplus beer, some of it in commercial establishments like taverns (Unger 2004, 34–35; Williams 2001, 244, 262–263).

The organization of monastic brewing appears to reflect a distinctly rationalized orientation to the craft. This orientation, I believe, is rooted in the Rule of St. Benedict that directed the ascetic behavior of monks toward an active life of work. The layout of St. Gall, for example, while idealized, highlights the impressive scale and advanced technique that was intended, at the very least, with the institutionalization of Benedictine asceticism. These factors, combined with the specific innovations listed above, highlight how medieval monks could be viewed as the original revolutionaries of modern beer making. While commercial brewing operations developed in urban centers toward the end of the Middle Ages and became highly scientized and industrialized in the nineteenth century, this trajectory toward progressive rationalization (that continues apace today) owes a small but significant debt to the religious asceticism of monastic communities, well over a thousand years ago.

Conclusion

The craft beer movement in the United States has been transformative, not just from an economic or industrial point of view but culturally as well. Compared to the everyman image traditionally associated with beer drinking, "craft" beer drinking involves a technical, erudite sophistication that has become a celebrated aspect of contemporary beer culture. With its quality control metrics, stylistic experimentation, academic degrees, professionalized associations, formal competitions, and judging certifications, I have aimed to show how the production and consumption of craft beer are highly rationalized. While it may be tempting to view these developments as functionally necessary for economic success or as part of a clever marketing strategy, I believe they also highlight a much broader sociological process—the rationalization of society. As Max Weber and others have argued, scientific and technical rationalization is the primary means of pursuing progress in the modern world. Therefore, employing all these sophisticated brewing techniques not only fosters mass production in efficient, calculable, predictable, and controlled ways, but also reflects a progressive enhancement that seeks to continuously perfect the craft.

This rationalized approach has conferred a high degree of legitimacy on craft brewers, valorizing their skill and the product they produce, but it is not entirely new. The scientific and industrial revolutions transformed many industries in a progressively rationalized manner, in addition to beer brewing. Following Weber's lead in *The Protestant Ethic*, I believe the rationalization of beer has religious origins that date back even further, to the ascetic organization of monastic communities in the early Middle Ages, as highlighted by the famous Plan of St. Gall and recent historical scholarship on medieval brewing. Nonetheless, further research in this area needs to uncover more evidence of monastic brewing operations and how they were organized and explore how their techniques potentially shaped the rise of secular brewing institutions that followed. Regarding the craft beer movement, this particular study could be complemented by interviews or surveys with different craft brewers to obtain more fine-grained information about how and why they brew in particular ways and to what degree they perceive their "craft" as different from big, commercial brewing. Similar methods could be used to ask consumers what they find appealing about craft beer (as compared to commercial beer) and how the various technical aspects of craft beer are meaningful and relevant.

NOTES

1. See the Brewers Association (https://www.brewersassociation.org/statistics/market -segments) for specific information about the size and scope of different craft beer producers.

2. These regulations are governed by the Alcohol and Tobacco Tax and Trade Bureau (TTB) of the U.S. Department of the Treasury. For more details, see https://www.ttb.gov/beer/beer -labeling.shtml. Beer label requirements can also vary from state to state.

3. This is not to say that commercial brands have ignored the success of the craft beer movement. For example, some have co-opted the technical sophistication of craft beer with slogans such as "triple hops brewed" (Miller Lite), "beech-wood aged" (Budweiser), "frost-brewed" (Coors Light), or "cold filtered" (Miller Genuine Draft). They have also created faux craft brands such as Blue Moon and Leinenkugel (both by MillerCoors), and Shock Top (by Anheuser-Busch) or have acquired craft breweries themselves, such as 10 Barrel in Bend, Oregon, Blue Point in Patchogue, New York, Elysian in Seattle, Washington, and Goose Island in Chicago, Illinois (all now owned by Anheuser-Busch). On the other hand, a 2015 advertisement by Budweiser called "Brewed the Hard Way" suggests a renewed focus on the everyman image of beer drinking that mocks the snobby, discriminating aspects of craft beer culture.

4. See Unger (2004, chapter 2) for a discussion of brewing in ancient Mesopotamia and Egypt.

5. "University Courses at TU Berlin," Research and Teaching Institute for Brewing in Berlin (VLB), accessed October 20, 2016, https://www.vlb-berlin.org/en/university-courses.

6. "Courses and Programs at the TUM School of Life Sciences Weihenstephan," Technical University in Munich, accessed October 20, 2016, http://www.wzw.tum.de/index.php?id=46&L=1.

7. "Brewing Schools & Organizations," Brewers Association, accessed October 20, 2016, http://www.brewersassociation.org/education/schools-organizations.

8. "Fermentation Science Option," Oregon State University, College of Agricultural Sciences: Food Science and Technology, accessed October 20, 2016, http://oregonstate.edu/foodsci/fermentation-science-option.

9. "Vision & Mission," Master Brewers Association of the Americas, accessed October 20, 2016, http://www.mbaa.com/about/vision/Pages/default.aspx.

10. "Title List A to Z," Master Brewers Association of the Americas, accessed October 20, 2016, http://www.mbaa.com/store/Pages/atoz.aspx.

11. "About ASBC," American Society of Brewing Chemists, accessed October 20, 2016, http://www.asbcnet.org/membership/about/Pages/default.aspx.

12. "Methods of Analysis," American Society of Brewing Chemists, accessed October 20, 2016, http://methods.asbcnet.org/toc.aspx.

13. "Purpose," Brewers Association, accessed October 20, 2016, http://www.brewersassociation.org/brewers-association/purpose.

14. "About CBC," Craft Brewers Conference and BrewExpo America, accessed October 20, 2016, http://www.craftbrewersconference.com/conference/about-the-craft-brewers-conference.

15. American Homebrewers Association, accessed October 20, 2016, http://www.homebrewersassociation.org.

16. "Events Calendar," American Homebrewers Association, accessed October 20, 2016, https://www.homebrewersassociation.org/aha-events/calendar/?event_id=16.

17. "Rank," Beer Judge Certification Program, accessed October 20, 2016, http://www.bjcp.org/membergd.php#rank.

18. "Style Guidelines," Beer Judge Certification Program, accessed October 20, 2016. http://www.bjcp.org/stylecenter.php.

19. Both aroma descriptions are longer in the original and are used in abridged form here.

20. See Nelson (2005), Unger (2004), and the 2012 issue of *AVISTA Forum Journal* on medieval brewing.

21. See "Bibliography on the Plan of St. Gall," Carolingian Culture at Reichenau & St. Gall, UCLA Digital Library, http://www.stgallplan.org/en/bibliography.html, for a summary of historical research.

REFERENCES

Adair-Toteff, C. 2010. "Max Weber's Notion of Asceticism." *Journal of Classical Sociology* 10: 109–122.

Beer Judge Certification Program, Inc. 2015. *Beer Style Guidelines*. Accessed July 1, 2015, http://www.bjcp.org/docs/2015_Guidelines_Beer.pdf.

Benedict of Nursia. 2011. *The Rule of Saint Benedict*. Edited and translated by Bruce L. Venarde. Cambridge, MA: Harvard University Press.

Bernstein, Joshua M. 2013. *The Complete Beer Course*. New York: Sterling Epicure.

Boli, John. 2006. "The Rationalization of Virtue and Virtuosity in World Society." In *Transnational Governance*, edited by Marie-Laure Djelic and Kerstin Sahlin-Andersson, 95–118. Cambridge: Cambridge University Press.

Bostwick, William. 2014. *The Brewer's Tale: A History of the World According to Beer*. New York: Norton.

Brewers Association. 2014. *2014 Beer Style Guidelines*. Accessed July 1, 2015, http://www .brewersassociation.org/wp-content/uploads/2014/06/2014_BA_Beer_Style_Guidelines _FINAL.pdf.

Carroll, Glenn R., and Anand Swaminathan. 2000. "Why the Microbrewery Movement? Organizational Dynamics of Resource Partitioning in the US Brewing Industry." *American Journal of Sociology* 106: 715–762.

Collins, Randall. 1986. "The Weberian Revolution of the High Middle Ages." In *Weberian Sociological Theory*, 45–76. Cambridge: Cambridge University Press.

———. 1998. "Introduction." In *The Protestant Ethic and the Spirit of Capitalism*, by Max Weber, vii–xli. Los Angeles: Roxbury.

Cornell, Martyn. 2003. *Beer—The Story of the Pint: The History of Britain's Most Popular Drink*. London: Headline.

Elliott, Michael A. 2012. "Monastic Asceticism and the Rationalization of Beer-Making in the Middle Ages." *AVISTA Forum Journal* 21: 55–61.

Ellul, Jacques. 1980. *The Technological System*. New York: Continuum.

Glover, Brian. 1997. *The World Encyclopedia of Beer*. London: Anness.

Hindy, Steve. 2014. *The Craft Beer Revolution: How a Band of Microbreweries Is Transforming the World's Favorite Drink*. New York: Palgrave Macmillan.

Horn, Walter, and Ernest Born. 1979. *The Plan of St. Gall* (3 vols.). Berkeley: University of California Press.

Jackson, Michael. 2000. *Great Beer Guide: 500 Classic Brews*. New York: Dorling Kindersley.

———. 2008. *Great Beers of Belgium* (6th ed.). Boulder, CO: Brewers Publications.

Kaelber, Lutz. 1996. "Weber's Lacuna: Medieval Religion and the Roots of Rationalization." *Journal of the History of Ideas* 57: 465–485.

Kehoe, Megan. 2014. "Beer Tasters Have Tough Work: Deschutes Uses Sensory Panel to Test Flavor," *Bend Bulletin*, January 24, 2014.

Meyer, John W., John Boli, and George M. Thomas. 1987. "Ontology and Rationalization in the Western Cultural Account." In *Institutional Structure: Constituting State, Society, and the Individual*, edited by George M. Thomas et al., 12–32. Newbury Park, CA: Sage.

Mosher, Randy. 2009. *Tasting Beer: An Insider's Guide to the World's Greatest Drink*. North Adams, MA: Storey.

Nelson, Max. 2005. *The Barbarian's Beverage: A History of Beer in Ancient Europe*. New York: Routledge.

Oliver, Garrett. 2003. *The Brewmaster's Table: Discovering the Pleasures of Real Beer with Real Food*. New York: HarperCollins.

———, ed. 2012. *The Oxford Companion to Beer*. Oxford: Oxford University Press.

Papazian, Charlie. 2003. *The Complete Joy of Homebrewing* (3rd ed.). New York: HarperCollins.

Price, Lorna. 1982. *The Plan of St. Gall in Brief*. Berkeley: University of California Press.

Rao, Hayagreeva. 2009. *Market Rebels: How Activists Make or Break Radical Innovations*. Princeton, NJ: Princeton University Press.

Ritzer, George. 2013. *The McDonaldization of Society* (7th ed.). Thousand Oaks, CA: Sage.

Slavin, Philip. 2012. "Ale Production and Consumption in Late Medieval England, c.1250–1530: Evidence from Manorial Estates." *AVISTA Forum Journal* 21: 64–74.

Smith, Gavin. 2014. *Beer: A Global History*. London: Reaktion Books.

Smith, Gregg. 1995. *Beer: A History of Suds and Civilization from Mesopotamia to Microbreweries*. New York: Avon Books.

Snyder, Benjamin H. 2013. "From Vigilance to Busyness: A Neo-Weberian Approach to Clock Time." *Sociological Theory* 31: 243–266.

Unger, Richard W. 2004. *Beer in the Middle Ages and the Renaissance*. Philadelphia: University of Pennsylvania Press.

Various. 2015. "The Plan of St. Gaul." Carolingian Culture at Reichenau & St. Gall, UCLA Digital Library. Accessed July 1, 2015, http://www.stgallplan.org/en/index_plan.html.

Watson, Bart. August 12, 2015. "What's the Next IPA?" Brewers Association. https://www.brewersassociation.org/insights/the-next-ipa.

Weber, Max. 1978. *Economy and Society* (2 vols.). Edited by Guenther Roth and Claus Wittich. Berkeley: University of California Press.

———. 1904–1905/2009. *The Protestant Ethic and the Spirit of Capitalism* (4th ed.). Oxford: Oxford University Press.

———. 1920/2009. "Prefatory Remarks to Collected Essays in the Sociology of Religion." In *The Protestant Ethic and the Spirit of Capitalism* (4th ed.), 205–220. Oxford: Oxford University Press.

Williams, David H. 2001. *The Welsh Cistercians*. Herefordshire: Gracewing.

CHAPTER 4

Entrepreneurial Leisure and the Microbrew Revolution

The Neoliberal Origins of the Craft Beer Movement

J. NIKOL BECKHAM

Introduction

The microbrew revolution describes a period in the American brewing industry—from the mid-1960s through the mid-1980s—when smaller producers returned in noteworthy numbers to the American brewing landscape. Though commonly considered to be synonymous with the beginning on the craft beer movement in the United States, this chapter holds the two developments to be conceptually distinct. Such a distinction is, to a large degree, already encoded in the distinction between the terms *micro* and *craft*. *Micro* refers primarily to small production volume. The term *craft* is far more flexible with regard to volume and also refers to a particular ethos and/or practice of brewing beer. Though few would have predicted it at the time, the microbrew revolution was the antecedent and opening overture to the contemporary craft brewing movement, currently an exploding cultural force and at the end of 2014 a $19.6 billion industry that experienced 22% growth from 2013 to 2014 alone (Brewers Association 2015). More importantly, the microbrew revolution marked a break in the status quo established by the nation's rapidly globalizing, corporate breweries. Bolstered by widespread interest in imported and premium products—from cars and coffee to sushi and Super Mario Brothers—microbrewed beers reintroduced Americans to the diversity of traditional beer styles, rekindled a creative spirit with respect to the art and business of American brewing, and birthed the ethos of innovation that continues to sustain American craft beer culture.

Homogeneity and standardization of product and an intense focus on marketing and branding made Budweiser, Miller, Coors, and Pabst the largest beer brands in the United States, and in the case of Budweiser and Miller, the world. However, the uncanny extent of this standardization left the door wide open for enterprising microbrewers. The U.S. post-Prohibition microbreweries defined themselves in opposition to the qualities that came to define the brewing industry's twentieth-century landscape. Microbrewers created products that were decidedly local, positioned as anticorporate, unapologetically flavorful, communally consumed in brewpubs, largely unavailable in grocery stores and other retail outlets, and crafted to contribute to the experiences of enjoying and appreciating beer. These microbreweries did not advertise, package extensively, or distribute broadly, but they cultivated a culture of appreciation in beer drinkers that fostered loyalty and justified a higher price point (effectively setting microbrews apart from existing commercial offerings as a distinctive product). And while the timing of the microbrew revolution coincides with the general growth in the popularity of niche markets in consumer product economies during the 1970s and 1980s, the microbrew revolution unfolded in ways that left structural openings for the more progressive cultural–economic formations that have emerged in the past two decades as part of the craft brewing industry (see, for example, Beckham 2014a). Far more than a niche market, the American craft beer industry is now putting significant pressure on the corporate brewing industry and its prevailing methods of production, distribution, and consumption.

The microbrew revolution was, without question, a rupture in the status quo of a post-Prohibition brewing industry that is often vilified as being so corporate in nature that the making of beer was no longer its primary function. Though intended to be damning, this characterization is justified. As of 1976, the price/cost breakdown of commercially brewed beer in the United States reflected expenditures on advertising that were equal to ingredient costs. In the same year, packaging expenditures began to exceed, more than twofold, those for ingredients and labor and production combined (Tremblay and Tremblay 2005). Many have argued that the priorities reflected in this approach to brewing resulted in the ruination of American beer. However, the revolution itself was largely an extension of the dominant cultural–economic ideology of the late twentieth and early twenty-first centuries. Namely, the neoliberal cultural paradigm not only fueled the spread of laissez-faire economic policy, encouraged privatization, and made possible the extensive financialization of commodity markets, but also sparked a nearly religious valorization of entrepreneurship in American culture (Marttila 2012). That is to say, while the microbrew revolution is commonly perceived to be the result of attitudes and actions that were fundamentally opposed to the currents that carried "big beer" (and thus deemed to be revolutionary), it was enacted within the same frame of capitalist neoliberalism that ensured the success of big beer. Importantly, this enactment was not expressed as a commitment to an overarching economic philosophy, but rather was performed as a set of individual cultural practices that relied upon a slippage between the meanings of work and leisure (Foucault 2008). Nonetheless, in the telling and retelling of its recent history, the microbrew revolution continues to be framed as a watershed moment, created by the radical and resistant acts of a handful of pioneers—a framing that has been instrumental in inspiring and sustaining the character of the craft brewing movement that followed. This chapter considers how narratives about the microbrew revolution have served as origin stories for the contemporary craft brewing industry and its attendant craft beer culture; it posits that these stories perform a unique kind of cultural work.

The Cultural Work of Origin Stories

As is the case with many popular American historical accounts, ranging from the drafting of the Constitution of the United States to the mass production of the automobile, contemporary histories of the microbrew revolution are crafted as hagiographies of a group of "founding fathers." The popular histories of the pioneering men who ushered in the microbrew revolution are part of the rhetorical tradition of origin stories. Origin stories are crafted and retold across a range of discursive domains, in popular fiction, theology, politics, and scientific texts. And while origin stories share common features—they address important aspects of the unknown, provide explanations for the way things are at present, and distinguish the conditions that preceded significant events, actions, and choices—this analysis is less concerned with the content of these stories and more with the cultural work that is accomplished in their telling. Joanne Harriet Wright, a scholar of political origin stories, asserts that their value "lies partly in their telling. . . . [They] serve an important function in helping societies organize their ideas about themselves and about their universe" (2004, 7). The origin stories of the microbrew revolution, then, can be explored for the ways in which they have helped to organize and give meaning to the acts of brewing and drinking beer outside of the structure erected by large corporate breweries.

Wright suggests that most origin stories "at least hint at a theory of human nature" (2004, 6). This claim is particularly salient in the case of origin stories that make use of the founding fathers trope, as these accounts spotlight individual qualities and values that are presumed to be virtuous, and as such, lead to success. Origin stories not only articulate a logic for the way things are, but also make clear a vision of the way things should be. In doing so, they perform three important kinds of cultural work. First, origin stories have a naturalizing function. In the context of the kinds of origin stories that populate the American imaginary (for example, the myth of George Washington's cherry tree or the biographical story of Oprah Winfrey's ascent to fame from poverty and childhood trauma), this is a particularly productive function. Such narratives are overwhelmingly fixated on the exceptional accomplishments of remarkable individuals. Consequently, these stories serve to naturalize the exceptional. This is not to suggest that the exceptional is rendered unremarkable in the narrative space of origin stories. Rather, it suggests that the exceptional is effectively removed from the domain of the uncommon. Exceptional becomes a natural and expected part of life. Significantly, this facilitates the ability to hear and repeat stories of exceptional circumstances and accomplishments as if they are part of the natural order of things, resulting in the untroubled telling and retelling of historical accounts that belie the need for investigation or the provision of explanatory context. Origin stories are also "infused with, and driven by, power" to the extent that they perform the work of authorizing and conferring authority upon certain interpretations of social life, while notably discarding others. Finally, origin stories serve to provide simplified solutions to complex social and cultural problems, as they are by design abstracted from the complexity of cultural history as it was experienced (Wright 2004).

Given the unique functions of origin stories, the accounts of the American microbrew revolution that are widely circulated, published, and revered among members of contemporary craft beer culture do not merely describe a series of events. They were, at their inception, intrinsic to the success of the revolution and continue to serve brewers and drinkers of craft beer today. The differences between the scale, methods, and products of the operation of microbreweries and those of the American brewing giants, provided tangible evidence of the stark divergence between these two approaches to commercial brewing. However, the microbrew revolution's origin stories serve brewers and drinkers by positioning small-scale brewing and its products as not just different from but also fundamentally opposed to the activities and products of the macrobreweries that dominated (and continue to dominate, though under a set of far more tenuous circumstances) the late twentieth-century American brewing industry. The oppositional tenor of these narratives puts into contrast the cartoonish "old money" presumption of the corporate brewing giants and the pluckiness of a group of under-resourced (in comparison to multibillion-dollar globalized entities) underdogs—utilizing the rags-to-riches storyline of any number of popular American narratives.

In the origin stories of the microbrew revolution, the revolution's founding fathers—Jack McAuliffe, founder of New Albion, the nation's first post-Prohibition microbrewery; Fritz Maytag, pioneer of Anchor Steam Brewing Company, the nation's first regionally and nationally successful microbrewery; Ken Grossman, creator of Sierra Nevada, perhaps the best known of the first wave of craft brewers; and Jim Koch, creator of Boston Brewing Company and Samuel Adams Boston Lager, one of the nation's oldest and most iconic craft beer brands—share a number of commonalities, most noticeably a passion for good beer and a dissatisfaction with corporate offerings that drove each to pursue the production of a different class of commercial beer. They also shared an approach to the business of brewing, referred to as entrepreneurial leisure—the transformation of leisure pursuits into businesses and occupations (Ides 2009). This analysis will consider how the performance of entrepreneurial leisure, both in the contextualized history of the microbrew revolution and in its abstracted origin stories, allowed the revolution to simultaneously exemplify and profit within the dominant economic paradigm, capitalist neoliberalism, and continue to represent an oppositional resistance to that paradigm so intoxicating that it fuels the culture of smaller-scale brewing some 30 years later.

Origins in Context

Before examining the craft beer industry's origin stories, the cultural–economic contexts in which the microbrew revolution occurred should be considered. From the time federal Prohibition ended in 1933 through the end of the approximately 20-year period that marked the microbrew revolution, the American brewing industry experienced a transformation that can be described as extreme industry compression. This compression of the industry occurred along two dimensions—contraction (i.e., a significant decline in the number of breweries in operation) and consolidation (i.e., a significant shift in market share to fewer and fewer top performers). Prior to federal Prohibition in the United States, the national brewing industry was characterized by a mixture of regional and local breweries, with the majority of the industry's market share divided among small brewing operations that would today be characterized as microbreweries. It is estimated that 4,131 breweries operated in the United States in 1873, a high-water mark that has yet to be eclipsed by the contemporary craft brewing industry. In 1934, the year after Prohibition was repealed, only 765 of the more

than 2,000 breweries that operated just before Prohibition returned to operation. Within months, roughly 200 more closed their doors. By 1983, exactly
50 years after Prohibition was repealed, the number of breweries in operation
in the United States stood at just 89, the lowest total since the colonial era. Perhaps
more significantly, only 44 firms controlled these 89 breweries, the industry
had reached all-time production highs, and the top four breweries—Anheuser-
Busch, Miller, Coors, and Pabst—were responsible for 92% of all domestic beer
production (Tremblay and Tremblay 2005).

Four critical changes were symptomatic of, and contributed to, the dramatic
post-Prohibition compression of the American brewing industry—the nation-
alization of the industry, the overwhelming adoption of the American adjunct
lager, the change in geographies of consumption from public to domestic spaces,
and the transition from a guild-based to a corporate model of operation for the
nation's breweries. Each of these changes, in turn, can be located in the context
of broader cultural–economic changes. The emergence of a national brewing
industry and coincident demise of local and regional brewers is aligned with a
nationalizing mood observable in the United States more broadly. The standardization of product to the American adjunct lager is closely tied with the
innovation of cost-saving mass-production technologies. The shift in geographies
of beer consumption from public to private spaces is intimately connected
with the explosion of modern branding and the emergence a new kind of
consumption-enabled, privatized domesticity. And lastly, the change from a
guild-style to a corporate business model in the brewing industry was one indicative of the changes in the composition of American businesses in general
(Beckham 2014b).

By 1970, the American brewing industry almost exclusively produced a fairly
bland, unadventurous, and (as most beer aficionados would argue) poor-quality
product. Moreover, the average American's knowledge of beer rarely diverged
from the light-colored, thin-bodied, mildly flavored, effervescent American adjunct lager. While the stagnancy of product offerings prior to the microbrew
revolution allowed the nation's largest breweries to enjoy success in a competitive oligopoly that for much of the twentieth century reinforced barriers to
entry that kept small brewers out of the trade. It also provided the context in
which change would be received as profitably revolutionary.

Much like previous instances when the complexion of the American brewing industry changed significantly, a policy decision on the part of the federal
government acted as a catalyst and condition of possibility for change. On
October 14, 1978, President Jimmy Carter signed H.R. 1337 into law (Library of
Congress, n.d.). By February 1979, the legislation was in effect, exempting from

excise taxation beer brewed at home for personal or family use, effectively legalizing the homebrewing of beer. Though this act was largely seen as the resolution of an incidental omission in the Twenty-First Amendment, it did generate a spike in interest in homebrewing. This growing interest in handcrafted beers supported the growing presence of American microbreweries. As a result, many of the microbreweries (and later, craft breweries) that entered the market in the late 1980s and 1990s were founded by former homebrewers who were brought to the hobby by changes in federal law.

During the 1970s and 1980s, a handful of brewpubs and microbreweries entered the market; many did not succeed. By the mid-1980s, however, the microbrew revolution was afoot and gaining support from the growing interest in imported beers. By the end of the 1990s, a number of the successful start-up American microbreweries of the 1970s and 1980s had grown into regional and national mainstays.

The Contingency of Entrepreneurial Identities

The origin stories of the architects of the microbrew revolution, briefly summarized below, are abstracted from the previously described context. Though this analysis could include a number of other influential individuals (most notably, Charlie Papazian, homebrewing advocate and founder of the American Brewers Association), the entrepreneurial narratives of Jack McAuliffe, Fritz Maytag, Ken Grossman, and Jim Koch are most consistently told and retold in relation to the return to success of the American microbrewery.

The Revolution's Founding Fathers

The New Albion Brewing Company, founded in 1976 by Jack McAuliffe in Sonoma, California, is by most accounts the first American microbrewery to operate in the modern era. It did not succeed, closing its doors in 1982, but McAuliffe is credited with providing the blueprint for microbrewery operation that was taken up and executed successfully by his contemporaries. Born in Caracas, Venezuela, McAuliffe was the son of an FBI agent stationed in South America during World War II. He returned to the United States as a child, attended technical school as a teen, and eventually began an engineering career in the U.S. military, serving as a technician for naval submarines. In a version of events that would be repeated for other craft beer entrepreneurs, in particular Brooklyn Brewery co-founder Steve Hindy, McAuliffe developed a taste for flavorful beer and was introduced to homebrewing while stationed abroad (Hindy and Potter 2005; Leonard 2013). Upon returning to the United States, McAuliffe studied physics at the University of California at Davis and began a career as an optical engineer in Silicon Valley. Shortly thereafter he relocated to the Sonoma Valley, where he would eventually start New Albion. Narratives differ on McAuliffe's reasoning for the move. In one telling, friends asked McAuliffe to assist in the construction of their home. By the time the project was completed, some three years later, McAuliffe was firmly entrenched in the community. Another version credits McAuliffe with a more business-motivated savvy, stating that he specifically located in Sonoma with a brewery plan in hand, hoping to take advantage of lower expenses and the vibrant local food and wine scene (Hall 2012; Ogle 2006).

Ultimately, New Albion did not succeed and McAuliffe returned to his first career as an engineer, "designing industrial control systems for sewage treatment facilities and factories that produced aluminum car wheels" (Leonard 2013). The formula for the start-up and operation of his brewery however, would be quickly disseminated to men like Ken Grossman, Fritz Maytag, and Jim Koch, all of whom found success by avoiding McAuliffe's mistakes (Leonard 2013). In particular, accounts of McAuliffe's contribution focus on the ingenuity with which he constructed his brewery. Beer writer Jay R. Brooks (2011) recounts, "McAuliffe was the first person to not only build a brewery from scratch but do it almost entirely by himself from scavenged equipment. He scoured salvage yards for scrap metal, old dairy tanks and anything he could use to build New Albion. In those days, there were no domestic brewing equipment companies."

Fritz Maytag, a contemporary of McAuliffe's, is at the center of another of the craft brewing industry's most repeated origin stories. Upon hearing about the impending closure of San Francisco's floundering Anchor Steam Brewery, Maytag, a directionless young Stanford graduate, rushed to secure 51% ownership in the brewery for a few thousand dollars, saving it from eminent bankruptcy (Ogle 2006). After a few years he secured full ownership of the brewery and steered Anchor brewing to regional success.

Maytag was recently celebrated in *Inc. Magazine* as one of the "26 most fascinating entrepreneurs." Recognized for "setting limits," the *Inc.* profile applauds Maytag for being a man who "knew nothing about beer-making or business" when he purchased a majority stake in the brewery but who was able to max out the brewery's production capacity in just four years (Burlingham, n.d.). As the story goes, rather than take on investors and increase his production to match demand, Maytag rationed the supply of beer to customers. "Size, he believed, was the enemy of quality. 'This was not going to become a giant company' Maytag said, 'not on my watch'" (Burlingham, n.d.). In a move that is said to have inspired the collaborative ethos of the contemporary craft beer movement, Maytag fostered the community of microbrewers cropping up in the San Francisco region, allowing surging demand to be met collectively. " 'It was a great relief,' says Maytag. . . . 'It's not any fun when you can't produce enough to satisfy people.' " (Burlingham, n.d.).

Southern California native and homebrewer, Ken Grossman's story begins with a cycling trip down the north coast of California. He reportedly made an early stop in Chico and fell in love with the college town, opening a homebrew supply store and laying the plans for his microbrewery. Regarded as something of the "mad scientist" of the revolution's architects, Grossman's habit of driving around the state to collect equipment from dairy farms and scrap yards to re-purpose as equipment for his brewery is said to be a continuation of a childhood fascination with taking things apart and putting them back together. Unsurprisingly, his visits to McAuliffe's New Albion Brewery are said to be some of the most influential road trips he undertook.

With $50,000 in personal loans from friends and family, Grossman and then-partner Paul Camusi rented a warehouse and in 1980 launched Sierra Nevada Brewing Company. Grossman is not only one of the most visible founding fathers of the microbrew revolution; his story is one of the most extensively and frequently retold. It has been canonized in the growing microgenre of autobiographical brewery start-up nonfiction. Grossman's book *Beyond the Pale* (2013), joins Dogfish Head Craft Brewery founder Sam Calagione's *Brewing Up a Business* (2011), Lagunitas Brewing Company founder Tony Magee's *So You Want to Start a Brewery?* (2014), Stone Brewing Co. founder Greg Koch's *The Craft of Stone Brewing Co.* (2011), and Brooklyn Brewery founder Steve Hindy's *Beer School* (Hindy and Potter 2005) as definitive sources for entrepreneurial brewery lore. In spite of this notoriety, one of the more frequent themes in Grossman's origin story is a quiet tenacity and famous humility. Charlie Bamforth, reviewer and professor of Malting and Brewing Sciences at the University of California, Davis, wrote, "In my many years in the brewing industry, nobody has impressed or inspired me more than Ken Grossman. His tale is astonishing: how he rose from brewing in the proverbial bucket to being the genius behind the world's most beautiful brewery. Ken is a legend, yet remains one of the most unassuming people in the business. Quality attitudes, responsibility, fairness, and hard work with an underlying enjoyment in seeking the best: these are the attributes of the Sierra Nevada success story that Ken tells in this brilliant book" (as cited in Grossman 2013).

Jim Koch is credited with reviving an old family recipe for a flavorful lager in his kitchen that eventually would become the perennially popular Samuel

Adams Boston Lager. Koch, who earned a Bachelor of Arts, Master of Business Administration, and Juris Doctor from Harvard University, left a high-paying position as a management consultant with the Boston Consulting Group to co-found the Boston Beer Company in 1984. In a popular story that is retold in some of the brewery's advertising, Koch went door-to-door offering samples of his beer to Boston bars and restaurants, building a loyal customer base for his brewery.

Koch's story is somewhat different from those of his contemporaries in that it centers not on what he was able to build from scraps, but on what he gave away in order to realize his dream. Koch not only abandoned a successful consulting career to found one of the East Coast's first microbreweries, he also parted ways with the an extensive family history of producing the kinds of commercial beers that Samuel Adams was intended to unseat, investing a significant amount of personal money into the start-up of his brewery (Epstein 2012). The investment paid off. The Boston Brewing Company has for two decades been the largest American craft brewer. With the sale of Anheuser-Busch to Belgium-based InBev in 2008, it became the largest American-owned brewery in operation. As of 2013, Koch became the first billionaire who made his fortune in craft beer (Satran 2013).

Understanding Entrepreneurs

Social and critical cultural theorists have advocated for the understanding of all social identities and subject positions—be they delineated by race, gender, class, sexuality, age, or ability—as contingent upon contextual factors that are external to the individual. Du Gay (1996) argues that economic identities, like that of the entrepreneur, function no differently. He underscores the role of difference in the formation of contingent economic identities. Du Gay suggests "a contingent identity only constitutes itself in relation to that which it is not." To examine an economic identity, then, is to trace the processes whereby it struggles against an outside that simultaneously denies that identity and provides its condition of possibility. Though an antagonistic rendering of identity construction such as du Gay's threatens to minimize the significance of collaboration and community building in that process, it is useful in this discussion for bringing attention to the ways that expressions of power coalesce to form the articulated set of elements that constitute entrepreneurial identity. The activity of entrepreneurship is constitutive of the identities of those who engage in this activity—and it is, most importantly, marked by who the entrepreneur is not.

The following is a brief and cursory overview of a vast and robust organizational literature. Rather than exploring the socially constructed, individually enacted, and collectively embodied identities of the American industrial worker, white-collar manager, and entrepreneur in detail, it focuses broadly on the ways each identity antagonizes, and in doing so defines, the others, and the subsequent consolidation of power within entrepreneurial identity. The contingent American entrepreneurial identity that helped to form the basis of the cultural–economic context in which McAuliffe, Maytag, Grossman, and Koch came to embody that identity, is an extension and negation of the contingent identities of the American worker and the white-collar manager.

The producing industrial subject (whose experiences were the focus of Braverman's [1974] germinal *Labor and Monopoly Capital*) is the basis for the identity of the American worker, native to the dominant capitalist context that has characterized the United States for past hundred years. For the greater part of the twentieth century, the figure of the American worker was perceived to be mythologically engaged in a losing struggle against an emerging managerial elite who used increasing mechanization and science-backed managerial strategies in a relentless pursuit of organizational efficiency. For Braverman and others, the reorganization of labor that is the result of the coordinated application of mechanization and managerialism resulted in the de-skilling and alienation of workers, who were subsequently pacified by emerging discourses on job satisfaction. In this way, Braverman frames the antagonism between the identities of workers and the managerial elite as a struggle between two mutually exclusive impulses: the quest for meaningful autonomy on the part of workers via the retention and utilization of theirs skills and the struggle to manufacture consent on the part of the managerial sector.

What is excluded from these narratives is a consideration of the ways that the identity of the American worker was historically established in relation to other identities outside of the workplace. These extra-workplace relations do as much to define the American worker as his relationship to the managerial class. My use of the pronoun he draws attention to a particularly important aspect of the identity formation of the American worker. It is largely taken for granted that the American industrial worker was already defined as a white male who worked a 40+-hour week at the time of Braverman's inquiry and in those that followed (du Gay 1996). "Rather than being a universal, gender-free 'individual' . . . the 'modern worker' is a male breadwinner who has an economically dependent wife to take care of his daily needs and look after his home and children. . . . The stable public identity of the 'modern worker' is therefore established through the positioning of the woman as 'other' within the domestic sphere" (du Gay 1996). Such an acknowledgment is in no way revelatory. It is referenced here in order to draw attention to the ways in which this relational antagonism is not only maintained in the formation of managerial identity, but also consolidated and exacerbated within it. That is to say, if the contingent identity of the American worker is decidedly not female and not nonwhite, the character of the white-collar manager and entrepreneur are even less so.

The character of managerial identity is, in significant ways, dependent upon and defined in opposition to the character of the American worker. Whereas the worker, as the executer of tasks, comprises the bottom of the food chain in a managerial hierarchy, managerial identity is defined by a capacity to execute bureaucratic, if not pedantic, managerial control. Thus, managerialism is production-focused and rule-bound (Down and Warren 2008), but enacted within discourses of greater freedom and creativity. Even as the Western workplace transitions to what some have called a "postbureaucracy"—a workplace in which discourse and consensus replace rules and mandates—control remains a central aspect of the performance of managerial identity. The postbureaucratic workplace is typified by "self-managing" employees who are empowered and trusted to pursue organizational goals with minimal supervision (Costa and Saraiva 2012). Managerial identity, therefore, has shifted focus from the management of people to the management of organizational culture and the maintenance of preferred technologies of the self (Foucault 1992).

Literature on entrepreneurial identity frequently cites its mythic, heroic, stereotypical, and often clichéd nature. Anderson and Warren (2011) add that, "entrepreneurial meanings are not free-floating, but are anchored in a modernist project that somehow tomorrow will be made better entrepreneurially than today." Thus, the entrepreneur is thought to be self-motivated, competitive, autonomous, bold, energetic, creative, productive, innovative, and above all antibureaucratic. Moreover, this list of traits is understood to justify the component of entrepreneurial identity that is most salient to this analysis, a valorized willingness to shoulder perceived risk and the tendency to understand that risk in the frame of personal responsibility.

Though often associated with financial risk (loss of personal assets, threat of extreme indebtedness, etc.), the risk tolerance of entrepreneurial identity might also be thought to be a product of its affinity for change. Indeed, the foundational contribution of the entrepreneur is a capacity to do things better by doing them differently, where difference represents divergence from the safety of the known and the proven. Entrepreneurial identity is, in this way, a profound reversal of managerial identity—insofar as managerialism is a kind of stewardship over the very aspects of organizational practice and culture that represent constraints to be overcome by the entrepreneur. Entrepreneurial identity also stands in stark contrast to the identity of the American worker, as both the champion of a character that is fundamentally "unmanageable" and the embodiment of the lost autonomy that defines the American worker. Thus, in terms of both business practice and organizational identity, the entrepreneur symbolizes the future of business, by charismatically displacing the now of business. "Enterprise rhetoric privileges entrepreneurs as change masters, to challenge the power of established elites—to be the architects of Schumpeterian creative destruction" (Anderson and Warren 2011).

The history of the American brewing industry from Prohibition to the microbrew revolution saw this drama of antagonism played out to the letter, as skilled tradesmen and apprentices (from brewmasters to barrel makers) were replaced by menial laborers who in turn were subsumed by an exploding white-collar managerial force at the nation's largest breweries. Historically, the brewing industry's labor force has been one of the most extensively organized and has formed and maintained some of the oldest American labor unions. Before Anheuser-Busch was purchased by Belgium-based InBev, it was known for having one of the most bloated and expensive executive forces, whose antagonistic relationship with its laborers was far more than theoretical.

Consider the following example from Julie MacIntosh's (2010) chronicle of the hostile takeover of Anheuser-Busch. In the early years of the tenure of August Busch III (colloquially known as "The Third") as CEO of Anheuser-Busch, he was confronted with an imminent Teamsters strike over pay negotiations. Rather than cede to the union's demands, The Third chose to staff his production floor with the company's white-collar middle management. The incident not only touched off what would be a combative relationship with organized labor for years to come, but also illustrates the divisiveness at the heart of these two organizational identities. "It was a disaster—an absolute disaster," said Bill Finnie [a 26-year Anheuser-Busch executive]. "The union people absolutely hated management in general and August in particular, and it was reciprocated. So August did not start off on day one on the right foot."

Finnie spent the first six hours of every day cleaning soggy beechwood chips out of the brewery's giant metal tanks, crawling into them through a two-foot hole while grasping a toilet plunger and a rake. Then he and the other midlevel executives would spend four or five hours at their desks in the office. One of his subordinates, graduate of the notoriously cerebral Massachusetts Institute of Technology, suffered that summer from a general lack of handiness and physical coordination. "He drove a forklift, and I think that he had some pretty serious accidents," Finnie said. "It was pretty ugly. But at lunch, they'd bring us really fresh beer in gallon milk jugs, and it was the best-tasting beer you've ever had in your entire life." The company ultimately paid each of the while-collar workers a $1,000 bonus for their loyalty. (MacIntosh, 2011). The bemusement apparent in Mr. Finnie's recollection of the incident and the fact that white-collar workers were rewarded with a cash bonus for performing the unheralded daily tasks of laborers who were actively fighting for higher wages, speaks volumes about the ways in which managerial identity was formed in the disavowal of the identity of brewery floor workers.

Du Gay (1996) writes, "If every identity is dislocated to the extent that relies upon a constitutive 'outside,' which simultaneously affirms and denies that identity, then it follows that the effects of dislocation will never be unambiguous. . . . If dislocation unhinges stable identities, it also opens up the possibility of new articulations: the construction of new identities and the production of different social subjects." The entrepreneurial microbrewer represents one such new articulation, unique in that it also represents a doubling back. Insofar as the identity of the American worker and the entrepreneur are both defined in the negation of bureaucratic managerialism, there is something of a parallel between the desires of the brewery floor worker and the fulfillment of the successful microbrewer. Where the worker is defined by a loss and desire for autonomy and creative self-actualization, the entrepreneur is defined by the self-directed realization of that autonomy. The entrepreneur is thus a truly heroic figure, specifically for the laborer for whom he represents the unattainable realization of desire.

Within the brewing industry, this was not only an abstract heroism. Microbrewers not only shared the historic laborer's disdain for the open corporatism of "big beer," but they also embraced the lost ethos of craft—making it central to the formation of their entrepreneurial project. Far from a return to the identity of the worker as apprenticed craftsman, the entrepreneurial microbrewer represents a reinscription of privilege and power into a craft-based identity. Significantly, this reinscription was performed within the discursive space of leisure, rather than labor—imbuing the demanding physical requirements of the brewmaster's trade with an element of choice that is not native to the producing subject; rather, it is more emblematic of the consuming subject at play.

Entrepreneurs at Play

Thus far, this discussion has focused on entrepreneurial identity with regard to labor and the organized spaces of waged work. When leisure is found to be a formative part of the calculus of entrepreneurship, it is often considered to be both a rare and decidedly contemporary phenomenon. However, there is a lengthy epistemological precedent for the conflation of labor and leisure, of work and play. Leisure, like labor, is a historical concept that emerges in discourse and cultural practice at different times, in different contexts in world history (Hunnicutt 2006). Common themes, however, have come to dominate the discourse of Western leisure and can be traced to origins in the Greco-Roman empire. Most critical to the concept of leisure as it is currently understood, is its various and complicated relationships to the notion of labor or "work." According to Hunnicutt's expansive history of Western leisure, there is no etymological record of the term *work* in its modern connotations existing prior to the advent of the slave state in the ancient Greek empire. As the social continuum became more stratified, the activities that were appropriate for men of status and the activities that men of status had the power to delegate to servile populations became significant. Control, then, was critical to work's articulation in classical Greek society. As slavery continued to define work and depreciate the status of subsistence labor, leisure came to be defined as a corollary condition—a freedom conferred by the ability to exercise power over others.

Hunnicutt (2006) points to leisure's questions, those inquiries that emerged as the result of widespread conditions of leisure among the privileged classes. Unfettered by the requirements of work, the elite were inspired to speculate what was possible for the dominant class—what were the things that were worth doing in and of themselves? In answering leisure's questions, sport, fine arts, doing politics, making music, and engaging in conversation as leisure activities, became representative of Greek social life. To this end, leisure was the generative and binding force of early Western society.

A significant transformation took place with the fall of Greek society and the rise of the Roman Empire. The desirability and social status of agrarian life was restored in large part, as the vision of simple, frugal pastoral existence became an object of romantic imagination. Simultaneously, urbanization became increasingly conflated with corruption and alienation. Leisure then, ceased to be an opportunity to enter civic life and rather became the opportunity to retreat from the crowd in the pursuit of solitude and simplicity. As such, leisure shifted from the public sphere into the domain of the individual. While these ideological shifts in Roman society at large are significant, changes in Christian values and church doctrine were most central to the emergence of modern conceptions of work and leisure.

The formation of Benedictine Order within the Roman Catholic Church brought the first of Christianity's two major contributions to the modern notion of work. As a privileged class that was both physically and dogmatically isolated from the responsibilities of work, the monks of the Benedictine Order pursued manual labor in search of balance for time spent in contemplation and prayer. Work became a means to the end of spiritual virtue. The Protestant Reformation reinforced this notion and marked Christianity's second major contribution to changing the value of work. The protestant work ethic emerged from the belief that all people were called by God to work; idleness was among the severest of early Protestant sins. As the Middle Ages came to a close, the valuation of work and leisure had been essentially reversed, an ideological development ripe for the rapid entrenchment of modern capitalism (Hunnicutt 2006; Rojek 1985).

Implicated with the rise of modernity and the efficiency of Western imperialism, capitalism has been established as a global economic system, ideological formation, and system of social interaction. The Protestant work ethic, now secularized, has been rearticulated as the spirit of neoliberal capitalism. Leisure's questions are now work's questions, and the most common answers to those questions suggest that acquiring a "good job" and making money are two of the most important things that are worth doing in and of themselves. Leisure now requires justification as it becomes increasingly subordinated to work and no longer holds its position as the glue of civic life, nor as the space where representative cultural practices are developed. Simultaneously, leisure grows more and more dependent upon leisure goods and services, as popular leisure activities are more and more closely conflated with consumption.

With this historical shift, leisure, as defined in the context of neoliberal capitalism, is not only dependent upon labor as a defining condition (i.e., leisure is understood as that which is not labor), but it also defers to labor as a justification (one is not entitled to leisure without labor), a model of operation (the pursuit of hobby and leisure is increasingly career-like), and the source of economic resources required to participate in increasingly consumption-oriented leisure activities.

In light of this paradigmatic shift, the emergence of entrepreneurial leisure as a heroic expression of neoliberal subjectivity is a comprehensible, if not predictable, development. The foundational narratives of the microbrew revolution mark small-scale brewing as an act of entrepreneurial leisure, a cultural practice of the self-actualized economic subject at play, in opposition to macrobrewing as an act of bureaucratic labor, a cultural practice of the economic subject who is complicit with institutional control. In this way, the microbrew revolution's success can be understood in part as the result of a mystique cultivated around a group of men who were ambitious and resourceful enough to "get paid to play" and to capitalize upon the productive consumption of fans/customers who enthusiastically invested in this vision.

The Radical Neoliberalism of the Microbrew Revolution's Founding Fathers

The preceding discussion suggests that popular narratives about the American microbrew revolution's founding fathers have served as origin stories for the contemporary craft brewing movement. These origin stories have been crafted and retold using the oft-repeated trope of the founding father that followed an against-all-odds, rags-to-riches path to great (and deeply rewarding) success. These accounts are dependent upon contemporary understandings of entrepreneurial identity, which is heroically rendered in its negation of the identities of the American industrial worker and the white-collar manager. Significantly, the unique entrepreneurial identity of small-scale brewers is cast and understood in the context of leisure, granting these innovators an even greater measure of anticorporate mystique and shoring up their position in the industrial history of American brewing as having provided the courageous oppositional resistance to the bureaucratic economism of the nation's multinational brewing corporations needed to spark the craft brewing movement.

As was previously alluded to, these origin stories perform cultural work. They naturalize the exceptional, confer and express power, and simplify the complexity of lived history in ways that have both supported and shaped the contemporary craft brewing movement. In addition to cultivating the vision of the microbrew revolution as heroic entrepreneurial leisure, the revolution's origin stories also serve to obscure the significant role that conditions of social privilege play in enabling the practice of entrepreneurial leisure. More specifically, this process—the codification of entrepreneurial leisure in stories of origin—exclude in their telling, but were entirely dependent upon, two preexisting conditions. The first condition that the architects of the microbrew revolution possessed the means to occupy and thus successfully subvert the managerial identities that dominated breweries like Anheuser-Busch in the 1960s, 1970s, and 1980s. The second condition is that the founding fathers also benefited from the ability to justify and eventually use the pursuit of leisure to lend credibility to the products and brands they produced. This second point is not inconsequential. The leisure of all identities and subject positions is not considered credible and valuable; the leisure of entrepreneurial subjects in particular blurs the boundaries between labor and leisure in ways that render both activities productive and profitable. Consequently, the use of the rags-to-riches narrative arc in histories of the microbrew revolution's trailblazers is not only sloppy, but also somewhat historically misleading. Though the revolution's central figures are justifiably regaled as anti–"big beer" renegades who shattered the hegemony of a proto-Orwellian corporate brewing industry, it is also accurate to say that the founding fathers of the microbrew revolution were white men of significant means and privilege—men who pushed aspects of white-collar managerialism, neoliberal self-actualization, and a ethic of justificatory risk to an illogical extreme and found success.

The story of McAuliffe's short-lived career as a professional brewer serves as a prototype of a now common story in the rapidly growing body of popular, professional, and scholarly writing on small brewery entrepreneurship. McAuliffe and nearly all of the notable craft beer entrepreneurs who followed his lead were in possession of university educations, specialized training, and successful careers in private industry. In the space of the revolution's origin stories, however, these preexisting conditions are not narrated as the necessary means to their success as entrepreneurs—assets that provided financial resources, the basis for credit and purchasing power, access to investors, expertise to navigate legal environments, technical know-how, and more. These resources are instead cast in the light of personal sacrifice and heroic risk tolerance, hallmarks of the neoliberal ideology of self-reliance. McAuliffe was the first in a line of men who would be regaled for quitting their real jobs to pursue a passion for making beer.

In the establishment of another central theme of these entrepreneurial narratives, McAuliffe's homebrewing practices followed the trajectory of serious leisure—the steady pursuit of an amateur, hobbyist, or career volunteer activity that captivates its participants with its complexity and challenges (Koch 2011). Serious leisure is distinguishable from casual leisure—leisure that is "immediately, intrinsically rewarding, relatively short-lived, requiring little or no special [knowledge or] training to enjoy it"—in that its rewards are often deferred, require the acquisition of special competencies, and often inspire sustained financial investment (Stebbins 2001). As such, homebrewing as serious leisure is part of a critical double articulation to the brewing industry in the microbrew revolution's entrepreneurial narratives—on one hand granting legitimacy to the "hobby" in business circles, and on the other, allowing the very labor-intensive process of professional brewing to be continuously read as leisure. As a result, the formula for the identity of the microbrewing entrepreneur was established in McAuliffe's origin story as a well-educated, technically competent, problem-solver. In its retelling, attention is repeatedly drawn to the fact that he used engineering skills gained in his first career to fabricate the brewery. As such, the microbrew revolution's quintessential entrepreneur was less a blue-collar "beer man" who learned to play the business game and more a talented specialist who was willing to get his hands dirty for the love of a hobby.

Maytag's story shares many of these elements. His Stanford education also set him apart as a talented newcomer to the practice of brewing who, at least by surface indications, possessed the tools to succeed in the world of big business but chose instead to pursue the path of profitable leisure. Interestingly, Maytag's family heritage plays a remarkably small role in his entrepreneurial narrative. He is the great-grandson of Maytag Corporation founder Frederick Louis Maytag I and heir to the appliance giant's family fortune. Popular accounts of Maytag's start at Anchor Brewing Company fail to state whether or not, or to what degree, Maytag was assisted by financial contributions from his substantial family wealth. However, it reasonable to conclude that many of the riskier moves in his history are arguably better explained in the light of a significantly reduced likelihood of personal ruin. The question has been rendered effectively moot. The exceptional nature of his "aimless college graduate buys a brewery on a whim" plotline is naturalized within the narrative form of American origin stories, rendering unnecessary the investigation of contextualizing factors that may have contributed to his success.

Though brewing only a few years after McAuliffe and Maytag, Grossman is most frequently cited as the founder of the first U.S. craft brewery, and his narrative embodies the ground-up, do-it-yourself ethic that has animated the opening of more than 3,400 small American breweries in the past 25 years (Brewers Association 2015). Grossman's story is also the narrative that relies least upon the notion of brewing as leisure. Rather, his contribution to the microbrew revolution is more often than not framed as an exemplar of perseverance and ingenuity. Unsurprisingly then, Grossman is the figure in this collection of narratives that least closely aligns with entrepreneurial identity. He arguably possessed the least in the way of traditional entrepreneurial assets and (ironically) possessed some of the most applicable hands-on experience in the making of beer, as a long-time homebrewer and retailer. His story's presence within the collective story of the microbrew revolution's founding fathers carries significant weight, however, defining for the group an aura of self-made success that is uniquely the product of dogged individual persistence.

Though Jim Koch's biography contains significant points of divergence from the narrative tropes already established by popular interpretations of the experiences of McAuliffe, Maytag, and Grossman, Koch's story is nonetheless shaped to be consistent with the rest of the group. Case in point, Koch's departure from a successful career at the Boston Consulting Group often overshadows the fact that he is the sixth-generation of firstborn sons in an established German brewing family—the first after five generations who did not (immediately) assume a career as a brewmaster. Thus, Koch's founding of the Boston Brewing

Company and development of Samuel Adams is largely interpreted as a departure from the corporate world and pursuit of a passionate leisure activity, though it is more accurately a return to a family trade with pre-Prohibition origins.

Discussion

This analysis of the biographies of the founding fathers of the microbrew revolution was not intended to minimize the significance of their individual accomplishments. They ventured into an industrial climate in which the precedents for their business models were long forgotten. They faced a number of practical and formidable constraints—small-batch brewing equipment simply did not exist and had to be fabricated; the few suppliers of ingredients made sourcing raw materials a challenge, and those who did source often only did so in quantities that were untenable for a small brewer; and banks and investors were skeptical of brewing operations whose models of operation flew in the face of everything that was known about commercial beer. It is also important, however, to recognize that the practice of entrepreneurial leisure that underscored the microbrew revolution was dependent upon the access to and/or possession of a white-collar managerial identity that could be abandoned and superseded by a romanticized entrepreneurial identity. The fact that this new identity was steeped in the understanding of brewing as leisure generated a wealth of narrative traction that in no small way has contributed to the mystique of micro-brewing and craft brewing as the "rebellious" careers of those who dare to pursue their passions. The cultural work of these narratives has contributed to the value of dozens of microbrewed beer brands and inspired the thousands of craft brewing entrepreneurs who followed.

The microbrew revolution demonstrates how particular subject positions constitute particular kinds of economic activity. In this case, the subject defined by entrepreneurial leisure appropriated and redefined the techniques required to make a small-scale brewing operation solvent in a corporate climate defined by macrobreweries with international scope. A principal contributor to the entrepreneurial identity that revolutionized the American brewing industry was its reliance upon the dominant expression of contemporary capitalism, that being neoliberalism. It is within the frame of neoliberal self-discipline that resources and flexibility conferred by social and institutional positions of privilege are privatized into the space of personal risk. And it is within the frame of neoliberalism that *Homo economicus* does not just implicate ostensibly noneconomic activities—such as leisure—into the calculus of capitalist profit making, but is also read as heroic for doing so. Though the microbrew revolution is frequently heralded as anticorporate, it did (and continues, through retelling, to do) much to reinforce the logics of the dominant capitalist regime by asserting that the most estimable form of leisure activity is that which generates a profit—that rebelliousness does not resist the corporate imperative, but rather extends it by making money at play.

REFERENCES

Anderson, Alistair R., and Lorraine Warren. 2011. "The Entrepreneur as Hero and Jester: Enacting the Entrepreneurial Discourse." *International Small Business Journal* 29 (6): 589–609.

Beckham, J. Nikol. 2014a. "Drinking Local: Sustainable Brewing, Alternative Food Networks, and the Politics of Valuation." In *Food and Everyday Life*, edited by T. Conroy, 105–127. Lanham, MD: Lexington Press.

———. 2014b. "The Value of a Pint: A Cultural Economy of American Beer." Ph.D. thesis, University of North Carolina at Chapel Hill.

Braverman, Harry. 1974. *Labor and Monopoly Capital: The Degradation of Work in the Twentieth Century*. New York: Monthly Review Press.

Brewers Association. 2015, March 16. "Craft Brewer Volume Share of US Beer Market Reaches Double Digits in 2014." https://www.brewersassociation.org/press-releases/craft-brewer-volume-share-of-u-s-beer-market-reaches-double-digits-in-2014.

Brooks, J. R. 2011, September 30. "Brooks on Beer: Jack McAuliffe, Craft Beer Pioneer." *San Jose Mercury News*. http://www.mercurynews.com/food-wine/ci_19014448?nclick_check=1.

Burlingham, Bo. n.d. "26 Most Fascinating Entrepreneurs: Fritz Maytag, Anchor Brewing, Inc." Accessed July 25, 2015, http://www.inc.com/magazine/20050401/26-maytag.html.

Calagione, Sam. 2011. *Brewing Up a Business: Adventures from the Founder of the Dogfish Head Craft Brewery*. Hoboken, NJ: Wiley.

Costa, Alessandra de Sa Mello, and Luiz Alex Silva Saraiva. 2012. "Hegemonic Discourse on Entrepreneurship as an Ideological Mechanism for the Reproduction of Capital." *Organization* 19 (5): 587–614.

Down, Simon, and Lorraine Warren. (2008). "Constructing Narratives of Enterprise: Clichés and Entrepreneurial Self-Identity." *International Journal of Entrepreneurial Behavior and Research* 14 (1): 4–23.

du Gay, Paul. 1996. *Consumption and Identity at Work*. Thousand Oaks, CA: Sage.

Epstein, J. D. 2012, November 15. "Revolutionizing the Beer Culture in America: Brewmaster Relates How Samuel Adams Ignited a Movement." *Buffalo News*, B6.

Foucault, Michel. 1992. "The Use of Pleasure." *The History of Sexuality* (vol. 2). Translated by R. Hurley. Middlesex: Penguin.

———. 2008. *The Birth of Biopolitics: Lectures at the Collège de France, 1978–79*. Translated by G. Burchell. New York: Palgrave Macmillan.

Grossman, Ken. 2013. *Beyond the Pale: The Story of Sierra Nevada Brewing Co.* Hoboken, NJ: Wiley.

Hall, J. 2012. "New Albion Brewing: The Rise and Fall of New Albion Brewing Led the Way for the American Craft Beer Revolution." Accessed June 12, 2014, http://www .craftbeer.com/featured-brewery/new-albion-brewing.

Hindy, Steve, and Tom Potter. 2005. *Beer School: Bottling Success at the Brooklyn Brewery.* Hoboken, NJ: Wiley.

Hunnicutt, Benjamin K. 2006. "The History of Western Leisure." In *A Handbook of Leisure Studies*, edited by C. Rojek, S. M. Shaw, and A. J. Veal, 55–75. New York: Palgrave Macmillan.

Ides, Matthew Allan. 2009. *Cruising for Community: Youth Culture and Politics in Los Angeles, 1910–1970.* PhD thesis, University of Michigan, Ann Arbor.

Koch, Greg. 2011. *The Craft of Stone Brewing Co.: Liquid Lore, Epic Recipes, and Unabashed Arrogance.* Berkley, CA: Ten Speed Press.

Leonard, Devin. 2013, March 29. "Jack McAuliffe, Father of American Craft Brew, Brings Back New Albion Ale." *Bloomberg Businessweek.* http://www.businessweek.com/articles /2013-03-29/jack-mcauliffe-father-of-american-craft-brew-brings-back-new-albion-ale.

Library of Congress. n.d. Bill Summary & Status: 95th Congress (1977–1978) H.R.1337. Accessed January 1, 2015, http://thomas.loc.gov/cgi-bin/bdquery/z?d095:H.R.1337.

MacIntosh, Julie. 2011. *Dethroning the King: The Hostile Takeover of Anheuser-Busch, An American Icon.* Hoboken, NJ: Wiley.

Magee, Tony. 2014. *So You Want to Start a Brewery: The Lagunitas Story.* Chicago: Chicago Review Press.

Marttila, Tomas. 2012. *The Culture of Enterprise in Neoliberalism: Specters of Entrepreneurship.* New York: Routledge.

Ogle, Maureen. 2006. *Ambitious Brew: The Story of American Beer.* New York: Harcourt.

Rojek, Chris. 1995. *Decentring Leisure: Rethinking Leisure Theory.* Thousand Oaks, CA: Sage.

Satran, Joe. 2013, September 10. "Jim Koch, Sam Adams Beer Creator, Becomes Craft Beer's First Billionaire." *Huffington Post.* http://www.huffingtonpost.com/2013/09/10/jim-koch -sam-adams-billionaire_n_3901890.html.

Stebbins, Robert. A. 2001. "Serious Leisure." *Society* 38 (4): 53–57.

Tremblay, Victor J., and Carol Horton Tremblay. 2005. *The US Brewing Industry: Data and Economic Analysis.* Cambridge, MA: MIT Press.

Wright, Joanne Harriet. 2004. *Origin Stories in Political Thought: Discourses on Gender, Power, and Citizenship.* Toronto: University of Toronto Press.

PART II

Space and Place

CHAPTER 5

Crafting Place

Craft Beer and Authenticity in Jacksonville, Florida

KRISTA E. PAULSEN AND HAYLEY E. TULLER

Introduction

In contrast to much of Jacksonville, which is typical of sprawling southern cities (Lloyd 2012) dominated by big-box retailers and chain restaurants, King Street is at the center of a walkable neighborhood of historic residences and locally owned businesses. In the past six years, craft beer destinations have proliferated here, and it has become known as *the* local destination for craft beer in Jacksonville—by one count, some 550 taps in a less than one-mile strip—and for associated types of hip urban consumption. King Street is now variously known as the "Brewery District," "Beer Central," and the "Craft Brew District" and is publicized to both locals and tourists as an entertainment destination.

As King Street has transformed, so have understandings of Jacksonville's character (Molotch et al. 2000). Jacksonville has long struggled to assert a distinct and recognizable identity, particularly in comparison to other well-known Florida cities such as Miami and Orlando. Local entrepreneurs, including those central to King Street's craft brewing scene, point to this as a source of frustration but also an opportunity. As we detail in this chapter, craft brewing, with its strong connection to the local, provides a means to identify and promote distinctive qualities of place.

At the urban and regional scale, craft brewers and bar owners play a part in announcing just what this city is about. They also affect the creation of place at the neighborhood level, through the construction of breweries, taprooms, and bars. Our aim in this chapter is to detail the role of craft beer and associated entrepreneurs in the simultaneous construction of place at these two scales, and to examine how authenticity informs this transition.

Beer, Bars, and Authentic Urban Places

Scholarship on the relationship between craft brewing and place emphasizes the industry's reliance on symbols and stories associated with the home places of microbreweries. Cultural geographer Wes Flack's (1997) work on microbreweries and "neolocalism" drives much of this research. Flack argued that akin to farmers' markets and local festivals, microbreweries self-consciously assert "the distinctively local," in contrast to big-box stores and other consumption spaces that are exceedingly generic (1997, 38). Schnell and Reese (2003) extend this line of inquiry, noting that microbreweries are responding to consumer demand not only for beer, but also for local distinction itself. This is reflected in the ways these breweries connect products to places (e.g., naming beers after local places, events, industries, or folklore and often privileging the esoteric) as well as their efforts to affirm local distinction through support of other local businesses and preservation initiatives. In the current era of globalization and homogenization, Schnell and Reese stress that people still crave a sense of place, so the work of creating places must be active, conscious, and ongoing.

This place making occurs in part through the creation of spaces for the consumption of beer. Not all microbreweries are particularly distinct. Indeed, as Flack (1997, 49) noted, many have conformed to a "cookie cutter approach" that may erode local distinction, and "The successful formula of gutting and renovating a historic building to brew five or six shades of the amber spectrum behind a Plexiglas wall has become all too common." Moreover, heritage and authenticity may become commodified through their incorporation into consumption spaces. Examining the trajectory of brewpubs in Toronto and Ottawa, Matthews and Picton (2014, 339) argue that, "The amenity of heritage has proven itself to be a lure for middle-class patrons in their quest to seek out authentic urban experiences, and accordingly a useful model for developers seeking to profit from post-industrial lands." In Toronto's Distillery District and Ottawa's LeBreton Flats, historic associations with alcohol production became fodder for developers seeking to promote these places to gentrifiers.

While much of the focus on craft beer and place has come from cultural geographers, a number of sociologists have examined the role of bars and similar consumption spaces in remaking place. Bars are often among the first commercial establishments associated with gentrification. This is in part because entrepreneurs establish places where members of the transforming community—particularly artists, musicians, and others with unconventional jobs and hours—can gather (see Lloyd 2006; Zukin 2009). In his examination of Lower Manhattan, Richard Ocejo identifies bars as "both signposts and catalysts" of gentrification:

New, hip commercial establishments generate local buzz in a neighborhood and signify that it is transforming. Bars have a mutually reinforcing relationship with gentrification: new businesses like bars accommodate the needs of middle-class residents at the same time they attract new ones. (2014, 3)

Part of the attraction of bars in gentrifying areas—for both entrepreneurs and patrons—is the distinctive characters of the neighborhoods they occupy. For example, Ocejo's informants stressed how, compared to other neighborhoods, Lower Manhattan "still felt like New York," a place of diversity and even danger (2014, 133). And because bars are associated with leisure and escape, they are particularly well positioned to connect middle-class consumers to out-of-the-ordinary places and experiences. Writing on the explosion of theme pubs, Brown and Patterson (2000) suggest that patrons want predictable and immediate access to unique and authentic experiences. Local history can provide the raw material for these "authentically" different and safely risky experiences, whether an Irish-themed pub (Brown and Patterson 2000) or a Lower Manhattan whiskey bar that salutes the Gangs of New York (Ocejo 2014).

Bar owners' engagement with "authentic" elements of gentrifying neighborhoods is only one example of how qualities of once-distressed places are made to appeal to affluent consumers and residents. Christopher Mele (2000) pointed to qualities of the East Village such as noise, street traffic, and the availability of drugs, that might repel some but that proved alluring to groups of a particular taste culture, and Richard Lloyd (2006) has noted the appeal of grit to artists and other neo-bohemians taking up residence in gentrifying areas. In his work on the creative class, Richard Florida (2002) claimed that this segment of well-educated, well-compensated, and mobile workers were particularly interested in authentic places, augmented by robust music scenes and tolerance for diverse groups.

Sharon Zukin (2009, 2010) argues that the expansion of "hegemonic global urbanism" has brought with it a celebration of the "urban village" (Zukin 2009, 546). Middle-class urbanites clamor for the simplicity and connection to history offered by small shops and historic structures of "urban villages," and regard spaces of production (such as industrial Williamsburg, Brooklyn) as particularly authentic. At the same time, newcomers to these districts still want "a good latte or a magazine store that carries *Wired* or the *New York Times*" (Zukin 2010, 19). New retailers then follow the demand. Consumption is thus instrumental in the transformation of working-class and ethnic neighborhoods into gentrified districts where structures and symbols suggest an unchanging history, but where populations and cultures are in flux (Zukin 2010). As Japonica Brown-Saracino (2004) observes, many affluent settlers of these types of neighborhoods are aware of the remaking power of their consumption patterns, and they seek to buffer these by actively preserving certain establishments. These "social preservationists," as Brown-Saracino calls them, bestow symbolic value on these landmarks and the consumption associated with them, authenticating their own tenure in the process.

Tourism, too, both capitalizes upon and challenges urban authenticity. As Gotham (2007) finds in his examination of New Orleans, the type of promotion associated with tourism can emphasize the distinct qualities associated with a place, and motivate their preservation. At the same time, the specific types of development that tourism brings—whether t-shirt shops or global hotel chains—may undermine authenticity through homogenization. In Chicago, Grazian (2003) finds that tourists and others who are looking for an "authentic" blues experience seek out clubs and acts that match their idealized preconceptions, which often feature black musicians and black neighborhoods. The city of Chicago is happy to promote the blues as part of the city's distinctive local culture, but it often does so through awkward and somewhat generic strategies.

Our study links these lines of inquiry, examining how a gentrifying district dedicated to the consumption and production of craft beer has gained traction as an "authentic" urban place. The aim is not to make a case for King Street's authenticity, but rather to reveal how the increasing salience of authenticity, as well as related notions of identity and distinction, have set the occasion for remaking this district and the city. We attend to the role of brewers and bar owners in affirming qualities of locality and history, as well as their desire to remake both the neighborhood and the city of Jacksonville. As we will show, this process depended on the distinct spatial qualities of the King Street district, as well as the conscious aims of key players in the craft brewing scene.

Methods

This chapter relies on data collected through first-hand observation, archival research, and interviews. The observations began asystematically, as both authors have lived near the site for a number of years (Paulsen since 2000, Tuller since 2006). Our residence in and use of the district predates its current incarnation, and as well-educated, middle-class, urban, white women, we are arguably part of the demographic to which these new consumption spaces cater. It was our informal conversations about King Street's transformation that motivated this project. Our observations became more systematic as we took on the writing of this chapter, including purposeful examinations of the production and consumption spaces discussed here, as well as visiting associated events and festivals. We added to this an examination of electronic and print media accounts, promotional materials generated by the bars, restaurants, and breweries, as well as discussions in relevant blogs and online forums.

The interviews were intended to locate people that have shaped the King Street district and to understand their perspectives on the place and its recent changes. We accomplished this by employing nonprobability sampling methods (Berg and Lune 2011), specifically a mix of purposive and snowball sampling, to secure interviews with key individuals in the district's craft beer scene. When recruiting participants, we pursued people who predated the recent block rejuvenation, those who were on the wave of the change, and finally those who were latecomers to the scene. Tensions and suspicions linked to conflicts over the district's redevelopment are ongoing in the area (e.g., tensions with regard to noise, parking, and other conflicts arising as more bars opened near a residential area) and complicated recruitment, and it became necessary to convince key figures that we were not journalists seeking an exposé but social scientists hoping to see the neighborhood through their perspective. In achieving this level of trust it was critical to find a gatekeeper who could vouch for our discretion. Once located, access became possible with diligent work in building rapport.

The four interview participants included women and men, all white, and all either owners of establishments, partners, or high-level employees. All presented as solidly middle or upper income and had widely varying tenure in the neighborhood, ranging from years before the establishment of the area as a craft beer destination to within the past year. We have obscured our subjects' names and refer to them based on their roles: brewery owners and staff are referred to as "brewers," and bar owners are referred to as such. In some instances, we have also obscured distinctions between individual speakers. While we recognize that this diminishes the differences of experience and perspective among informants, and distances our data from individuals, given the scene's small size we saw no other way of protecting our subjects' confidentiality.[1]

Interviews were semistructured, based around questions of how these key figures decided to enter into their business and how they selected locations, as well as the design of the consumption space and the branding process. Questions also included those about the change these people had seen in recent years and how they felt about it. Finally, we probed how they saw their customers and what their businesses meant for the neighborhood and the city. Interviews were conducted by Hayley Tuller and recorded with the respondent's permission for later transcription and analysis. Based on the preferences of the respondent, the interviews took place at either the craft brew establishments or other local places, such as coffee shops. Interviews conducted in the relevant establishments included some off-mic interactions as respondents pointed out and explained features of the space or artifacts of production, and these were recorded in memo form. Transcripts and memos were then reviewed for emergent descriptive and analytic themes (Berg and Lune 2011), which became central to our analysis.

Findings

The Transformation of the King Street District

Developed primarily between 1901 and 1929, and located just two miles south of downtown, Jacksonville's Riverside-Avondale neighborhood is typical of early, streetcar suburbs (Warner 1978; Wood et al. 1996). The older section, Riverside, was the first major development built after Jacksonville's Great Fire of 1901; Avondale, an early planned community marketed to the discerning 1920s home buyer, came shortly after and is slightly further from downtown. Now known as Riverside-Avondale, the area is dominated by historic structures including large, stately homes in a mix of architectural styles, modest bungalows, a number of small-scale apartment buildings and commercial spaces, and numerous churches. While the area includes a number of more contemporary structures—many from the 1960s and 1970s, when suburban flight, expansion of a local hospital, and freeway construction plans (ultimately unsuccessful) threatened to remake the neighborhood as a more commercial space—historic buildings set the tone. The area is included on the National Register of Historic Places, and since 2008 it has been protected by a city zoning overlay designed to preserve its historic character.

Our area of interest, King Street, bisects the neighborhood, running from the St. Johns River on the street's southeastern end, north and under Interstate 10, and terminating at Beaver Street. Along the way, it spans three neighborhoods: Riverside (including North Riverside), then Lackawanna, and Mixon Town on the other side of the interstate. Nearer the river, Riverside is primarily white and middle to upper-middle class; as one follows King Street north, the neighborhood becomes poorer and more predominantly black (over 85% in the Census tract that includes Lackawanna and Mixon Town).[2] Our study area is demographically mixed, including young professionals, "hipsters," and families. Riverside has long been home to Jacksonville's LGBT community and much of the city's countercultural scene—distinguishing the neighborhood as a tolerant and progressive space within a culturally and politically conservative city.

Riverside-Avondale is peppered by small-scale retail centers dating to the 1920s. In Riverside is the edgy Five Points, known for hip and vintage clothing shops, trendy restaurants and bars, and tattoo parlors; Avondale is home to The Shoppes, a two-block strip of upscale restaurants and high-end clothing and décor boutiques. King Street's business district runs from Riverside Avenue to College Street and spreads laterally for a block along Park Street (see figure 5.1). King Street is midway between Five Points and The Shoppes, both literally and figuratively. It has long contained a mix of restaurants, small shops, and commercial services typical of neighborhood commercial districts: a national drugstore chain, bank, veterinarian, insurance broker, lingerie store, comic book store, florist, two antiques malls, and European Street, a restaurant-bar that has long featured "beers of the world." The customer base is mainly local, though a large Catholic hospital, located where King Street meets the St. Johns River, also provides customers. Before the recent transformation, the King Street business district was perhaps best described as utilitarian, and it lacked the clear identity of either Five Points or Avondale's Shoppes. The "Brewery District" moniker has written over this previously nondescript area, and many of its commercial spaces now feature craft beers and associated types of consumption.

In addition to two breweries, the King Street district is now home to 13 bars and restaurants we characterize as part of the "Brewery District" (see figure 5.1 and table 5.1). These include restaurants that feature a number of craft beers (Pele's Wood Fire, an upscale pizza restaurant, had 49 taps[3]; the other pizzeria, Carmines, has only a few, but features the local brews in its bar specials); as well as bars and package stores (Beer:30, a "Craft Beer Emporium," and Riverside Liquors, which recently moved from Five Points). These places all date from 2008 and later (most opened in 2012) and cater to an urban market that includes those with substantial financial or cultural capital. They foreground the local in ways now part and parcel of hip cosmopolitan consumption, such as touting the local and "slow" qualities of their fare. For instance, the menu for Lola's Burrito Joint, at Park and King, emphasizes the food's home-cooked quality (and lists some fifty beer varieties)[4]; and the Blind Rabbit, on King and College, notes the provenance of its seafood on the menu. Others reference local history in their names and/or décor. The Silver Cow, a self-described "watering hole" features 30 domestic craft and imported brews on tap and select upmarket menu items (or, as they call them, "ruminations"). The name of the establishment invokes Jacksonville's history, albeit in an oblique way. *Silvertown* was a black district eventually enveloped by Riverside, and *Cowford* was the original name of Jacksonville.

Ten years ago it would have been hard to imagine anyone coming to King Street to drink a beer. European Street drew a consistent crowd, and Park Place

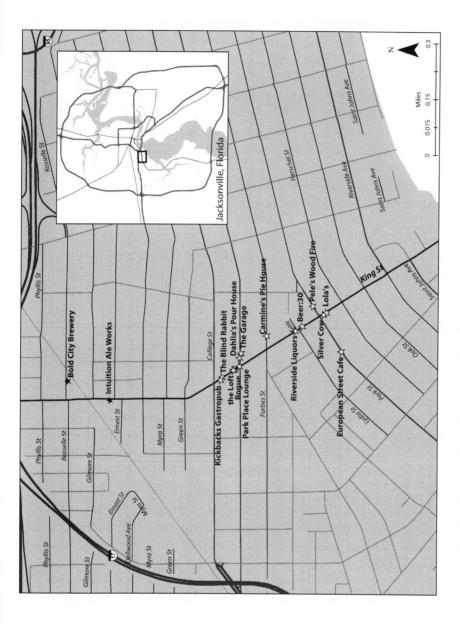

Figure 5.1. King Street, with Craft Beer Establishments. Figure by David Wilson, University of North Florida Center for Instruction and Research Technology Lab.

Table 5.1. King Street Brewery District Timeline

1970s?	Park Place Lounge	Bar/club
1992	European Street Cafe	Sandwiches, "beers of the world"
2005	Kickbacks	Sports bar, extensive beer offerings added in 2007; Goozlepipe and Guttyworks addition in 2014; now >200 taps
2008	Bold City Brewery	Brewery and taproom
2010	Intuition Ale Works	Brewery and taproom
2010	Loft	Bar/club
2010	Rogue	Bar/club
2011	Carmine's Pie House	Pizza and 25 taps
2012	Beer:30	Package store
2012	Dahlia's Pour House	Tavern; 85 taps
2012	The Garage	Bar and restaurant; 16 taps
2012	Lola's Burrito Joint	Burritos and 54 taps
2012	Pele's Wood Fire	Upscale pizza and 50 taps; closed 2015
2014	Blind Rabbit	Burger and whiskey bar; opened as Salty Fig in 2012
2014	Riverside Liquors	Package store
2014	Silver Cow	Craft beer bar; >25 taps

Lounge, at King and Post, served as a neighborhood bar for the area's LGBT population (we have heard informally, but repeatedly, that it was the *only* bar "back in the day"). A few small restaurants sold beer, primarily in bottles, but these kept limited hours, had few tables, or both. Arguably, the first mover in the transformation we chronicle here is Kickbacks. Kickbacks began unassumingly enough as a gay-friendly, smoke-free (before all bars in Florida that serve food were made smoke-free by statute) neighborhood bar and restaurant. While the beer list has been strong since 2005 (60 taps; then 84 in 2007), the initial draws were plenty of TVs and lively team trivia nights. Over time, Kickbacks continued to expand its taps, building a brand identity around its extensive variety of novel brews. Then in 2014, Kickbacks opened the steampunk-themed annex "Goozlepipe and Guttyworks," effectively tripling the size of the venue and upping the tap count to over 200. The eclectic decor of the Kickbacks expansion—part Belgian abbey brewery, part steampunk—embraces the work of local artists across two floors, making it destination dining and a major anchor of the Brewery District.

Local culture writer Stephen Dare (2013) cites the popularity of Kickbacks as pivotal in turning around the King Street corridor:

> The simple fact that there were people walking back and forth from the restaurant to their cars ended up being a real crime deterrent in the neighborhood, as police were called when things happened, and the cops began to patrol through the area more frequently and with more purpose due to the number of people dining there past 2 in the morning . . . Without any public commendation or apparently notice, the management (and customers) of Kickbacks managed to do what decades of community watch programs failed to do. They made King Street safe to walk down.

Prior to this time, Dare characterizes King Street above Park as home to a few edgy and artsy clubs, gay street hustlers, and drug dealers. Post-Kickbacks, King Street began to attract the foot traffic that Jane Jacobs (1961) and legions of followers have associated with safety and vibrancy. Moreover, Kickbacks affirmed the existence of a substantial market eager to consume craft and imported beers served in diverse, neo-bohemian environments.

Among the transformed spaces, and particularly in those that struggled, we can see just how the King Street district has defined itself and its market. For example, at the corner of Post Street is The Garage. The structure was initially an automotive tire shop, and in 2009 it became Walker's Wine Bar. With exposed brick, plenty of natural light, and a few well-placed chandeliers, Walker's typified upscale loft-style aesthetics and should have appealed to the neighborhood's relatively affluent and well-educated residents. However, the business struggled, and never developed a significant following. In 2011, the owners rebranded the space as The Garage, a bar with an all-over darker, grungier ambience that harkens to the building's initial purpose through auto-related memorabilia and accessories (if you bring your dog, she or he will be offered water in an oil pan). The establishment's tagline, "Est. 1929," emblazoned on the menus, creatively ignores the location's various incarnations since it serviced neighborhood cars, and gives the impression that the space has always been auto-themed. The new "concept" has been a hit, and The Garage draws a large, diverse crowd of regulars, afternoon patio denizens, and weekend-night destination drinkers. A similar pattern can be seen up a block at the Blind Rabbit, formerly the Salty Fig. The Salty Fig opened in 2012 as a brick-and-mortar incarnation of the popular local food truck of the same name, billing itself as a "gastropub," albeit one requiring reservations and serving \$20+ entrees (glazed quail, anyone?). While business seemed brisk at first, the establishment faltered, and the owners downscaled the concept. The Blind Rabbit now touts itself as a "whiskey bar" with a substantial menu centered on various interpretations of hamburgers and Southern home-cooked classics.

Just four blocks north of the dense strip of bars are Jacksonville's first two craft breweries: Bold City Brewery and Intuition Ale Works. These opened in 2008 and 2010, respectively, about one block from each other near King and Rosselle (see figure 5.1). Here King Street's commercial district tapers off, yielding to single-family homes and apartment buildings, then transitions to small-scale industrial spaces as King Street meets the railroad tracks. As we discuss below, it is the industrial quality of the spaces here that attracted the breweries. The presence of the breweries and their taprooms pulls patrons toward a part of Riverside that had not been not routinely trafficked by white, middle-class consumers. Organized events such as festivals, as well as the Riverside Avondale Night Trolley (which carries revelers through the neighborhood the first weekend night of every month) and the Jacksonville Ale Trail (which packages eight area breweries as a tourist attraction), further promote and solidify the identity of King Street, including the breweries, as a craft beer consumption destination.

The breweries arrived at a key moment—when King Street's nightlife (if one could call it that) included only two bars and one beer-heavy restaurant. Their presence, as well as their taprooms and events, and the expansion of Kickbacks' tap list, provided a coherent theme around which redevelopment could occur. Arguably, because these were working breweries they lent valuable authenticity to what might have otherwise been regarded as a hollow entertainment district or theme environment (see, for example, Sorkin 1992, Judd and Fainstein 1999; see also Matthews and Picton 2014). Together, the breweries and bars that came after solidified the identity of King Street as Jacksonville's "Beer Central," "Brewery District," or the other monikers that began to call attention to this distinct agglomeration (see, for example, Bull 2012).

Spaces of Production and Consumption

The north end of King Street offers the types of spaces that breweries require: small industrial buildings with features such as loading docks, high ceilings, and floor drains. However, rather than being tucked away in a district that is *solely* industrial, these spaces are more or less adjacent to establishments dedicated to consumption. As such, the King Street breweries succeed as both production and consumption spaces and have facilitated the success of the exclusively consumption spaces down the street.

At the time breweries such as Bold City and Intuition Ale Works moved into their north King Street sites, King Street's beer consumption scene was relatively modest. Kickbacks was in place, but not the half dozen or so other bars that now pepper the strip. The area, near a well-traveled set of railroad tracks and Interstate 10, had a number of vacant and disused structures and lots. Together, the vacant properties, industrial sites and transportation infrastructure degrade the surrounding neighborhoods, which are substantially poorer and more racially mixed than areas closer to the river. Our brewery informants conveyed some anxiety about the neighborhood when they arrived. One summed up her impression upon first seeing the prospective site as, "Dang! This is like—*sketchy* over here! Like, are people gonna come?" However, the spaces available suited beer *production*. When asked how one brewery found its location, a brewer stated:

> We looked all over Jacksonville. Now remember, again, we didn't have a lot of funds. My son found this location. . . . They did welding in this building. He found it, and it had the drains in the floors. I was just like, "Mmmm, I don't know, location!" But it was all that we could afford. . . . Our first priority is to the brewery and distribution. . . . So, because it had the right . . . space and the drains, we said, "Okay. This is where we'll do it."

Given the inflexible spatial demands of beer production, concerns regarding the safety and appeal of this part of the neighborhood were allayed.

Another informant noted the need to balance a space's production facilities with its symbolic resources. For this brewer, it was important that the space convey the kind of message and meaning associated with the brewery's product:

> I wanted to go with an old building. I wanted a brick building that had some cool bones to it, and something that *looked* like a brewery. . . . I'd have real estate people that wanted me to go in these, like, brand new kinda light industrial flex space things that are, you know, stucco. And I just figured, I don't want that. I don't want that vision, or what people would think of our brewery like that.

While the logistical constraints of brewing were important, they didn't trump aesthetics and their central role in building the brewery's identity. Brick was part of the desired aesthetic, and this brewer cited other breweries in old brick buildings (Goose Island, Sam Adams, and Brooklyn Brewery) as informing his vision. When pressed on why he preferred older buildings, this informant finally specified, "An older building is more authentic."

Aesthetics are equally, if not more, important in the taprooms. The brewers we interviewed were keenly aware that their taprooms needed to be hospitable and inviting spaces and that these spaces had the power to convey meanings associated with their products.[5] One brewer described their customers and taproom as having "a family feel." Another brewer, displaying sociological savvy, said of his taproom:

> I just wanted for people to just come in and hang out and drink cool beer and talk. And not just be in a sports bar, not be somewhere people just sit and stare at a TV. To just interact. So, like, they talk about that "third place." You know, it's home, business, and me wanting to be that third place where people come and just hang out.

Taprooms can also be means of connecting the product to place. One of these taprooms is decorated with the brick associated with pubs and older industrial spaces, and photographs of the brewer's conception of Florida. This is a Florida of marshes, palmettos, and pines, distinct from the variants of Florida found further south. The other brewery's taproom features pictures of the Jacksonville skyline over the years and a homey bulletin board with snapshots of patrons and staff. The beer names featured on tap handles and menus also connect product to place (just as Schnell and Reese [2003] observed): I-10 IPA is named for the interstate connecting Jacksonville to California; there's a King Street Stout; Mad Manatee IPA honors the creatures that inhabit northeast Florida springs and rivers; and 1901 Red Ale is named for the year of the city's great fire.

In addition to having retail taprooms, the breweries host festivals and events that draw patrons to the establishments and provide further opportunities to craft the brand's image. For instance, each hosts an anniversary party, and Bold City has music and food trucks many weekends, especially when the trolley is running. Intuition Ale Works used to host a number of events, including fundraisers for local causes, but has ceased because of conflicts with some vocal neighbors.[6] This motivates the search for a new, larger, and more events-friendly site, as events are understood to be central to sustaining the brewery's public image. In the words of one informant:

> Well, when you think about it, most craft breweries are kinda in an industrial area. You kinda have to have a festival to get people there, as a destination. . . . Because you're not going to just walk by it, and say, "Oh, I'm gonna pop in this place." It needs to be a destination for you to get there.

This brewer's observation that pedestrians don't typically "pop into" a brewery illustrates the challenge that brewers face in integrating into a sublocality such as a neighborhood. The spatial demands of production and consumption—particularly casual consumption—are in tension. In short, it's difficult to be accessible to both forklifts and pedestrians. By spatially connecting industrial and commercial sections of greater Riverside, King Street has facilitated both consumption and production of craft beers, and the cultivation of this distinct agglomeration.

Remaking Place

While our informants had many reasons for undertaking their craft brew enterprises, among them was a desire to make Jacksonville, and Riverside, into a different kind of place. In their observations, as well as ours, and in the grumblings of some public leaders (Gibbons 2004; Kritzer 2013, 2014), Jacksonville lacks a number of qualities that might distinguish it from other southern cities, particularly in terms of attracting young, educated, and mobile talent. As local business writer Ashley Gurbal Kritzer stated in a 2014 article on Jacksonville's simultaneous search for a brand and "soul":

> Without a strong brand, it's difficult for [engineering firm president Steve] Halverson and other business leaders to recruit the workforce of the future. That's why the city is fighting to create a brand attractive to millennials—those between 18 and 35—in hopes of building a sustainable, vibrant economy and attracting the companies competing for that workforce.

Jacksonville's identity is widely regarded as nondescript and up for grabs; what center there is relies on sports (such as the NFL team the Jacksonville Jaguars, or the area's numerous golf courses and events) or its geography (Ross and Donges 2014).

This lack of identity, and the capacity of food and drink to affirm local identity, registered with several of our informants. As one brewer stated,

> When I moved to Jacksonville I was struggling to find what that meant here. And I knew from visiting craft breweries in Australia and Boston and places before that you walk into a craft brewery and they all have a different personality, they all kinda speak to the neighborhood that they're in. . . . It just fascinated me that that was kinda an application of, like I said, food and culture. That maybe we can use this as something to

give Jacksonville an identity. Something that we just didn't have when I moved here.

For this brewer, who elsewhere in the interview discussed food as a way to involve one's self in a local culture, the brewery presented an opportunity to fill in the blanks of Jacksonville's place character. Another brewer explicitly cast this lack of identity in a comparative frame, noting that friends who had relocated from Jacksonville to other places did so in part because those cities (e.g., San Francisco, New York, Charlotte) had more to offer the young professional. He observed:

> I mean, these areas that have culture, have the nightlife, have the lifestyle that someone who's young and wants to live is going to appreciate it. I just want Jacksonville to be like that. I want us to have the cool restaurants, I want us to have the local products, I want us to have a culture that is appealing to a young professional.

While we are struck by the irony of localism as something that can be copied from other cities, given the permeation of Florida's (2002) "creative class" rhetoric into popular discussions of what makes places appealing, we are not surprised to hear this.

Official Jacksonville has also embraced craft beer as a means of assigning a hip, appealing, and locally grounded identity to the city. Visit Jacksonville, the local Convention and Visitor's Bureau, sponsors the Jax Ale Trail (n.d. a, b), designed to provide locals and residents alike with a fun and structured way to access the burgeoning craft beer scene (visitors who have their "passport" stamped at multiple breweries earn prizes such as t-shirts). The website for Visit Jacksonville (n.d. a) carefully positions the city and its beer scene as legitimate, but still approachable: "The local craft beer scene has doubled in the past few years and it continues to expand. . . . In Jacksonville, we are pioneer hipsters . . . minus the Brooklyn attitude." Promoting craft beer alongside food trucks and locally sourced restaurants, Visit Jacksonville now can proclaim that Jacksonville is as authentically local as anywhere else.

Conclusion

The rise of Jacksonville's King Street District illustrates how, in the current moment, craft beer can act as a catalyst for redevelopment. Ten years ago King

Street was up for grabs, with empty commercial spaces and no distinct identity. Its transformation proceeded slowly at first, gaining momentum as the two breweries and the expansion of pioneering bar Kickbacks suggested a coherent identity. The presence of the breweries and bars reinforced the attraction of each, culminating in a strip with over 500 taps per mile. King Street's transformation is in part a reflection of national consumption trends. Craft beer is seemingly everywhere, and cities are increasingly expected to have their own local brews. At the same time, gentrifying neighborhoods are displacing suburbs and downtowns as entertainment and consumption destinations, especially for affluent and well-educated urbanites. King Street illustrates both of these forces at work, and in so doing, provides insight into how qualities of space and the production of things facilitate the production of places.

First, King Street points to ways that space, and scale in particular, facilitate the integration of production and consumption. Residential, commercial, and industrial spaces are in close proximity here, owing to the transportation technologies available when the area was developed in the early twentieth century. The scale of the area's industrial spaces provided a good fit for upstart breweries. Today, scale and proximity allow patrons to walk from brewery to bar, establishing the breweries as not only local to Jacksonville, but also local to this neighborhood. Just as the production of art, fashion, and food in Williamsburg, Brooklyn, lent authenticity to neighborhood's galleries, clubs, shops, and restaurants (Zukin 2010), we offer that the production of craft beer here allows King Street to promise greater authenticity than that of other "entertainment districts," particularly those that primarily serve tourists.

This engagement with authenticity is amplified through brewers' adaptive reuse of spaces and self-conscious attention to architectural and decorative features that communicate a particular version of urban life and of Jacksonville. Taking aesthetic cues from other craft breweries, they seek to create inviting spaces in which patrons can connect to the locale and to one another. The bars and restaurants that have succeeded here are those that emphasize local and historic connections, allying themselves with the "preservationist" ethos of this historic neighborhood. In so doing, brewers and business owners employ a vocabulary of symbols, architectural styles, typography, naming schemes and branding that reference the hyperlocal, much as the social preservationist also does (Brown-Saracino 2004). While on one level they seek to preserve these narratives in order to leverage them as guarantees of their own authenticity and right of tenure, in a deeper sense, they are also commodifying them. Employing this symbolic language to make their product distinct, they are bringing to market a form of consumption through which even newcomers can display respect for the "roots" of the neighborhood. Through this discursive process of brewing, marketing, and consumption, brewers and consumers engage in a project that fundamentally remakes King Street.

These strategies reflect contemporary consumption trends that valorize the local, the slow, and the historic. Another trend will likely displace this one. But for the moment, craft beer production and consumption are facilitating a distinct type of urban redevelopment in which structures are not only retained and reused, but also their histories are exhumed and celebrated. In a place like Jacksonville, this is a departure from practices through which sprawl and urban renewal erased the past and generated an indistinct present.

The Brewery District's capacity to remake place extends beyond King Street. The city, too, was something of a blank canvas—to the brewery personnel interviewed here, and to boosters seeking to attract an educated workforce. Jacksonville's sprawl-and-mall development did little to distinguish it, and the city suffered by comparison to places that could articulate a distinctive culture or heritage. With its tradition of celebrating locality (Flack 1997; Schnell and Reese 2003), craft beer provided a mechanism for granting the city two important identities. One is its own identity, rooted in historic buildings and connected to Jacksonville's nature, culture, and heritage. There is a second identity, too: Jacksonville increasingly touts itself as a legitimate player among cities that celebrate the authentic and the local. It remains to be seen whether craft beer and other dimensions of locally based production and consumption will continue to warrant the attention of boosters and whether this will have any real impact in luring young professionals. But for the moment, craft beer can take some credit for both the remaking of a neighborhood and the articulation of a distinct sense of place.

NOTES

1. Confidentiality was key to our research design, as presented to and approved by the University of North Florida Institutional Review Board. This project was granted exempt status as UNF IRB #662827-1 on October 10, 2014.

2. U.S. Census: Race—QT-P3, Race and Hispanic or Latino Origin: 2010 Census Summary File 1; Income—DP03 ACS 2010 5 year estimate Duval County.

3. As we wrote this, Pele's Wood Fire closed and was purchased by a local restaurant group. The new venture, called Il Desco, opened in late 2015 and features "modern Italian" fare in a more upscale atmosphere. The beer list now includes 12 taps, with an emphasis on artisanal cocktails.

4. http://lolasburritojoint.com/menu/beverage-menu/ and http://lolasburritojoint.com/about -our-food, accessed November 5, 2014.

5. The taprooms also provide a valued source of income. Breweries may sell drafts and growlers on site, and the brewers we spoke with emphasized the centrality of this revenue to their

businesses, as it returns far more income than packaged beer sales (cans, bottles, kegs, which, in Florida, must be routed through a distributor).

6.   While the two breweries are only a block apart, their siting is quite different. Intuition Ale Works is surrounded on most sides by residences; while Bold City is surrounded by other industrial spaces.

REFERENCES

Berg, Bruce, and Howard Lune. 2011. *Qualitative Research Methods for the Social Sciences.* Upper Saddle River, NJ: Pearson.

Brown, Stephen, and Anthony Patterson. 2000. "Knick-Knack Paddy-Whack, Give the Pub a Theme." *Journal of Marketing Management* 16: 647–662.

Brown-Saracino, Japonica. 2004. "Social Preservationists and the Quest for Authentic Community." *City and Community* 3 (2): 135–156.

Bull, Roger. 2012, August 24. "Riverside's King Street Becoming Jacksonville's Beer Central." *Florida Times-Union.* http://jacksonville.com/entertainment/food-and-dining/2012 -08-24/story/riversides-king-street-becoming-jacksonvilles-beer.

Dare, Stephen. 2013, February 7. "Against the Odds: Miracle Successes on King Street." *Metro Jacksonville.* http://www.metrojacksonville.com/article/2013-feb-against-the-odds -miracle-successes-on-king-street/page/#.VFvuSOf94XU.

Flack, Wes. 1997. "American Microbreweries and Neolocalism: 'Ale-ing' for a Sense of Place." *Journal of Cultural Geography* 16 (2): 37–53.

Florida, Richard. 2002. *The Rise of the Creative Class: And How It's Transforming Work, Leisure, Community, and Everyday Life.* New York: Basic Books.

Gibbons, Timothy J. 2004, February 16. "Jacksonville Has Much to Do to Attract Young, Creative Workers. It Seems to Be Heading in the Right Direction." *Florida Times-Union.* http://jacksonville.com/tu-online/stories/021604/bus_14805915.shtml#.VQ7hYbPF_pA.

Gotham, Kevin Fox. 2007. *Authentic New Orleans: Tourism, Culture, and Race in the Big Easy.* New York: New York University Press.

Grazian, David. 2003. *Blue Chicago: The Search for Authenticity in Urban Blues Clubs.* Chicago: University of Chicago Press.

Jacobs, Jane. 1961. *The Death and Life of Great American Cities.* New York: Random House.

Judd, Dennis R., and Susan S. Fainstein, eds. 1999. *The Tourist City.* New Haven, CT: Yale University Press.

Kritzer, Ashley Gurbal. 2013, September 27. "220 Riverside Project Aims at Luring the Creative Class." *Jacksonville Business Journal.* http://www.bizjournals.com/jacksonville /print-edition/2013/09/27/220-riverside-project-aims-at-luring.html?page=all.

———. 2014, March 14. "Wish You Were Here: Inside Jacksonville's Quest for the Workforce of the Future." *Jacksonville Business Journal.* http://www.bizjournals.com/jacksonville/print -edition/2014/03/14/wish-you-were-here-inside-jacksonvilles-quest-for.html.

Lloyd, Richard. 2006. *Neo-Bohemia: Art and Commerce in the Postindustrial City.* New York: Routledge.

———. 2012. "Urbanization and the Southern United States." *Annual Review of Sociology* 38: 483–506.

Matthews, Vanessa, and Roger M. Picton. 2014. "Intoxifying Gentrification: Brew Pubs and the Geography of Post-industrial Heritage." *Urban Geography* 35 (3): 337–356.

Mele, Christoper. 2000. *Selling the Lower East Side: Culture, Real Estate, and Resistance in New York City*. Minneapolis: University of Minnesota Press.

Molotch, Harvey, William Freudenburg, and Krista E. Paulsen. 2000. "History Repeats Itself, but How? City Character, Urban Tradition, and the Accomplishment of Place." *American Sociological Review* 65 (6): 791–823.

Ocejo, Richard. 2014. *Upscaling Downtown: From Bowery Saloons to Cocktail Bars in New York City*. Princeton, NJ: Princeton University Press.

Ross, Melissa, and Patrick Donges. 2014, January 2. "Despite Size and Attractions, Jacksonville still in Search of Identity." *WJCT News First Coast Connect*. http://news.wjct.org /post/despite-size-and-attractions-jacksonville-still-search-identity.

Schnell, Steven M., and Joseph F. Reese. 2003. "Microbreweries as Tools of Local Identity." *Journal of Cultural Geography* 21: 45–69.

Sorkin, Michael, ed. 1992. *Variations on a Theme Park: The New American City and the End of Public Space*. New York: Hill and Wang.

Visit Jacksonville. n.d., a. "Good Times Are Brewing in Jax!" Accessed March 19, 2015, http://www.visitjacksonville.com/itinerary/good-times-are-brewing-in-jax.

———. n.d., b. "Jax Ale Trail." Accessed May 12, 2015, http://www.visitjacksonville.com /jax-ale-trail.

Warner, Sam Bass. 1978. *Streetcar Suburbs: The Process of Growth in Boston, 1870–1900*. Cambridge, MA: Harvard University Press.

Wood, Wayne W., Stephen Joseph Tool Jr., and Joel Wright McEachin. 1996. *Jacksonville's Architectural Heritage: Landmarks for the Future (Revised Edition)*. Gainesville: University Press of Florida.

Zukin, Sharon. 2009. "Changing Landscapes of Power: Opulence and the Urge for Authenticity." *International Journal of Urban and Regional Research* 33: 543–553.

———. 2010. *Naked City: The Death and Life of Authentic Urban Places*. New York: Oxford University Press.

CHAPTER 6

Ethical Brews

New England, Networked Ecologies, and a New Craft Beer Movement

ELLIS JONES AND DAINA CHEYENNE HARVEY

Introduction

> With over sixty breweries to visit, there is plenty of award-winning beer right around the corner. Many of these world-class breweries feature ingredients from Massachusetts such as locally grown and malted grains, fresh hops, and indigenous yeast strains. Valley Malt, the region's first micro-maltster in Hadley, works with area farmers who supply organic grains. Hops grown at Four Star Farm in Northfield and Clover Hill Farm in Hardwick are also used in many local brews. Specialty ingredients from Bay State growers include apples, blueberries, herbs, honey, maple syrup, pumpkin and even cranberries, peaches and oysters!
> —Massachusetts Craft Brewers Trail Brochure (2015).

The brewers and owners of New England craft breweries whom we interviewed viewed what they do as part of a larger national movement. Some compared this movement to the slow food movement, describing what they do as a return to tradition or a as providing a creative outlet; their beers were to be measured not by consistency—though that was something to aim for—but rather quality and diversity. Others favored the language of locavorism and described their commitment to sourcing local ingredients, their role in the community, and keeping their products in the region. Still, some brewers had adopted larger sustainability goals, such as resource conservation, using renewable energy, and closed-loop production (i.e., "farm to table beer").

All of the brewers and owners we met and spoke with, however, agreed that something special was happening now with craft beer in New England. Despite some of them being well connected in the national craft beer scene, they argued that New England craft beer is different. They pointed to other regional products and industry, like maple syrup, lobster, and Ben and Jerry's ice cream, that have a distinctive New England quality. They likewise noted the demand for community-supported agriculture and farmers markets. For them, New England was the prime place for the craft beer revival.

For this chapter, we spoke with representatives from nine breweries. Most of the time these conversations consisted of us talking with the head brewer, but we also were able to interview owners on a couple of occasions. We selected breweries who promoted their environmental work or work in the community on their websites. We also used convenience sampling, as we live and work near two breweries. Interviews lasted on average 40 minutes and were recorded and transcribed.

In this chapter, we look at the relationship between craft beer, geography, and ethics. In particular, we examine the burgeoning movement within the craft industry in New England to promote regional products and to sell locally. To do so, we focus on how craft brewers frame their beer in reference to large corporate breweries and as part of a "networked ecology"—a group of independent systems that build up a particular infrastructure (Varnelis 2008). Ultimately, we argue that in presenting themselves this way, New England breweries are part of a larger movement that is focused on producing ethical beer.

How David Frames Goliath: Responding to Big Beer

By 2007, the top two beer producers, Anheuser-Busch InBev and MillerCoors, accounted for 75% of the U.S. market of beer, with the ten largest producers reaching over 92% (Elzinga 2011). In addition, as Toro-González et al. (2014) demonstrated, most beer consumers are exceedingly brand-loyal despite the minimal taste variation offered by the large beer producers. It is in this context that contemporary scholars regard craft brewing in the United States as a new social movement arising in response to the colonization and domination of a small but significant piece of American food culture by a handful of large beer producers generating a relatively McDonaldized product (Carroll and Swaminathan 2000; Rao et al. 2000).

Most social movements, in the process of offering up an alternative model to that provided by the status quo, construct oppositional narratives that allow individuals to consider how the dominance of a group of institutions is destructive on multiple levels to the public being courted. This is just what we would expect to find in the craft brewing movement in New England; instead, what we discovered was an almost unanimous nonconfrontational response to "big beer." Consistently, the craft brewers we interviewed expressed almost no anger toward, no critique of, or any condemnation for these dominant competitors, their practices, or their beer. We heard the following sentiment over and over again—not better or worse, but different:

> I don't have the hatred [towards big beer] that you sometimes see or the knee jerk reactions that I do see in general. (Ben, Wormtown)

> A lot of people always say, especially craft beer enthusiasts, that Budweiser is crap. It's just different. (Bryan, KBC)

Even when a critique was offered, the speaker backpedaled. For example, even though Phil, the owner of the Cambridge Brewing Company, referred to macrobeer as "yellow fizzy crap," he quickly followed up by saying that there is nothing wrong with it, he just does not drink it anymore. And when the owner and head brewer at the People's Pint both referred to Coors and Budweiser as not particularly good, they in turn agreed that both beers are okay, but that there are simply too many really good beers to drink and eventually explained away the difference as simply being that of being a cook versus a chef. Likewise, many brewers noted that the macrobrewers were very consistent—a quality prized by all brewers. The younger brewers or newer breweries, in particular, seem to almost have a reverent awe for how macrobreweries make beer.

This refusal to adopt a somewhat standard anticorporate narrative often heard in circles of related (locavore, slow food, sustainability) movements is quite striking. To make sense of this, it's important to consider a few potential contributing factors. First, a number of brewers seemed to be placing a special emphasis on reaching out to mainstream beer drinkers in order to teach them about what craft beers have to offer rather than to "other" customers loyal to their macrobeer brand. In this way, customers are seen as students that have come to learn the language of craft beer rather than consumers that must pick a side in a cultural war.

> It's great to try to get those Budweiser and Coors Light drinkers kind of off that path. And that's what our beers are, they're transition beers.
> —Shaun, Rapscallion

> We understand that there's an audience for their beer, and we don't want to alienate anybody . . . so we thought it was important to have a beer as light as Budweiser. (Bryan, KBC)

Almost all of the brewers we spoke with mentioned the necessity of having at least one transition beer, or what Ogle (2006) calls "gateway beers." Some of the craft brewers we spoke said their goal was to have a "big tent brewery." Phil at Cambridge Brewing Company noted that while they have a number of experimental styles (such as Red God with seven different hop varieties and Banryu Ichi—a Sake Hybrid that comes in at 14% ABV), they make sure to always have "normal" beers (IPAs, stouts, blondes) on draft. Bryan, the head brewer and owner of KBC, in response to a question about making organic beer, looked around the bar, and then quietly explained that he would not do it because his working-class customers would interpret it as an effort to be trendy. When it was pointed out that a few of his beers, where he uses local ingredients and organically grown grains, are technically organic, he explicitly referenced his transition beer and noted that the organic beer would seem like a contradiction next to it, but later explained that consumers looking for that would probably realize it anyway.

Second, Ben at Wormtown Brewing asserted that larger brewers are not even on the radar of craft brewers, as what they produce is just in a completely different category, like attempting to compare fast food to food at a nice, local restaurant.

> I look at them in a similar way that you might look at a national restaurant chain or a packaged food provider at the supermarket versus someone who is locally doing it. It's just different things. One of the comforts that arises from American macro-lagers is that the person that's drinking it is reassured that every time they drink that beer no matter where they are: (1) it's available, and (2) it's going to taste the same. The first time I read that is when they talked about the McDonald's chain and stopping on a highway and you know what you're going to get and that's reassuring to people. That's just not my type of thing. (Ben, Wormtown)

Ben went on to emphasize that these larger companies have actually helped craft brewers by driving technological innovation in brewing equipment and creating new varieties of hops that are now available for craft brewers to use in their own beers. Other brewers simply said it was like comparing apples to oranges. Bryan at KBC went to the greatest lengths to explain what he saw as a clear distinction between "big beer," or macrobrewers, and craft brewing. He pointed out that craft breweries themselves come in a variety of sizes that are deemed to be important distinctions within the microbrewing world. He asserted that there are roughly five sizes of craft breweries (with the top size in some dispute among brewers) and gave one or more examples of each in Massachusetts.

- Regional (Samuel Adams, Boston Beer)
- Large Local (Wormtown, Jack's Abbey, Night Shift)
- Medium Local (Rapscallion)
- Small Local (Idle Hands, Brewmaster Jack)
- Nano (KBC, Old Colony, 3 Cross)

Macrobreweries remain undifferentiated. Bryan's inability to offer categories of macrobeer demonstrate that he has never even thought of macrobeer in the same way he thinks of craft beer.

Furthermore, a number of craft brewers worried about becoming too big. While none of the craft brewers we interviewed were in danger of being categorized as a macrobrewer, most said they had no plans for expansion, expressing an implicit desire to avoid being thought of as too big:

We are staying true to the Vision of Stoneman where "Less is More" and of building a sustainable family business whose collective goal is to produce 100% locally/regionally sourced ingredients for beer - one barrel at a time. In other words, we are proud of being one of the smallest breweries in the Northeast and we plan on staying small.

—Stoneman Brewery Newsletter, February 2015.

As Paxson (2013) notes, much of the romantic pastoralism of craft production in New England involves keeping the "ecology of production" down to scale. Scaling up means in some way selling out, compromising on quality, or running the risk of being compared to corporations.

Third, we may find some plausible explanations in small pockets of social movements literature. In the budding research on the craft brewing movement itself, Taylor Richard Johnson (2013) argues that while the early stages of the craft brewing movement may be characterized as a kind of counterculture, microbreweries have now established themselves as promoting change from well within the system. In the wider literature on new social movements, scholars have identified what they have alternately called a noncontentious ideology (Brigham 1990), a no-enemy approach (Jones 2002), and an accommodative consciousness (Hosseini 2006), to describe how social movements find it advantageous to offer alternatives to the status quo without demonizing it in the process. And if we reach back to some of the earliest literature on new social movements, we find scholars like Jurgen Habermas and Alain Touraine proposing that these kinds of movements are more concerned with expanding individuality, reproducing authentic culture, and improving quality of life than with winning the battle for money, power, and information (Habermas 1981; Touraine 1992).

Finally, it is important to note that while those in the craft brewing movement may not frame themselves as being in opposition to "big beer," the reverse is not true. Rao et al. (2000, 264) note that, like other similar movements, the craft brewing movement experiences significant push back from those institutions directly benefitting from the status quo: "social movements in hierarchical fields face similar problems in terms of resistance when powerful actors first try to quash them and then infiltrate or imitate them to defuse challenges to their authority."

This process of quashing, infiltrating, and imitating is all a part of the present response being generated by larger brewers as a way to slow the progress of the movement. A 2015 Super Bowl television advertisement from Anheuser-Busch InBev, for example, took direct aim at the craft beer movement by proclaiming Budweiser as "proudly a macrobeer," which is for "people who like to drink beer brewed the hard way." The advertisement goes on to encourage "drinking not dissecting" beer and advising viewers to "let them sip their pumpkin peach ale," portraying "them" (craft beer enthusiasts) as somewhat pasty-faced, pseudo-masculine, intellectual elites in opposition to "us" (the viewers) hardworking, real Americans just looking for beer to share the good times with friends.

In addition, at least half of our brewers noted that craft breweries like Goose Island (Illinois) and Elysian Brewing (Washington) were being purchased by larger beer companies (in this case, by Anheuser-Busch InBev) as a way to gain a foothold in the emerging marketplace. Finally, brands like Blue Moon (Anheuser-Busch InBev) and Shock Top (MillerCoors) often mimic some of the flavors, labels, and narratives of craft beers while essentially being produced at the same manufacturing facilities as their more widely recognized brands. These are sometimes referred to as "macro posers" (Johnson 2013), and they are policed by craft beer drinkers and identified as imposters (Carroll and Swaminathan 2000) within the movement.

The brewers we spoke with thus saw themselves as different from macrobrewers and indifferent to the various machinations macrobrewers were employing to discredit the microbrewing phenomenon. Part of this indifference involved an ethical orientation to others in the beer community, including customers, but this even extended macrobrewers. It was apparent in their desire to stay small and not scale up, but it was most obvious in how they talked about place and people, which we discuss below.

Networked Ecologies

The ecology of New England has long had a schizophrenic identity. On the one hand it has been dismissed as rocky, infertile crag (Black 1950; Haystead and Fite 1955) and on the other its bucolic landscape has served as a point of reflection on the relationship between civilization and nature (Thoreau and Cramer 2004). As Bell (1996) notes, these disparate identities reveal a sort of moral geology. They allow us to tell and listen to stories about the landscapes of New England; socially constructed landscapes that reveal long-held ideologies regarding people and environment.

These stories of the New England landscape are again being told in conversations about the craft beer movement in New England. As Justin Korby, head brewer and owner of Stoneman Brewery in Colrain, Massachusetts explained, New England's history of cottage industry and pastoral heritage makes it the perfect place for the emergence of a craft beer movement. Korby and other brewers noted that New England food culture, while not necessarily distinct, nonetheless has a much-valued authenticity. In his work on Vermont, Hinrichs (1996) asserts that it is not so much what but where it is produced that matters. The brewers that we spoke to emphasized that what they could produce was less a cultural product and more of a material practice—making beer in a specific place. Hence, if we want to interpret how this conversation on New England craft beer is being conducted, we have to stress the New England part of it and to some degree deemphasizes the beer.

Paxon's (2013, 31–32) ecology of production focuses on craft producers, and in her case, cheesemakers. She describes this particular ecology as "an assemblage of organic, social, and symbolic forces put into productive play in the service of a post-pastoral form of life [which] encompass nested spheres of productive activity: first, the multispecies on a farm; and second, how that farm activity is made possible, organized, and constrained by broader social, economic, and legal forces." Thus, the ecology is comprised of people and place, animals and bacteria. In our analysis of the craft beer movement, we extend her concept and synthesize it with work in architecture—which has its own vocabulary of place.

Varnelis (2008) uses the term *networked ecologies* to describe the interdependent systems that make up the infrastructure of Los Angeles. These systems, which include environmental, land use, communication, and service delivery are networked and produced by a complex array of technologies, laws, political systems, and people. Varnelis describes these ecologies as "balls of yarn after visitation by a litter of kittens" (2008, 15); they are messy and often difficult to discern. While much less messy and at times easier to discern, the term is both evocative and illustrative for describing the craft beer movement in New England.

Combining Paxson's focus on the production of food and Varnelis's focus on interdependent systems, we describe New England's craft beer movement as a networked ecology. We situate this ecology as a return to New England's cottage industry and early pastoral life, but also as a part of new social movements that focus on slow food, locavorism, and environmental sustainability. These ecologies include the production of local grain and hops, the building of the first micromaltster in New England, and the use of regional ingredients from local farmers. They also, however, go beyond systems of production to include consumers—as the majority of the beer from the brewers we interviewed limit their distribution to New England, with many limiting it to a particular state. Chris, the head brewer at The People's Pint in Greenfield, Massachusetts, describes what these ecologies do for the beer:

> Barley that is grown in this valley, especially that is used for malting, has a very specific flavor to it, and it comes from the couple types of bacteria that develop because of the high level of moisture in the area on the actual husk of the barley. So during the malting process you get this development of flavor that happens that is unique to this area. And um, it's sort of a fascinating example of the wine concept of "terroir" in beer . . . and once you know what that flavor is you can pick it out a mile away . . . and then the hops have their own character too . . . and where this farm is in Northfield it sits in the Millersville River Valley, it's in Connecticut, along the Connecticut River, you get this sort of fog that lasts longer in the morning, and so the flavor development in the hop cones themselves is sort of related to that late day fog . . . and so you can get like a cascade hop rhizome from Washington state that is genetically identical to the one they are using in Washington state and you park it in a you know moist river valley and [it's completely different] . . . and it's fun to brew this beer because I can't make it again . . . that's what is fascinating about it.

Many of the brewers we spoke with discussed the uniqueness of New England when describing their beer. As Chris notes above, he couldn't make the beer again. While a challenge, it also presents opportunities to feature beers that evoke an idea of New England.

Ben Roesch, Master Brewer at Wormtown Brewery in Worcester, Massachusetts, began his career as a homebrewer, taking forestry courses at the University of Massachusetts at Amherst. He describes visiting, as part of his course work, saw mills, sugar shacks, and orchards and taking home handfuls of "souvenirs" to add to his homebrew. After college, he worked at a local farm, and when he left to brew at Cambridge Brewing Company he encouraged them to buy pumpkins from the farm. Later, at Nashoba Winery, he used their farmed peaches for a lambic. Bringing these practices with him to Wormtown he still includes at least one local ingredient in each beer. Other brewers noted that having a cranberry saison or a cranberry porter was a necessity for making a New England Beer. Shaun Radzuik, head brewer at Rapscallion in Acton, Massachusetts, exchanges smoked hops from B.T.'s Smokehouse in Sturbridge, Massachusetts, for beer to be used in B.T.'s onion rings. Other brewers used local oysters or blueberries for their beer to claim authenticity and identity. Thus, in addition to the reliance on regional farmers, these networked ecologies of craft beer include a unique interaction between different producers and have actually begun to drive production and industry.

Andrea and Christian Stanley started Valley Malt in 2010, the first micro-maltster in New England. The three pillars of their business are: (1) grow local, (2) choose organic, and (3) craft tradition. They began production after realizing that the craft beer industry in New England was becoming a bit crowded and that the lack of local suppliers was actually constraining brewers in their attempt to brew local beer. They stress that what they are interested in doing is building a sustainable food movement in New England (the name of their farm is "Slow Tractor Farm"). In partnering with local farmers and working with local groups such as Grow Food Northampton, which is now the largest community farm in New England, Valley Malt has quickly become part of the networked ecology.

Justin Korby credits Valley Malt with leading him to become a craft brewer. "What drove me to create Stoneman Brewery was that I was in an opportunity to make almost one hundred percent local beer, as a business plan . . . all locally sourced and that's unheard of and the opportunity isn't really available to other people." Andrea pulled Justin into craft beer production by providing him with off-grains, grains that either did not turn out the way they should have or experimental batches produced when Valley Malt was just learning how to malt.

In turn, Korby uses his brewery as a way to showcase Valley Malt and local grain production. Other craft brewers we spoke to explained these interactions as central to what makes New England craft beer unique.

Chris, from The People's Pint, for instance highlights his willingness to work with other brewers on projects. He speaks of this willingness as being part of a community, a "beer culture" with "crazy, frenetic energy." Justin, from Stoneman Brewery, with whom Chris has collaborated on a number of projects, started a Beer Share Series in 2014. In this series, Justin often works with other brewers to come up with a recipe for a new beer, which he then brews at Stoneman. The beer is then featured at another brewery at a release party, often People's Pint, and the remainder is bottled and sold exclusively at a local food co-op, River Valley Market. Likewise, Ben at Wormtown, who opened at a new location in spring 2015, is helping a new brewer, who now leases Wormtown's original space, adapt his recipes as he increases production. These interactions even extended to larger brewers as Cambridge Brewing Company uses Harpoon Brewery's keg-cleaning equipment, while maintaining smaller ties by using Ipswich Ale Brewery's bottling equipment and Wachusett Brewery's canning equipment.

The attention of brewers to the local and to community goes beyond the rhetorical. While craft brewers do frequently reference the imagery of pastoral New England to explain their motives, they also engage in material practices that affirm the social roots of what they see as a "genuine cuisine" (Mintz 1996). Here nostalgia and the desire for new products combine to drive production (Appadurai 1996; Peace 2011), but the means seem far more important the ends. Korby's mantra of "Grow Beer" would have been unthinkable in New England only a few years ago. It is only through these networked ecologies that growing beer and growing the New England craft beer movement have been possible. For these brewers, these interactions and interdependencies create ethical assemblages that reveal a particular way to make beer (Paxson 2013). In addition to a unique terroir—a concept not usually associated with beer, these brewers hope that their beers also reveal these ecologies and hence the people who help grow, produce, and consume their beer.

Conclusion

The first locavore movement in the United States likely started as a boycott of English barley and hops (Bostick 2014). In a return to its roots, today New England has local grain and hops growers and a micromaltster—with others in the works. Yet despite a burgeoning craft beer scene, the craft brewers we interviewed, for the most part, had few plans to scale up. A few noted their worries about a crash in the craft beer market as a reason to be cautious about expanding, but most noted a symbiotic relationship with local suppliers and thus their place in the local ecology of production. Their desire to produce an ethical product, inscribed in what they see as a moral geography, influences not only how they make beer, but also why they make beer. As Justin Korby and others noted, they would not be making beer unless they could make it the way they do, and perhaps more importantly, make beer with the people they do.

From a social movements perspective, New England's craft beer movement seems to be locating itself at the nexus of three related social movements:

1. Slow food (quality, diversity, tradition, creativity, regionality).
2. Locavore (local farms, local businesses, community cultivation).
3. Environmental (reduce, reuse, recycle, renewable energy).

In this way, then, New England is both catching up to European brewers who have long stressed locavorism and also imitating winemakers here and abroad who distinguish themselves through their specific terroir. Several of the brewers we interviewed talked about the concept of terroir without fully invoking the concept. When these three movements were brought up in the interview, brewers acknowledged the similarities to what they were doing, but at the same time refrained from explicitly linking themselves to any particular movement. We speculate that brewers see these movements as global in scope and thus, even though complementary to how they make beer, nonetheless threatening to their place in the local ecology.

Moreover, their approach to beer consumers reflects more of a nonoppositional, educational framework than what we might typically expect in such a competitive market sector. In this sense, craft brewers are tapping into a similar value-added (or values-added) segment targeted by organic and fair trade producers. And yet, New England craft brewers are particularly sensitive to the potential class divisiveness that is often attached to these labels, and they seek to avoid narrowing their own potential consumer audience by actively reaching out to mainstream beer consumers in such a way that they feel immediately welcomed rather than possibly alienated. Their place in the ecology of New England beer also often puts them into direct contact with farmers and local business owners. Hence, the majority of local brewers are able to connect with both working-class drinkers and foodies.

Macrobrewers see potential gain in exploiting this class issue (as evidenced by the anti–craft brew Super Bowl advertisement), but the craft brewers have not taken the bait. It may be that the craft beer movement is the tortoise in this race for the American beer drinker's palate, slowly but surely capturing a small, but increasing share of the beer marketplace, and, perhaps in the process, quietly building a revolution in which small businesses, local communities, culinary innovation, and the planet itself is a little better off because of it.

REFERENCES

Appadurai, Arjun. 1996. *Modernity at Large: Cultural Dimensions of Globalization*. Minneapolis: University of Minnesota Press.

Bell, Michael M. 1996. "Stone Age New England: A Geology of Morals." In *Creating the Countryside: The Politics of Rural and Environmental Discourse*, edited by E. Melanie DuPuis and Peter Vandergeest, 29–64. Philadelphia: Temple University Press.

Black, John. 1950. *The Rural Economy of New England*. Cambridge, MA: Harvard University Press.

Bostick, William. 2014. *The Brewer's Tale: A History of the World According to Beer*. New York: Norton.

Brigham, William. 1990. "Noncontentious Social Movements: 'Just Say No To War.'" In *Peace Action in the Eighties: Social Science Perspectives*, edited by Sam Marullo and John Lofland, 155–166. New Brunswick, NJ: Rutgers University Press.

Carroll, Glenn R., and Anand Swaminathan. 2000. "Why the Microbrewery Movement: Organizational Dynamics of Resource Partitioning in the American Brewing Industry after Prohibition." *American Journal of Sociology* 106: 715–762.

Elzinga, Kenneth G. 2011. "The US Beer Industry: Concentration, Fragmentation, and a Nexus with Wine." *Journal of Wine Economics* 6 (2): 217–230.

Habermas, Jurgen. 1981. "New Social Movements." *Telos* 49: 33–37.

Haystead, Ladd, and Gilbert C. Fite. 1955. *The Agricultural Regions of the United States*. Norman: University of Oklahoma Press.

Hinrichs, C. Clare. 1996. "Consuming Images: Making and Marketing Vermont as Distinctive Rural Place." In *Creating the Countryside: The Politics of Rural and Environmental Discourse*, edited by E. Melanie DuPuis and Peter Vandergeest, 259–278. Philadelphia: Temple University Press.

Hosseini, Seyed Abdolhamed. 2006. "Beyond the Practical Dilemmas and Conceptual Reductions: The Emergence of an 'Accommodative Consciousness' in the Alternative Globalization Movement." *PORTAL Journal of Multidisciplinary International Studies* 3 (1): 1–27.

Johnson, Taylor Richard. 2013. "I Drink, Therefore I Am: The American Craft Beer Movement in the Postmodern Age." PhD thesis, College of Arts & Architecture, Montana State University, Bozeman.

Jones, Ellis. 2002. "Social Responsibility Activism: Why Individuals Are Changing Their Lifestyles To Change The World." PhD thesis, Department of Sociology, University of Colorado, Boulder.

Massachusetts Brewers Guild Brochure. Accessed January 12, 2015, http://www.massbrewersguild.org/craft-beer/index.php/2014/03/2014.

Mintz, Sidney. 1996. *Tasting Food, Tasting Freedom: Excursions into Eating, Culture, and the Past.* Boston: Beacon.

Ogle, Maureen. 2006. *Ambitious Brew: The Story of American Beer.* New York: Harcourt.

Paxson, Heather. 2013. *The Life of Cheese: Crafting Food and Value in America.* Berkeley: University of California Press.

Peace, Adrian. 2011. "Barossa Dreaming: Imagining Place and Constituting Cuisine in Contemporary Australia." *Anthropological Forum: A Journal of Social Anthropology and Comparative Sociology* 21 (1): 23–42.

Rao, Hayagreeva, Calvin Morrill, and Mayer N. Zald. 2000. "Power Plays: How Social Movements and Collective Action Create New Organizational Forms." *Research in Organizational Behavior* 22: 237–281.

Thoreau, Henry D., and Jeffrey S. Cramer. 2004. *Walden: A Fully Annotated Edition.* New Haven, CT: Yale University Press.

Toro-González, Daniel, Jill J. McCluskey, and Ron C. Mittelhammer. 2014. "Beer Snobs Do Exist: Estimation of Beer Demand by Type." *Journal of Agricultural and Resource Economics* 39 (2): 174–187.

Touraine, Alain. 1992. "Beyond Social Movements." *Theory, Culture and Society* 9: 125–145.

Varnelis, Kazys. 2008. *The Infrastructural City: Networked Ecologies in Los Angeles.* New York: Actar.

CHAPTER 7

Atmosphere and Activism at the Great British Beer Festival

THOMAS THURNELL-READ

Introduction

While pubs, bars, and nightclubs have been at the center of long-running debates among academics, media, and policymakers with regard to drinking, drunkenness, and disorder, the emergence of beer festivals as a popular setting for the consumption of alcohol has been largely ignored. Indeed, beer festivals present a quite different physical and social setting for the consumption of beer, often in crowds considerably larger than even the most spacious bar or nightclub; therefore, understanding the atmosphere at such events offers valuable insights into the significant changes in the social and cultural practices of beer consumption that have taken place in recent decades. Allied to this are recent advances in academic analysis of what we might refer to as "affective atmospheres" (Shaw 2014; Thien 2005; Thrift 1996) and their particular application to understanding how drinking spaces are experienced as richly emotional, embodied, and sensory (Jayne, et al. 2010). Specifically, beer festivals are gatherings in a temporary location where a particular atmosphere is created in which the consumption of beer takes on a number of meanings. As this chapter will discuss, beer festivals bring together novice and expert beer consumers, brewery staff and other industry professionals, and a variety of volunteers often working behind the scenes to produce and sustain an open, convivial atmosphere. More specifically, it has been argued that beer festivals represent an important moment for the propagation of a sense of community centered on emergent and alternative forms of consumption.

While a number of discussions of the symbolic value of craft beer and real ale in relation to meanings of locality and identity exists (Daniels et al. 2009; Flack

1997; Thurnell-Read 2015b), the emphasis of this chapter will be on the specific spatial–social enactment of beer consumer practices at beer festivals. Because they are temporary establishments, beer festivals are particularly interesting events in which to explore atmospheres and the sensory, embodied, affective nature of drinking that they comprise. Beer festival spaces are, for a number of reasons explored below, conducive to a convivial, playful, and even carnival-esque social ambience. Further, the ephemeral nature of festivals, set up and taken down in a matter of days in exhibition halls, rugby clubs, village halls, hastily constructed marquees, and student union buildings also means that so-cial interactions that take place forge, albeit momentarily, a sense of community around a common practice and passion for craft beer and real ale.

This chapter draws on qualitative research on the British beer and pub con-sumer rights group the Campaign for Real Ale (CAMRA), and their flagship annual event The Great British Beer Festival specifically, to unpack these themes and consider what part beer festivals play in the craft beer revolution in the United Kingdom and beyond. It is argued that festival atmospheres create a space in which attendees are open to new tastes and may sample numerous new beers from a range of breweries. As festival attendees come into contact with the mate-rial product of beer itself but, also, with brewery staff and campaign activists, the atmosphere makes them receptive to a wider set of messages about alterna-tive leisure and consumption practices. Thus, in this space, CAMRA has found fruitful opportunities to recruit new members and to disseminate its messages relating to resisting corporate rationalization and homogenization of the beer industry. The latter part of the chapter will, therefore, consider how festivals contain moments of playful festivity but also, within this, moments for the pol-itics of consumer practice to be contested.

Atmospheres, Affects, and Drinking Spaces

Attempts to capture the specific and often vibrant atmospheres of the diverse environments in which the drinking of alcohol takes place are a characteristic of much academic work on the consumption of alcohol. An early example of this is *The Pub and the People*, a genre-defining study that emerged from detailed field research by the British social research organization Mass Observation (1987) during the late 1930s in the Northern English industrial city "Worktown," an anonymized Bolton. Expressed throughout the book are copious observa-tions on the sensory ambience of the public house; laughter, singing, heated conversations, boastful proclamations, interruptions, curses, and dismissals all abound (Mass Observation 1987). Drinking spaces of all kinds tend to make interesting subjects of academic studies because of these very qualities. Jayne et al. (2010) have shown the importance of embodied and sensory facets of drinking spaces by noting how the sounds, smells, moods, and feelings of a given drinking context are influenced by the physical layout and of the various presence and positioning of bodies, drink, tables, and chairs. Drinking environments do not occur by chance; rather, they are created by various actors who produce, consume, and regulate the character of both the settings themselves and the manner of behavior that takes place within them (Chatterton and Hollands 2003). One element of this has been the use of techniques of high-volume vertical drinking, where bars and clubs are characterized by the strategic use of sound and lighting, seating, and spatial layouts as part of "aesthetic processes aimed at encouraging alcohol-related excitement and excess" (Hayward and Hobbs 2007, 438). Since the 1980s in particular, such drinking spaces often have themes that center around a particular experience as a corporate strategy (Knowles and Howley 2000; Rountree and Ackroyd 2015).

In recent years, a rich body of conceptual work on the sociological nature of atmospheres has emerged. As Anderson notes in an influential article, "by creating and arranging light, sounds, symbols, texts and much more, atmospheres are 'enhanced,' 'transformed,' 'intensified,' 'shaped,' and otherwise 'intervened' (Anderson 2009, 80–81). It has been suggested that although perceived and experienced by individuals, such atmospheres can be said to be "coproduced" and "interactional" (Edensor 2012). These understandings of atmospheres have developed in close relationship with the development of the notion of affect. Thrift (1996, 6) describes *affect* as "a sense of push in the world," which acts upon us, making us feel part of the space we occupy in an essentially embodied and sensory way. Thus, a further notable characteristic is that such atmospheres are constituted by and felt through human bodies. As Reckwitz (2012, 254) suggests, affective spaces involve "the presence and arrangement of human bodies within particular settings" and prompts us to attune our analyses to "the number of bodies, their being gathered or separate, their being distant from or close to each other."

As such, we now have an increased academic understanding of how drinking environments are constructed and sustained. However, with the exception of Spracklen et al.'s (2013) study involving research at a local English beer festival, there have been few studies of beer festivals as social and cultural phenomena and as locations for the study of actual embodied consumption practices. Turning this understanding of atmospheres as being produced and dynamic toward the way in which beer festivals produce a particular drinking context and social atmosphere, this chapter will explore how beer festivals have provided an important vehicle through which real ale consumption has been sustained and expanded.

Beer Festivals and the Campaign for Real Ale (CAMRA)

The Campaign for Real Ale was founded in 1971 and coined the term *real ale*, which entered the *Oxford English Dictionary* in 1981 and is widely, if sometimes inaccurately, used in common parlance in the United Kingdom to define beer that is produced using natural ingredients and is allowed a secondary fermentation in the dispensing receptacle without the addition of extraneous gases. From the outset, CAMRA has offered consumers a voice in resisting various changes in the British beer industry. Principally, this has focused on challenging and, it was hoped, reversing the precipitous decline in sales of cask-conditioned beer being driven by the dominance of several large British breweries and their rapid conversion to pasteurized kegged, and typically heavily branded, beers. As such, the corporate rationalization and the profit motivated efficiency drives of big businesses were the original "enemy" of CAMRA (Watson and Watson 2012, 694). Over the years since, the organization has grown steadily: reaching 5,000 members in 1973; 30,000 in 1976; 50,000 in 1997; 75,000 in 2005; and passing the milestones of 100,000 and 150,000 members to much celebration in 2009 and 2014, respectively. With membership now standing in excess of 175,000 members, CAMRA rightly regards itself as the United Kingdom's leading organization representing beer drinkers and pubgoers and has even been described as Europe's most successful single-issue consumer group. Through the years, CAMRA has sought, through activities at local and national levels, to promote real ale to consumers by positioning cask-conditioned beer in relation to a range of notions about craft, skill, localism, and authenticity in contrast to mass-produced and heavily commercialized beers, which it has readily derided as bland, characterless and "fake."

Alongside its more directed campaigning activities, such as lobbying Parliament on matters relating to brewery and pub closures, the increase in the number and scale of beer festivals has been a striking feature of CAMRA's success as an organization. For example, while the January 1987 issue of *What's Brewing*, the campaign's monthly members newspaper, listed just six beer festivals for the coming months, with most of these offering between 20 and 40 beers, the first six months of 2015 listed 85 official CAMRA festivals, with even relatively modest festivals in regional towns and cities regularly offering over 100 beers and some regional events, such as that held in the northern city of Macclesfield, over 250. Notable in this growth has been the continued success of the Great British Beer Festival, or GBBF as the annual festival is affectionately known within the organization and among many attendees, which has long been thought of as a showpiece or flagship event for CAMRA, providing publicity to the campaign and widening the reach of its message. A reader's letter to *What's Brewing* following the 1978 Great British Beer Festival, the first of four to be held at London's Alexandra Palace over the subsequent years, reflected in relation to the 150 beers available that "many of these brews would have disappeared but for the work of the Campaign." The 1987 festival, held in the southern seaside town of Brighton, boasted a record (at the time) offering of 237 beers. By way of contrast and an illustration of the marked growth of the festival, the 2015 Great British Beer Festival offered over 900 beers from over 300 breweries, as well as over 90 ciders, and was attended by over 50,000 festivalgoers over the course of the week.

The Great British Beer Festival can therefore be regarded as an essential element of CAMRA's existence as an organization and, in other ways, as a litmus test of the health of the real ale movement in the United Kingdom. Indeed, it occupies a cherished position in CAMRA's organizational history, with chapters on the festival and its importance to the campaign featured in volumes produced to mark the 21st and 40th anniversaries of the campaign's existence. The author of the first of these reflects on the very first such festival by suggesting that "the simple message of good beer, brewed and served traditionally, accompanied by wholesome food had caught the imagination of the media and the public at large. Never before, or since, has the Campaign and the idea of real ale has such a high and favorable world-wide exposure" (Bishopp 1992, 59).

As such, conducting participant observation at the Great British Beer Festival, in August 2012 as a consumer and in August 2013 as a volunteer, was an important element of the wider research that I conducted between August 2012 and April 2014 involving 53 qualitative interviews with CAMRA staff, members of the National Executive and local branches, as well as brewers, beer writers, and student ale society members. Adding to this was archival analysis of CAMRA documents and publications dating from its formation in 1971 to the present and further participant observation involving attending two CAMRA Annual General Meetings and two regional conferences and numerous local branch meetings. I also conducted research with a university student ale appreciation society involving regular socials in the local area as well as trips to two cities for larger regional beer festivals and attendance of the society's own annual beer festivals on a number of occasions. Throughout the chapter, pseudonyms are used for all participants and, where necessary, certain identifying characteristics such as organization roles have been obscured in order to preserve participant anonymity.

"What Have You Had, Anything Good?": Festivity, Community, and Taste

Perhaps the most prominent feature of the beer festival atmosphere is the ubiquity of the taste and smell of beer. Taking that further, the air actually fills with the sound of people talking about the taste of beer and their perception of and appreciation for particular ales. For example, while conducting participant observation with the student ale society of a local university, the following scene was observed at the CAMRA National Winter Ales Festival in Manchester:

> A circle forms, each of us now with a pint. Glasses are raised to lips, heads are nodded. "How's that porter then?" "It's good, try it." Glasses are swapped. "That is nice. I do like a good dark beer. It's stronger than I thought, you can taste . . . what is it, 5 percent, 6?" "Its 5.6!" "Really nice." "How's that?" "Not too sure, it's growing on me."

While the scene and the comments, jotted down soon after as ethnographic field notes, are banal enough, the social interaction taking place is unique to beer festivals in that the group of a dozen students stand, rather than sit, and trade observations about the tastes of their beers and even physically swap glasses. Beer festivals are a place where the emphasis is on trying new flavors and sampling beers to which festivalgoers might not normally have access. As the circle grew and shrunk as different society members joined or departed to have their glasses refilled, a running commentary on the taste, style, quality, and variety of the beers was sustained, with several of the students adding ticks and scribbled notes to their festival program beer lists. Indeed, throughout fieldwork it was common to observe festivalgoers looking up from tasting notes and beer lists to announce to friends that they "have to try that" or "you don't see their stuff up this far" in relation to specific beers or breweries. As such, a primary appeal of the festival is the chance to access a range of beers more numerous and more diverse than any pub or bar would otherwise allow, but it also generates a sense of occasion and opportunity where festivalgoers seek out new tastes and share their opinions on the relative merits of the ales they sample.

Festivals are therefore also sites for the expression of knowledge and passion, which many CAMRA members, and real ale or craft beer consumers in general, have spent considerable time and effort to acquire and develop (for a discussion of ale appreciation as "serious leisure," see Thurnell-Read 2015c). Because many of the student ale society were relative newcomers to the field of craft beer and real ale consumption, it was also worth noting how many of those spoken to informally during fieldwork and more formally during interviews made reference to festivals as being moments of inspiration and initiation. One student, Justin spoke with glee, saying:

> The uni festival was amazing! I think I tried 40 or 50 beers over the three days. It was a great laugh and by the end of each night there was always some bad drunken singing [...] I'm really hoping this summer to get to the big one, the London one.

For Justin, and others, the appeal of festivals lay in adopting new behavior and acquiring new beer knowledge as well as a general sense of communal pleasure as evidenced by the nightly sing-along. Anthropologist Victor Turner (1982), for example, considered festivals and other moments of "social drama" to be characterized as moments of playfulness and creativity where new practices may emerge and alliances or antagonisms may be fostered.

Developing these observations further, it becomes clear that the atmosphere created at beer festivals is one that proves conducive to a sense of occasion and conviviality in which beer consumption take place. Thus, following Reckwitz's (2012) concern with "the presence and arrangement" of bodies as being central to the creation of atmosphere, we can note that crowds are a notable feature of beer festivals. Although most festivals will have some seating areas, it is the open floor spaces alongside the serving areas and beer stillage—where large groups gather to drink, talk, and, on occasion, laugh, sing, or cheer—that are central to the spatial context of most beer festivals. Typically, most beer festivals have both daytime and evening sessions and throughout the day the ebb and flow of the density of the festival crowds both indicates the rise and fall of festival atmosphere but also is, in itself, a constituent facet of the sense of the event. For example, one participant spoke of his strategy of "following the crowd to the best beers" by looking for points on the serving stands with longer queues and more densely gathered bodies as being indicative of the locations of the most interesting beers. Further still, a notable feature of the Great British Beer Festival is the lengthy lines that form as festivalgoers wait to sample winning beers following the announcement of awards such as, most notable, the Champion Beer of Britain or a particular brewery releasing a limited batch of a unique beer. As such lines form—as they did during fieldwork at Great British Beer Festival in 2013 for a limited release of a strong oak-aged "Reserve" beer made by London brewer Fuller's, which was being released a cask a day at specific times and, due to its strength and scarcity, only in one-third-pint measures—anticipation rises and, it was observed, numerous conversations between strangers took place spontaneously between those next to each other in line.

In addition to simply stocking a venue with large quantities of good beer, festival organizers propagate a convivial atmosphere and sense of occasion in a number of ways. For example, for many years the Thursday of the Great British Beer Festival has been designated as "Hat Day," with festivalgoers encouraged to wear novelty hats either brought to the festival, bought from one of the numerous merchandise stalls at the event, or, perhaps most fascinating, self-made by attendees. More generally, at many festivals, live music is performed by amateur and professional bands and stages are also used to make presentations of awards or raffles of brewery-related prizes. As such, the sounds of music, songs, and announcements joins that of the chatter and cheer of crowds and the clinking and occasional smash of glasses in adding to what Connell and Gibson (2003, 192) have referred to as the "aural architecture" of the space of the festival. Along with sound, taste and smell also add to the sensory landscape of the festival. Even small regional festivals usually offer a number of food stalls. The Great British Beer Festival provides an extensive and diverse food area, leading to the smell of fish and chips, pasties, pies and curries joining that of beer in the hall—what one fellow volunteer described as "that lovely old GBBF smell."

The choice and layout of venue is also evidently essential to beer festival atmospheres. Notably, in 2012 when the Great British Beer Festival returned to the London Olympia exhibition hall from the nearby Earls Court conference hall, where the annual event had been staged since 2006, many vocal commentators felt that Olympia's grand hall, with its high ironwork arched roof that allowed light to flood in, created a superior atmosphere to the darker, more enclosed, space of Earls Court. Further, given that the festival had previously been held at Olympia between 1992 and 2005, many regular attendees also felt that, as one fellow volunteer observed in 2013, GBBF returning to Olympia was like coming home. Light is also an important but often underanalyzed facet of atmosphere (Edensor 2012). Depending on the venue of the beer festival, many can be characteristically underilluminated or dingy. Other festivals are staged in spaces that invoke a wider sense of heritage and nostalgia. For example, the annual Bristol Beer Festival is staged by the city's local CAMRA branch each spring in Brunel's Old Station, a Victorian-era railway building designed by the acclaimed civic engineer Isambard Kingdom Brunel and now repurposed as a conference and events venue.

The scale and prominence of the Great British Beer Festival means that some of the larger businesses represented construct their own areas within the festival. In recent years, Weston's, a national cider producer, has sponsored a "cider orchard," consisting of a small seating area marked off by rural-style wooden fences and gates with hay-bale seating and a blackboard announcing the times of cider-tasting events. At the 2013 festival, Shepherd Neame, a regional brewery from Kent whose branding of their Spitfire Kentish Ale draws heavily on the county's association with the Battle of Britain and the British Air Force during World War II, constructed a vintage themed area where festivalgoers could dress in Royal Air Force–style clothing and pose for pictures wearing flying caps and goggles. Two breweries from Cornwall, England's most southwesterly county, provide interesting examples of these theme areas. The St. Austell Brewery stand featured screens and banners showing picturesque fishing villages, coastal scenes, and images of waves and surfers, while Skinner's Brewery has achieved relative notoriety among festival regulars for arriving at the festival each year with a sizable marching band led by a man in costume as "Betty Stogs," the eponymous Cornish "wench" of the brewery's leading brand of bitter.

A further notable feature of beer festivals, and the Great British Beer Festival in particular, is the presence of often large groups of staff from breweries from across the country and beyond, with many wearing branded clothing bearing the names and logos of their particular brewery or beers. One brewer, Stan, reflected during an interview that he always made the effort to attend the London event, saying: "It's a great way to keep up with what's happening, you get to meet old friends and make new ones too. Everybody there is united by this love of beer." Unpacking this comment further, we can see that to brewers such as Stan, beer festivals are a number of things: a chance to glean new ideas to inform his own brewing; an important means of establishing and maintaining social networks within the British brewery industry; and, more generally, a space in which to act the part of knowledgeable and passionate beer lover.

A number of breweries reported using festivals to showcase new beers; this often involves having brewery staff serving beers or just "hanging out" and talking to festivalgoers. Festivals were also seen as a chance, in one brewer's words, "to go off-piste and do something really fun." Brewers spoke in interviews of particular beer styles that might be difficult to sell in pubs and bars—mild, porter, old ale, and barley wine—selling well at festivals, and one brewer spoke of "twisting" one of his core brands by dry hopping it for a festival. Even the sole proprietor of what was, at just two-and-a-half-barrel capacity, the smallest brewery involved in the research, Ryan, spoke of beer festivals as one of the important stages for his beers. Indeed, beyond supplying the pub behind which his brewery was located in a former coffin workshop, he reflected that festivals were one of the few ways in which people could sample the product of his admittedly obscure brewery. He said that:

All the big beer festivals have my beer. This year Nottingham, Birmingham, all the big boys take it on at the festivals and that increases the knowledge that the beer is available but then if they want it again they have to come and get it from the pub.

Similarly, when Steve was interviewed not long after the opening of his brewery on the outskirts of his home city, he already knew that the local beer festival would be an important resource for him in testing new beers. He said that:

Yeah, I mean the [local] beer festival is late March, early April, next year and I would like to have possibly a Mild actually, a new beer that I can launch there, which does them a favor as they've been very supportive and obviously helps me launch a beer. That's probably be the first time I'll specifically try and time it so that it is launched at a beer festival. Plus you have a reasonable chance of it winning beer of the festival if you do that.

Thus, for many of the brewers interviewed, festivals were a chance to bring their beers to a wider audience and to connect with the local beer drinking community and therefore, even if they represented only a fraction of their overall sales, they were seen as important and worthy of their time and efforts. Geoff, for example, spoke of supporting a local beer festival through collaboration on a special festival ale. He said that:

You can almost be dismissive of them thinking "it's just a festival, isn't it," but the fact is that everybody walking into a beer festival is a beer drinker, everybody walking into a pub isn't a beer drinker. So, yeah they are important. We support and sponsor [local] beer festival and next month a group of their organizers for the festival are coming to the brewery and they brew a beer with me specifically for their festival. A unique beer, it's always a world premier at [local city] and after that it might be a mainstay to the portfolio but it isn't let loose anywhere before the [local] beer festival.

A final group that plays a significant role in the construction of the festival atmosphere are the numerous CAMRA members who volunteer to serve beer, wash glasses, and act as stewards, as well as staff tombola, pub game, and merchandise stalls. CAMRA estimates the combined labor value of volunteering within its organization, at beer festivals but also running local branch meetings and other campaigning activities, to stand in excess of $2.5 million per year (based on 2012 exchange rates). Thus, the accounts of volunteer festival staff offer interesting insights into the workings of the festival and the backstage elements that go into producing the events. Writing in a collection marking the 40th anniversary of CAMRA, a former National Chairman and organizer of multiple Great British Beer Festivals, reflected on her first involvement with the Great British Beer Festival in 1982 by saying that:

> I had one of the best weeks ever, I met some truly remarkable people, worked so physically hard I could barely stand up at the end of the shift, and was infected by the bug of the event (Waters 2011, 42).

Such sentiments were also expressed by others. During the Saturday morning shift of fieldwork as a volunteer at Great British Beer Festival 2013, a steward from Scotland described how he volunteers at a number of festivals each year, saying:

> I'm a chemical research scientist, I'm in the lab all day. I'd never be able to do all this before but I've been doing the stewarding and I'll talk to anyone you know, you have to. It brings you out of yourself. You could be managing a multi-million pound company and have all these skills but you come here and it's fun so you just work on a bar.

Pete, a key member of the CAMRA Head Office staff, reflected on this importance of sociability by saying that:

> A lot of people join CAMRA because of the sociability of it, they can go along to a festival, volunteer at a festival and you meet like minded people, you volunteer for the Great British Beer Festival and you work with a thousand people, you socialise with them, you have a good time.

Again, the atmosphere at the festival is understood as one where people come together to engage in their mutual appreciation of real ale in a fun and convivial context. Emily, a member of the national executive committee, with experience in festival organization at a national and local level, observed during an interview that:

I think a lot of the people who visit the beer festivals are not aware that the festival is organised and run by unpaid volunteers, they think "oh look they get a wage for this." That's why we have our big banners saying this festival is manned by unpaid volunteers, these people give a week of their holiday to do this, GBBF can be a week and a bit, so they do give up their annual leave for beer festivals.

The importance of volunteers working to produce and sustain the atmosphere of the festival was experienced first-hand through participant observation as a volunteer during the 2013 Great British Beer Festival. Thus, the following extract describes one of three shifts spent on the "Lucky Plucker," one of several tombola-style game stalls where festivalgoers can pay to draw raffle tickets and win prizes ranging from beer tokens, brewery-branded sweatshirts, and CAMRA books and beer guides to novelty hats, soft toys, and garden gnomes:

It's very slow for first hour and the three of us get to stand and chat or go for a walk and collect drinks. Things steadily pick up as people have a few drinks and make their way around the venue and into the side hall. Once the central seating has filled up more people near the stall, using the adjacent counter to lean and prop up drinks. If they get near enough we shake the ticket buckets at them. Most people play in groups. . . . As the afternoon progresses there is a steady stream of customers and by the evening we are continually serving. . . . Some large groups where one person plays and then others get drawn in more as it goes along. . . . We ring the hand-bell and cheer 'And another winner!' when someone wins. Towards the evening Keith the shift manager finishes and is replaced by Tim who adopts a different style, grabbing a pink cowgirl hat from the stand and pumping the horn to draw in more customers. As the hall fills we have to shout to be heard by customers. (Field notes, GBBF, August 14, 2013)

While other research has explored the role played by tour guides and other such individuals who facilitate and encourage drinking and drunkenness in pub and club settings (Thurnell-Read 2015a; Tutenges 2013), it is worth noting that at beer festivals numerous volunteers work not to encourage drinking but to add to and heighten the atmosphere and general sense of fun and festivity. As one fellow volunteer advised me on my first shift, "You just have to have a laugh with it, make a noise, and keep it fun."

Such examples illustrate the varied contributions made festivalgoers, organizers, and breweries to the atmosphere of the festival. In these examples, we see how beer festivals occupy a unique position in the consciousness of both real ale drinkers and real ale brewers. Beer festivals in general, and Great British Beer Festival in particular, provide spaces in which new tastes are developed, existing tastes are sustained, and a passion for good beer is performed.

"Ask Me about CAMRA": Mixing the Business of Activism with the Pleasure of Atmosphere

So far in this chapter, I have explored how it is through the combined interaction and work of different actors that the atmosphere at beer festivals is "coproduced" and performed as a space in which beer consumers can enact their passion for beer and important connections between beer consumers and producers can be fostered and sustained. As noted, this involves the sounds, sights, tastes, and smells of the festival, all of which are evidently important constituents of the beer festival as a particular drinking space. Further still, several interviewees spoke of festivals being one of the best occasions to recruit new members to CAMRA, as an organization, and to the leisure practice of real ale appreciation in general. For example, Oliver, a member of the CAMRA headquarters staff, noted the importance of festivals in bringing new adherents to the field of ale consumption. He said that:

> Those festivals are a really great way of introducing to real ale for the first time because people tend to as part of a group, that group will go because there is perhaps one advocate that is interested in real ale and drags their friends along and they are actually interested but haven't got to the festival to try a few beers and that can influence longer term drinking patterns so that really helps.

Beer festivals, especially larger showpiece events such as the Great British Beer Festival, are therefore an important means for CAMRA to attract new members and new consumers to real ale as well as to promote and disseminate various meanings associated with consuming real ale. This final section will consider how it is that whilst providing an atmosphere of festivity and conviviality, the festival space is also a site for important campaigning activities.

Given that much of CAMRA's campaigning work involves efforts to position real ale as more authentic than mass-produced beers (Watson and Watson 2012) and to associate real ale in relation to positive thinking related to localism, sustainability, and community (O'Brien 2006), it is no surprise that throughout its history, beer festivals have always been a means for CAMRA to increase the visibility of the organization and to further the aims of its campaigns. For example, at the first national beer festival, held in September 1975 in the Coventry Garden market (at that point prerestoration), CAMRA added significantly to its membership, with over 800 new members signing up and many immediately volunteering to help staff the event (Bishopp 1992, 59). Festivals have even provided a platform for direct campaigning. During the 1986 Great British Beer Festival held in Brighton, in southern England, 2,000 postcards preaddressed to the Home Secretary Douglas Heard complaining about restrictive public house licensing laws were distributed to festivalgoers. More recently, the 2012 Great British Beer Festival was used to generate support for a campaign petition relating to beer taxation and to make the eventual announcement that the petition had passed the 100,000-signature mark.

For senior CAMRA staff, the real success of events such as the Great British Beer Festival lay in the ability to balance the somewhat competing demands of furthering the various causes of the campaign and providing a convivial and light-hearted atmosphere that attendees would enjoy. As such, there is an apparent similarity to how Sharpe (2008, 223), in her study of how politics and leisure intersect at a community music festival, spoke of how "recognizing its potential for political and social influence, organizers decided early in its history to use the event as a forum for promoting a set of principles deemed worthwhile by the organization." As in Sharpe's (2008, 224) study, CAMRA "enacted its politics through the choices that were made in the staging, servicing, and organizing of the event." Typically, even a modest CAMRA local branch–organized beer festival will include a membership stand where festivalgoers can learn about the organization's campaign activities and sign up for membership, as well as a shop or stall selling CAMRA books and other materials related to the campaign.

Further still, one of the primary means by which the meanings and values associated with CAMRA's campaigning are disseminated at beer festivals is, again, in the important role played by staff. Thus, festival volunteers are encouraged to view themselves as advocates of the campaign and to be ready during their shift to talk about CAMRA to festivalgoers. Throughout my fieldwork on the Lucky Plucker stall, recounted above, it was common during quieter moments for some festival attendees, perhaps prompted by an "Ask me about CAMRA" badge pinned to my festival volunteer's t-shirt, would ask questions about the campaign and activism activities of CAMRA. CAMRA members who volunteer at beer festivals might therefore be said to be vital to the success of the event in performing the role of passionate people who can demonstrate to visitors how to feel about real ale (Bennett 2013).

In a similar manner to how Aspers and Darr (2011) suggest that the coming together of participants at trade shows allows for specific cultures to coalesce around certain activities, the Great British Beer Festival stands as an example of how the disparate elements of the alternative beer scene in the United Kingdom come together in the specific time and space of the festival. As Crouch (2000, 68) observes, leisure spaces "are sites of friendship and social engagement and become meaningful through the ways in which people are encountered." Beer festivals are, therefore, a good example of how leisure spaces are embodied and "lived in" as participants interact, exhibit commitment and passion, and share ideas, knowledge, and tastes. Drawing on Turner's (1982) notion of the essentially creative character of such moments of festivity, we can see that the beer festival space and the social interactions that take place there allow for, again in Turner's terms, a form of *communitas* to develop. Indeed, beer festivals can be seen to carry many of the characteristics of a "community of practice," where knowledge, identity, and community are all "situated" in the embodied social setting (Duguid 2005; Lave and Wenger 1991).

While there has been a striking growth in what might be described as an online community of beer consumers, beer festivals remain one of the moments when beer lovers come together to demonstrate their passion for beer (Clemons et al. 2006), as noted, there are few studies of beer festivals in this regard. However, interesting comparisons might be made to alternative food consumer networks where farmer's markets and food festivals act as sites where face-to-face interactions between consumers and producers help to reinstate the act of consumption with a sense of community and social embeddedness (de Solier 2013). More specifically, the Slow Food movement's use of sociable meetings or "convivia" as a time and space for various groups and individuals such as consumers, chefs, activists, farmers, and producers to meet and interact (van Bommel and Spicer 2011), bear striking similarity to the ways in which CAMRA beer festivals succeed in the mutually reinforcing tasks of playful social gathering and a more directive expansion of activism and campaigning goals. Just as such events allow foodies to enact and sustain their identity as being passionate, knowledgeable, and caring when it comes to food (Hayes-Conroy and Hayes-Conroy 2010; Cairns et al. 2010), beyond or, indeed, because of the evident festivity and conviviality at beer festivals such as the Great British Beer Festival, both atmosphere and activism can be achieved at one and the same moment.

Conclusion

This chapter has explored how beer festivals represent an interesting yet understudied example of how drinking spaces are shaped as affective atmospheres. Numerous factors influence the atmosphere of the festival, including the size and layout of the venue, the positioning and density of bodies, and the various strategies used to influence the sounds, smells, tastes, and sights of the festival. Importantly, as I have sought to demonstrate, the beer festival atmosphere is the culmination of inputs and efforts from a variety of actors: paid and unpaid festival staff; brewers and other staff from local, regional, and national breweries; and committed real-ale drinkers and relative novices. As such, beer festivals exemplify the renegotiation of relationships between beer producers, suppliers, and consumers that has been central to CAMRA and the real-ale movement in the United Kingdom and, more generally, craft beer globally. Beer festivals create an atmosphere that is a platform for small and independent breweries to present their beers and for new and old consumers alike to bond and enact pleasure and passion. Although temporary, beer festivals provide a specific moment and space that is a locus for a range of values and practices associated with craft beer consumption to be performed, shared, and disseminated. Because they are highly embodied and sensory in nature, beer festivals allow participants a form of "situated learning," where they can learn to exhibit passion, knowledge, and taste (Lave and Wenger 1991). As a former CAMRA National Chairman and festival volunteer and organizer with extensive experience reflects, at the Great British Beer Festival "all the different parts of the festival interlock and together become greater than the sum of the parts" (Waters 2011, 46).

REFERENCES

Anderson, B. 2009. "Affective Atmospheres." *Emotion, Space, and Society* 2 (2): 77–81.

Aspers, Patrick, and Asaf Darr. 2011. "Trade Shows and the Creation of Market and Industry." *Sociological Review* 59 (4): 758–778.

Bennett, Katy. 2013. "Emotion and Place Promotion: Passionate about a Former Coalfield." *Emotion, Space, and Society* 8: 1–10.

Bishopp, J. 1992. "Called to the Bar: An Account of the First 21 years of the Campaign for Real Ale." In *The Covent Garden Beer Festival*, edited by R. Protz and T. Millns, 58–60. St. Albans, UK: CAMRA.

Cairns, Kate, Josee Johnston, and Shyon Baumann. 2010. "Caring About Food Doing Gender in the Foodie Kitchen." *Gender & Society* 24 (5): 591–615.

Chatterton, Paul, and Robert Hollands. 2003. *Urban Nightscapes: Youth Cultures, Pleasure Spaces and Corporate Power*. London: Routledge.

Clemons, Eric K., Guodong Gordon Gao, and Lorin M. Hitt. 2006. "When Online Reviews Meet Hyperdifferentiation: A Study of the Craft Beer Industry." *Journal of Management Information Systems* 23 (2): 149–171.

Connell, John, and Chris Gibson. 2003. *Sound Tracks: Popular Music Identity and Place.* London: Routledge.

Crouch, David. 2000. "Places around Us: Embodied lay Geographies in Leisure and Tourism." *Leisure Studies* 19 (2): 63–76.

Daniels, Evan, Chandler Sterling, and Eli Ross. 2009. "Microbreweries and Culture in the Greater Madison Area." *Geography* 565: 12.

De Solier, Isabelle. 2013. *Food and the Self: Consumption, Production and Material Culture.* London: Bloomsbury.

Duguid, Paul. 2005. " 'The Art of Knowing': Social and Tacit Dimensions of Knowledge and the Limits of the Community of Practice." *The Information Society* 21 (2): 109–118.

Edensor, T. 2012. "Illuminated Atmospheres: Anticipating and Reproducing the Flow of Affective Experience in Blackpool." *Environment and Planning-Part D: Society and Space* 30 (6): 1103–1122.

Flack, Wes. 1997. "American Microbreweries and Neolocalism: 'Ale-ing' for a Sense of Place." *Journal of Cultural Geography* 16 (2): 37–53.

Hayes-Conroy, Allison, and Jessica Hayes-Conroy. 2010. "Visceral Difference: Variations in Feeling (Slow) Food." *Environment and Planning A* 42 (12): 2956–2971.

Hayward, Keith, and Dick Hobbs. 2007. "Beyond the Binge in 'Booze Britain': Market-led Liminalization and the Spectacle of Binge Drinking." *British Journal of Sociology* 58 (3): 437–456.

Jayne, Mark, Gill Valentine, and Sarah L. Holloway. 2010. "Emotional, Embodied and Affective Geographies of Alcohol, Drinking and Drunkenness." *Transactions of the Institute of British Geographers* 35 (4): 540–554.

Knowles, Tim, and Michael J. Howley. 2000. "Branding in the UK Public House Sector: Recent Developments." *International Journal of Contemporary Hospitality Management* 12 (6): 366–370.

Lave, Jean, and Etienne Wenger. 1991. *Situated Learning: Legitimate Peripheral Participation.* Cambridge: Cambridge University Press.

Mass Observation. 1987. *The Pub and the People.* London: Cresset Library.

O'Brien, Christopher Mark. 2006. *Fermenting Revolution: How to Drink Beer and Save the World.* Gabriola Island, BC: New Society.

Reckwitz, A. 2012. "Affective Spaces: A Praxeological Outlook." *Rethinking History* 16 (2): 241–258.

Rountree, C., and R. Ackroyd. 2015. "More Than Just a Shop That Sells Beer? JD Wetherspoon and the Pub Authenticity-Value Aesthetic." In *Biographies of Drink: A Case Study Approach to our Historical Relationship with Alcohol*, edited by M. Hailwood and D. Toner, 100–135. Cambridge: Cambridge Scholars.

Sharpe, Erin K. 2008. "Festivals and Social Change: Intersections of Pleasure and Politics at a Community Music Festival." *Leisure Sciences* 30 (3): 217–234.

Shaw, Robert. 2014. "Beyond Night-Time Economy: Affective Atmospheres of the Urban Night." *Geoforum* 51: 87–95.

Spracklen, Karl, Jon Laurencic, and Alex Kenyon. 2013. "'Mine's a Pint of Bitter': Performativity, Gender, Class and Representations of Authenticity in Real-Ale Tourism." *Tourist Studies* 13 (3): 304–321.

Thien, D. 2005. After or Beyond Feeling? A Consideration of Affect and Emotion in Geography." *Area* 37 (4): 450–454.

Thrift, Nigel. 1996. *Spatial Formations*. London: Sage.

Thurnell-Read, Thomas. 2015a. "Beer and Belonging: Real Ale Consumption, Place and Identity." In *Drinking Dilemmas: Space, Culture and Society*, edited by T. Thurnell-Read, 45–61. London: Routledge/BSA Sociological Futures.

———. 2015b. "'Just Blokes Doing Blokes' Stuff': Risk, Gender and the Collective Performance of Masculinity during the Eastern European Stag Tour Weekend." In *Men, Masculinities, Travel and Tourism*, edited by T. Thurnell-Read and M. Casey, 43–57. London: Palgrave Macmillan.

———. 2015c. "'Real Ale' Enthusiasts, Serious Leisure and the Costs of Getting 'Too Serious' about Beer." *Leisure Sciences* 38 (1): 68–84.

Turner, Victor Witter. 1982. *From Ritual to Theatre: The Human Seriousness of Play*. Baltimore: Paj.

Tutenges, Sebastien. (2013). "Stirring Up Effervescence: An Ethnographic Study of Youth at a Nightlife Resort." *Leisure Studies* 32 (3): 233–248.

Van Bommel, Koen, and Andre Spicer. 2011. "Hail the Snail: Hegemonic Struggles in the Slow Food Movement." *Organization Studies* 32 (12): 1717–1744.

Waters, P. 2011. "On the Road with the Great British Beer Festival." In *CAMRA at 40: Still Campaigning for Real Ale and Good Pubs*, edited by R. Protz, 42–46. St. Albans, UK: CAMRA.

Watson, Tony James, and Diane Heather Watson. 2012. "Narratives in Society, Organizations and Individual Identities: An Ethnographic Study of Pubs, Identity Work and the Pursuit of 'the Real.'" *Human Relations* 65 (6): 683–704.

CHAPTER 8

Neighborhood Change, One Pint at a Time

The Impact of Local Characteristics on Craft Breweries

JESUS M. BARAJAS, GEOFF BOEING, AND JULIE WARTELL

Introduction

Brooklyn Brewery occupies half a block along North 11th Street in the heart of Williamsburg, one of New York City's most rapidly changing neighborhoods. On most weekends, the tasting room is packed full of enthusiastic craft beer drinkers. Former industrial spaces nearby house gourmet restaurants, trendy bars, boutique hotels, and renovated residential lofts. Williamsburg was not always this way. Remnants of the area's industrial past are visible everywhere—large brick factory buildings fill entire city blocks and a still-active oil depot operates along the river inlet two blocks northwest of the brewery. Many consider Brooklyn Brewery to be the anchor institution of Williamsburg's revitalization, a popular narrative that, as we describe in this chapter, repeats itself with Wynkoop Brewing in Denver's LoDo neighborhood, 21st Amendment Brewery in San Francisco's SoMa neighborhood, and others across the country.

Shifting consumer preferences toward more flavor, more options, and more local products have fueled the growth of these three breweries and of craft beer in general. However, urban planning and policy have also influenced the success of craft brewing. Some cities have modified their zoning regulations and offered financial incentives that have allowed intrepid entrepreneurs to become first movers into economically uncertain locations (Best 2015; Hopkins 2014). In turn, these anchor establishments helped spawn new, smaller craft breweries, as the demand for high-quality local beer—and other niche products and services—has increased. Future growth of the craft beer industry is tied to the success of these new breweries. Upstart brewers tend to be small—often born of a homebrewing hobby—with the capacity and profit incentives to serve only a local market. Unlike the pioneering microbrewers before them that serve regional and multistate consumers, these newer brewers—such as brewpubs that produce beer only for the customers who patronize their restaurants—require smaller production spaces and thus are not limited to locating in industrial neighborhoods. Seeking to capitalize on a new market of place-based consumers, newer and smaller brewers may not be catalysts of urban revitalization so much as respondents to changing neighborhood demographics.

In this chapter, we explore the influence of neighborhood change over the past decade on where craft breweries are located. This study is the first to empirically examine the relationship between neighborhoods and craft breweries across the United States. Using U.S. Census data, we first describe the neighborhood characteristics of where craft breweries operate. We then look at neighborhoods to understand how changes in residential composition suggest factors influential in craft brewery location decisions. We also explore differences at regional and subregional spatial scales. We conclude with some suggestions for urban planning and policy as other cities turn to craft brewing as an opportunity for neighborhood revitalization, economic development, and tourism.

Craft Beer: People, Place, and Planning

People and Place

Although the demand for craft beer has increased rapidly over the past three decades, it has not grown uniformly across all demographic groups. Craft beer drinkers tend to have higher incomes than other beer drinkers, because, on average, craft beer commands a higher price than other domestic or imported beers (Tremblay and Tremblay 2011). Furthermore, in the recent past, craft beer drinkers have tended to be white, male Gen Xers (Tremblay and Tremblay 2005), but current trends indicate an increasingly racially and ethnically diverse, female, and millennial demographic profile (Watson 2014).

Several researchers have explored the link between place, demographics, and the location of craft breweries. Three main threads link these studies. First, the spatial geography of craft beer production in the United States is uneven on multiple scales. At a regional level, for example, the Pacific Coast states have seen major increases in production volume and brewing facilities over the past three decades, while there has been very little growth in the number of facilities in the southeastern United States over the same period (McLaughlin et al. 2014).

To some extent, this is a result of California's vanguard position in the rebirth of local brewing—many consider Anchor Steam in San Francisco, New Albion in Sonoma, and Sierra Nevada in Chico to be the modern founders of today's craft brewing industry (Acitelli 2013). At the state level, research has found a significant association between demographics and craft beer. Higher population levels predict more craft beer production, but controlling for population, traditional brewing culture is a stronger predictor (McLaughlin et al. 2014). Higher educational attainment and greater levels of happiness and well-being may also be associated with the amount of craft brewing at the state level (Florida 2012).

Cultural attitudes and affinities associated with place may impact craft beer production and consumption in a metropolitan area. For example, the values of residents who have helped to "keep Portland weird" may have also contributed to the explosion of the craft beer industry in that city (Cortright 2002). On the other hand, religious convictions and corporate influence are significant predictors of the low number of craft breweries in the southern United States (Gohmann 2016). Metropolitan-level influences on craft beer also vary by region. Factors such as the cost of living and the level of tolerance the population has for activities outside of cultural norms are significant predictors of craft breweries' presence in the South. Education levels and the amount of arts and culture in the metropolitan area are not significant predictors in the South, even though they are in other regions (Baginski and Bell 2011).

A second thread of research on craft beer and place focuses on the idea of local production. Cultural geographers have used the term *neolocalism* to describe the present-day phenomenon of the desire for the local: preferring the mom-and-pop shop on Main Street to the anonymity and sameness of the "big box" store (Flack 1997). Much as wine connoisseurs travel to wineries to experience the terroir of a vintner's product or foodies look to experience local flavors in new restaurants or farmers markets, craft beer drinkers seek out the local connection between their favorite beverage and the place where it was brewed.

Many craft breweries tie into local landmarks and lore through their beer names and labels. This can help newcomers share in the cultural history of a place through consumption of a distinctively local product (Schnell and Reese 2003), creating a common narrative of a certain neighborhood history as new residents move in. For example, the Great Lakes Brewing Company, based in Cleveland, Ohio, brews Burning River Pale Ale, whose label pays tribute to the infamous 1969 Cuyahoga River fire as a symbol of the city's industrial past and modern rebirth (Stradling and Stradling 2008). Oakland, California's, Linden Street Brewery ties into the local ethos by delivering its flagship product in kegs solely by bicycle to restaurants and bars in the city. The cargo bike that sits in front of its brewing facility serves as a visible symbol of local production and consumption, as well as its membership in the city's bicycle culture.

A third rationale for the connection between craft beer and place can be seen through the literature on gentrification. *Gentrification* does not have a unique definition, but generally refers to the process of middle-class professionals moving to disinvested central city neighborhoods, upgrading housing, and attracting new businesses that cater to the new neighborhood clientele. Often, this process coincides with the displacement of current residents and businesses, who tend to be poorer and from racial and ethnic minority groups. Some have argued that as a result of America's postindustrial economy, the newly enlarged occupational class of managers and technical professionals, usually considered the gentrifiers, has had a substantial impact on consumer tastes and housing preferences as they seek the culture and compactness of the central city (see, for example, Lees et al. 2008).

Some scholars have argued that in certain locations, the development of craft breweries can accelerate gentrification by playing on the industrial heritage of the past (such as old manufacturing sites), appealing to the "discerning" consumer class attracted to such amenities, and in turn anchoring subsequent development (Mathews and Picton 2014). In some respects, then, craft beer is entangled with the process of neighborhood change and may be either a leading indicator (as a pioneer of reinvestment) or a lagging indicator (as a response to changing tastes and local culture) (see, for example, Cortright 2002).

Urban Planning and Policy

Craft beer has become intertwined with city planning over the past decade for two related reasons. First, it is increasingly seen as an engine of local economic development and neighborhood vitality. Second, for reasons articulated in the previous section, craft beer is readily identified with its place of origin and attracts well-educated, affluent consumers. As a result, civic leaders and city planners increasingly look to the craft beer industry to play a role in neighborhood revitalization (cf. Hackworth and Smith 2001). Efforts to revitalize once-declining inner cities have emphasized the importance of the "creative class" and their demands in shaping reinvestment. Some have argued that because creative professionals drive the new economy, cities that wish to improve their economic performance should invest in the amenities that attract this class of people (Florida 2002)—museums, cultural activities, and perhaps craft beer.

Craft breweries are common first movers into economically depressed neighborhoods, often out of necessity. Larger breweries require expensive equipment and ample space. Inexpensive rent is essential to keep overhead costs low for this type of entrepreneurial light industry, much as Jane Jacobs (1961/1992) noted in her praise of aged buildings. Breweries may also produce unpleasant noise, odors, and considerable wastewater pollution, making them less likely to obtain permits in bedroom suburbs or upscale shopping centers. Nevertheless, with its large equipment and high fixed costs, a new brewery signals that someone is starting to invest long term in a place, more so than does a bar or restaurant. Smaller breweries may then follow. In turn, services move in, young families begin to settle, a community grows, and craft breweries become the canary in the coal mine for neighborhood change.

Significant anecdotal evidence suggests that this pattern is common. The 21st Amendment brewery in San Francisco is sometimes considered the "grand-daddy" of the South of Market neighborhood (Associated Press 2013b), which is rapidly changing as a result of the region's technology sector. The city of Oakland, California's, senior economic development specialist has argued that breweries revitalize struggling neighborhoods by serving as a magnet for new businesses while creating foot traffic and social activity (Somerville 2013).

Accordingly, city planners have recently begun to play an active role in fostering brewery openings and the inchoate neighborhood revitalization that trails them. Great Lakes Brewing opened in Cleveland's economically depressed Ohio City neighborhood in 1988. When it started attracting customers and other shops began to open nearby, the city repaved surrounding streets with cobblestones and invested millions of dollars in the redevelopment of a neighboring abandoned historic market hall (Associated Press 2013b). On the West Coast, Portland, Oregon's, development commission assists craft breweries with building renovations (Best 2015). Since 2000, Portland has spent $96 million on revitalization efforts in its Lents neighborhood, recently dedicating $1 million to building improvements and loans for a new brewpub (Boddie 2014).

City planners also play a role through permitting and land-use regulation. Craft breweries' amalgam of industrial and retail uses often necessitates special zoning, infrastructure, and government assistance (Perritt 2013). Some cities, including San Diego, Long Beach, Dallas, Charlotte, and Cincinnati, have introduced specific microbrewery land uses or more mixed-use designations to simplify development (Appleton 2012; City of San Diego 2015; May and Monk 2015; Peters and Szczepaniak 2013). The San Francisco Brewers' Guild recently stated that the biggest challenge facing their brewers was the long delay in acquiring permits from the Department of Building Inspection, due to a permitting logjam from the city's construction boom (Crowell 2013).

Today, many craft brewers explicitly view themselves as agents of neighborhood revitalization and change (see, for example, Bartlett et al. 2013; Flynn et al.

2014). In 1989, Boulevard Brewing opened in central Kansas City, Missouri. Rather than locating on inexpensive land at the urban periphery, the brewers wanted to contribute to the central city's urban vitality, referring to themselves as "committed urbanists" (Associated Press 2013a). However, urban breweries like Boulevard may sometimes become victims of their own success; the ensuing desire to be in the neighborhood can increase local rents and demand for space. Marquee breweries such as 21st Amendment and Brooklyn Brewery have begun to expand and relocate to less-expensive neighborhoods in their metropolitan areas (Associated Press 2013b; Li 2014), perhaps starting anew the cycle of neighborhood change elsewhere.

The news media, case studies, and development reports provide many of the details behind the effects of craft breweries and the economic transitions of neighborhoods in which they are located. In summary, craft brewing benefits cities by investing in struggling neighborhoods and adding an amenity to changing neighborhoods, and planners are willing to accommodate these new investments. Much of the information on a submetropolitan scale relies on anecdotal evidence or single case studies. There is little empirical evidence from these studies or others that assess the relationships between residential characteristics of neighborhoods and craft breweries.

Methods and Data

Craft brewing is related to neighborhood change and urban planning, but the nature of this relationship remains vague in the research literature. To address this, we explored the extent to which the changing residential characteristics of neighborhoods influence the location of new breweries. In other words, does urban revitalization predict the locations of these desirable assets? Given the cross-sectional nature of our dataset, it is not possible to assign a direction of causality to the relationship between craft brewery locations and neighborhood change—and, in fact, there may be a reciprocal relationship. Nevertheless, understanding associations between craft brewing and neighborhood change has policy implications, such as whether cities should create incentives for breweries to locate in disinvested neighborhoods if demographic changes encourage them to locate in revitalized neighborhoods otherwise.

Craft Brewery Locations

To understand the relationship between craft brewing and location, we obtained a unique dataset of craft breweries in the United States from PubQuest (2015), a company that maps craft breweries.[1] PubQuest compiles the brewery data from a variety of public and private sources and includes each U.S. craft brewery location open to the public, the address, and the type of brewery. Brewery types include brewery with tasting room, brewpub with on-site brewing and food service, and brew houses that are owned by craft breweries without on-site brewing. The dataset includes all craft breweries that were in operation at some time between 2006 and 2015. The dataset does not include production volume, though all breweries listed meet the Brewers Association definition of a craft brewer.

We aggregated the PubQuest data to the census-tract level to harmonize with U.S. Census socioeconomic variables. Census tracts are an imperfect spatial unit and may miss more localized relationships between neighborhood change and craft brewery locations. Nevertheless, they provide a consistent level of geography across the United States and are relatively stable over time (though, see discussion below). Socioeconomic data are more reliable at the census-tract level than at smaller spatial units, such as block groups. Thus, we defined neighborhoods using the census tract as the spatial unit.

Identifying Neighborhood Change

We measured change between the 2000 decennial Census and the 2009–2013 five-year American Community Survey (ACS) estimates. The ACS aggregates survey responses from each year of the five-year period into one dataset, so it allows for a rough comparison of 2000 and 2011 socioeconomic data. Literature on gentrification and displacement provided a starting point for variables appropriate to measure when trying to understand neighborhood change (see, for example, Freeman 2005; Newman and Wyly 2006). We selected variables on race and ethnicity, age, family structure, educational attainment, income, employment, housing age, median home value, and population density as independent variables. All dollar amounts are inflation-adjusted 2013 dollars.

Although we are primarily interested in how change in these variables is associated with craft brewery locations, we also included year 2000 values for each variable for which we examined change. In this way, we controlled for locations that may have experienced little change but had high or low values for each variable to begin with. We standardized census-tract definitions to the 2010 boundaries, using the Brown University Longitudinal Tract Database files (Logan et al. 2014). We included in our models only variables that are strictly comparable between the two datasets.

We estimated a series of logistic regression models, in which the dependent variable is whether a census tract has a new craft brewery. We estimated both standard and robust versions of the models. We defined *new* to mean whether a brewery opened in 2013 or later. In each model, we controlled for whether a craft brewery existed prior to 2013. Particularly in the early years of the craft brewing renaissance, brewers relied on existing knowledge of those who came before them in the industry (Acitelli 2013; Ogle 2006), so we expected to see a positive relationship between the presence of an older brewery and a new one. We also controlled for the census division in which the tract is located, as defined by the U.S. Census Bureau (2000). As we described earlier, existing research has shown an uneven geographic distribution of craft beer, with far greater prevalence in the western United States and far less prevalence in the southeastern portion of the country (Baginski and Bell 2011; Gohmann 2016; McLaughlin et al. 2014). Independent variables in the models are cross-sectional and paired together: one member of the pair measures change over time while the other measures the value in the base year.

Craft Beer and Neighborhood Change

Descriptive Statistics

As of March 2015, a total of 4,044 craft brewery locations, as we defined them, were in operation in the United States, approximately half of which (2,036) had opened in 2013 or later. The Pacific census division has the most craft breweries, with 884, while the East South Central division, which includes Alabama, Kentucky, Mississippi, and Tennessee, has the fewest, with 73 (figures 8.1 and 8.2). Most of the Pacific's breweries are in California, which has more than twice the number of craft breweries than the next-largest concentration in Colorado. Several states outside the West, including Michigan, New York, and Pennsylvania, also have a significant number of breweries. Breweries are not clustered at the neighborhood level across the United States—fewer than 4% of census tracts had one or more breweries, and 88% of those had only one. However, over 90% of census tracts with craft breweries are in urbanized areas or urban clusters as defined by the Census Bureau, which means that almost all breweries are near concentrations of at least 2,500 people.

Mean values for several demographic, housing, and employment variables using 2009–2013 ACS estimates are shown in table 8.1, categorized according to whether the census tract had at least one craft brewery location in 2015. Neighborhoods with craft breweries are about two-thirds as dense as those without (equivalent to densities of many inner-ring suburbs). Those neighborhoods tend to have more white residents, a higher proportion of people in the 25-to-34-year age range, fewer households with children, more education, a slightly lower

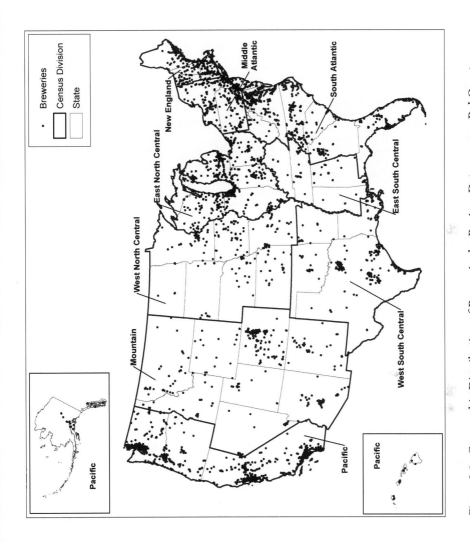

Figure 8.1. Geographic Distribution of Breweries by Region. Data sources: PubQuest (2015), U.S. Census Bureau (2000).

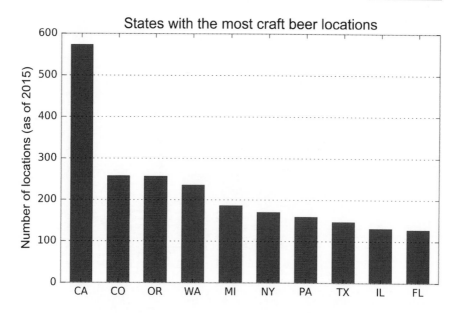

Figure 8.2. Craft Brewery Locations by State. Data source: PubQuest (2015).

median income, a higher proportion of people in professional or technical occupations, more new housing, and higher housing prices.

Effects of Neighborhood Change on New Breweries

Analytical results are shown in table 8.2. Coefficients and significance levels in both the standard and robust versions of the models were similar, so their interpretations did not change substantially. Thus, we show only the standard model estimates. Values in the table represent odds ratios; that is, the odds that there is a new brewery in the tract compared to the odds that there is not given the presence of the variable. Each of the first three models tests the influence of a different set of indicators on the location of new craft breweries.

The first model tests the influence of racial and ethnic categories. Breweries were more likely to locate in census tracts that lost racial and ethnic diversity over the decade we examined. Taken together, higher proportions of each of the racial and ethnic groups in the year 2000 were statistically significantly associated with a brewery opening. However, declines in the black and Latino populations between 2000 and the 2009–2013 ACS estimate predicts greater odds of a new craft brewing location. For each percentage point decline in the black and Latino populations, breweries were about 3% more likely to open.

Table 8.1. Mean Values per Census Tract

	With Craft Brewery	Without Craft Brewery
Population density (sq. mi.)	3,604	5,377
Non-Hispanic white	71%	63%
Black/African American	8%	14%
Hispanic/Latino	13%	16%
Age 24 or younger	32%	33%
Age 25–34	16%	13%
Age 35–44	*13%*	*13%*
Age 45–54	14%	14%
Age 55–64	*12%*	*12%*
Age 65 or older	14%	14%
Households with children	27%	33%
Earned bachelor's degree	34%	27%
Median income (2013 $)	54,585	56,834
Employed	90%	90%
Professional occupations	62%	59%
Housing built since 2000	15%	13%
Median housing age (yr)	43	42
Median house price (2013 $)	250,046	217,988

All differences significant at 95% confidence interval except those in italics.
Source: 2009–2013 five-year ACS estimates.

Model 2 tests the relationship between other socioeconomic indicators and craft breweries. The results give some credence to the idea that breweries are locating in places where they can cater to a younger urban professional crowd. An increase in the 25-to-34-year-old population and the proportion of older residents is positively associated with craft brewery locations. Fewer households without children in 2000 is also statistically significant. Both high levels of college-educated residents and increases in the proportion of people with college degrees predict the opening of a brewery, while the relationship is the inverse for income level. We hypothesized that craft brewing would appeal to a professionally employed population. However, change in this occupational classification is

Table 8.2. Logistic Regression Models of Neighborhood Change Impacts on Breweries[a]

	Model 1: Race/Ethnicity	Model 2: Other Socioeconomic Indicators	Model 3: Housing	Model 4: Full Model	Model 5: West Coast
		Odds Ratios (95% Confidence Intervals)			
Non-Hispanic white (%)	1.017*** (1.010, 1.025)			1.010*** (1.006, 1.014)	1.012** (1.001, 1.023)
Change in non-Hispanic white (pp)	1.001 (0.990, 1.012)			1.013*** (1.005, 1.021)	1.011 (0.991, 1.032)
Black/African American (%)	1.012*** (1.005, 1.020)				
Change in black/African American (pp)	0.970*** (0.957, 0.983)				
Hispanic or Latino (%)	1.013*** (1.006, 1.021)			1.013*** (1.008, 1.018)	1.012* (1.000, 1.026)
Change in Hispanic or Latino (pp)	0.977*** (0.965, 0.989)			1.010* (0.999, 1.020)	1.005 (0.983, 1.028)
Age 25 or younger (%)		1.000 (0.989, 1.012)			
Change in age 25 or younger (pp)		0.997 (0.981, 1.013)			
Age 25–34 (%)		0.998 (0.982, 1.014)		0.995 (0.980, 1.010)	1.037** (1.001, 1.075)

Change in age 25–34 (pp)	1.019**	1.031***	1.006
	(1.000, 1.038)	(1.013, 1.050)	(0.965, 1.050)
Age 35–44 (%)	1.088***	1.107***	1.071**
	(1.057, 1.121)	(1.081, 1.134)	(1.016, 1.129)
Change in age 35–44 (pp)	0.925***	0.914***	0.951*
	(0.898, 0.952)	(0.894, 0.936)	(0.903, 1.002)
Age 45–54 (%)	1.036**		
	(1.003, 1.070)		
Change in age 45–54 (pp)	0.963**		
	(0.932, 0.995)		
Age 55–64 (%)	0.873***	0.888***	0.921**
	(0.836, 0.912)	(0.864, 0.914)	(0.860, 0.987)
Change in age 55–64 (pp)	1.136***	1.124***	1.103***
	(1.093, 1.180)	(1.090, 1.159)	(1.024, 1.189)
Households with children (%)	0.953***	0.956***	0.955***
	(0.945, 0.961)	(0.948, 0.964)	(0.935, 0.974)
Change in household with children (pp)	0.994	0.994	1.004
	(0.985, 1.003)	(0.985, 1.003)	(0.984, 1.025)
Earned bachelor's degree (%)	1.026***	1.022***	1.014
	(1.019, 1.033)	(1.015, 1.029)	(0.996, 1.032)
Change in earned bachelor's degree (pp)	1.030***	1.026***	1.021**
	(1.022, 1.039)	(1.017, 1.035)	(1.000, 1.043)

(continued)

Table 8.2. (*continued*)

	Model 1: Race/Ethnicity	Model 2: Other Socioeconomic Indicators	Model 3: Housing	Model 4: Full Model	Model 5: West Coast
Change in median income (%)		0.994***		0.992***	0.988***
		(0.991, 0.996)		(0.990, 0.995)	(0.981, 0.995)
Employed (%)		1.011		0.999	1.060***
		(0.998, 1.024)		(0.984, 1.015)	(1.021, 1.102)
Change in employed (pp)		1.013**		1.004	1.030**
		(1.002, 1.024)		(0.993, 1.016)	(1.003, 1.058)
Professional occupations (%)		0.974***		0.979***	0.960***
		(0.966, 0.983)		(0.971, 0.988)	(0.939, 0.981)
Change in professional occupations (pp)		1.002		1.000	1.009
		(0.994, 1.009)		(0.992, 1.008)	(0.992, 1.027)
Housing built in past 10 years (%)			1.020***	1.013***	1.008
			(1.015, 1.025)	(1.007, 1.018)	(0.995, 1.021)
Change in housing built in past 10 years (pp)			1.011**	1.005**	0.997
			(1.007, 1.016)	(1.000, 1.010)	(0.985, 1.008)
Median housing age (yr)			1.036***	1.014***	1.004
			(1.031, 1.042)	(1.008, 1.019)	(0.990, 1.017)
Change in median housing age (%)			0.999*	1.000	0.999
			(0.998, 1.000)	(0.998, 1.001)	(0.995, 1.001)

Log of median home value (2013)		1.152***	1.570***	1.251
		(1.052, 1.261)	(1.323, 1.865)	(0.883, 1.786)
Change in median home value (%)		1.003	1.006*	1.008
		(0.991, 1.008)	(0.999, 1.012)	(0.993, 1.017)
Brewery before 2013	3.020***	5.265***	2.790***	3.317***
	(2.578, 3.527)	(4.540, 6.085)	(2.373, 3.268)	(2.490, 4.386)
Population density (per sq. mi.)	1.000***	1.000***	1.000***	1.000***
	(1.000, 1.000)	(1.000, 1.000)	(1.000, 1.000)	(1.000, 1.000)
Region (ref: New England) Mid-Atlantic	0.696***	0.606***	0.769**	
	(0.553, 0.876)	(0.482, 0.762)	(0.609, 0.972)	
South Atlantic	0.502***	0.752***	0.646***	
	(0.405, 0.624)	(0.604, 0.940)	(0.513, 0.816)	
East North Central	0.800**	0.864	0.894	
	(0.652, 0.985)	(0.705, 1.064)	(0.726, 1.107)	
East South Central	0.249***	0.410***	0.321***	
	(0.176, 0.347)	(0.289, 0.572)	(0.225, 0.452)	
West North Central	0.558***	0.687***	0.660***	
	(0.435, 0.716)	(0.535, 0.883)	(0.510, 0.853)	
West South Central	0.361***	0.492***	0.460***	
	(0.275, 0.471)	(0.372, 0.648)	(0.343, 0.614)	
Mountain	1.201	1.624***	1.206	
	(0.962, 1.504)	(1.294, 2.044)	(0.952, 1.533)	

(continued)

Table 8.2. (continued)

	Model 1: Race/ Ethnicity	Model 2: Other Socioeconomic Indicators	Model 3: Housing	Model 4: Full Model	Model 5: West Coast
Pacific	1.291**	1.349***	1.396***	1.350***	
	(1.047, 1.598)	(1.101, 1.661)	(1.141, 1.717)	(1.089, 1.680)	
Number of breweries	72,815	72,518	71,205	71,204	9,980
Log likelihood	−8,114.107	−7,682.520	−7,928.172	−7,518.136	−1,371.342
AIC	16,262.210	15,427.040	15,890.340	15,110.270	2,800.683

Note: *p<0.1; **p<0.05; ***p<0.01.

*a*Models 1–4 use nationwide data; model 5 is the West Coast model. AIC = Akaike information criterion; pp = percentage points.

statistically insignificant. Lower proportions of residents who were professionally employed in 2000 are associated with the presence of neighborhood breweries.

The third model tests the influence of housing factors on craft brewery locations, primarily as a proxy for urban growth and change. We find that areas with a higher proportion of new housing stock in 2000, an increasing proportion of newly built housing, and a decline in the median housing age predict craft brewing. At the same time, for every year the median housing age in the census tract increases, the odds of a new craft brewery location increase by 3.6%. The model indicates that census tracts with higher home values are likely to have breweries, although the change in home values is insignificant. We suspect this could mean that breweries are locating in census tracts with more infill development rather than those with expansive growth, indicating brewers' preferences for urban or central locations rather than outlying locations.

Model 4 tests the simultaneous influence of all three categories on craft brewery openings. To reduce issues of multicollinearity, we removed variables with variance inflation factors greater than 7. Most of the variables from the first three models remain significant, with a few notable differences. The black population in a census tract is no longer a significant predictor of breweries, though an increase in the white population becomes significant. Lower median incomes in a neighborhood have stronger effects on a brewery opening as compared with the models that do not control for race and housing variables.

In all model specifications, we controlled for whether the census tract had a craft brewery prior to 2013, the population density of the census tract, and the geographic region of the country. The effect of a previous brewery is strong: the odds of a new craft brewery opening in a census tract are 2.8 times greater if one had previously existed, when controlling for all other characteristics. The result suggests that older breweries act as catalysts for new breweries to colocate. Population density has a small but negative relationship with brewery locations: adding 100 additional people per square mile reduces the odds of a new brewery by about 1%. Consistent with other research (Baginski and Bell 2011), we found that the odds are significantly higher for breweries to open in the western United States and significantly lower in the southern United States.

A Closer Look: Brewing on the West Coast

Because of the distinctive regional variation in craft brewing locations and the role of pioneers in the western United States in establishing the new craft brewing movement, we reestimated our national model for California, Oregon, and Washington. These three states contain about a quarter of all craft breweries in the United States. We expected that, in addition to its unique history with respect to the craft brewing movement, relatively higher living costs compared to the rest of the country might change some of the relationships between neighborhoods and breweries. Results are shown in table 8.2 as Model 5.

Fewer relationships are significant in the regional model as compared with the national model. An increase in the proportion of people aged 55 to 64 and people employed predict new breweries in a neighborhood. Curiously, in both the West Coast model and the national model, an increase in the number of bachelor's degrees and a decrease in median income are associated with new brewery openings. We discuss this paradoxical finding further below. In addition, as in the national model, the presence of an older brewery remains a significant predictor of whether a new one opened in the previous two years. The results suggest a smaller influence on neighborhood change factors in craft brewing locations along the West Coast. It is possible that new craft breweries are unable to open in significantly changing residential areas because of other development pressures.

Discussion and Conclusion

Today's wave of urban revitalization efforts has been viewed by supporters as a way to increase a city's wealth and economic opportunities. Detractors, however, consider it gentrification with better marketing. There has been considerable anecdotal evidence that craft breweries are harbingers and even instigators of neighborhood change. Many cities today pursue craft breweries as potential job creators, catalysts for investment and development, and tourist attractors. Craft beer consumption is associated with higher socioeconomic indicators such as race, income, and education (Florida 2012; Tremblay and Tremblay 2005; Tremblay and Tremblay 2011) and, at larger spatial scales, population growth and diversification (Schnell and Reese 2014). This study is unique in that we looked at neighborhood-level characteristics, which better reflect the character of small craft brewers than regional- or state-level analyses can.

At a neighborhood level, we find a slightly different story than that told by previous researchers. Our data do not allow us to conclude that new craft breweries cause changes in neighborhood indicators, but we can see how they follow change. Our results are not entirely consistent with the story of gentrification in neighborhoods; changes in racial composition do not seem to be a draw for new craft breweries, nor do so-called creative-class occupations. On the other hand, areas that have a highly educated population, increasing education levels, lower and declining income levels, and an older but developing housing stock do appear to welcome craft brewing to the neighborhood. Perhaps we might speak of a link between craft beer and what one writer has recently called "yuccies"—young, urban creatives—who may not fit into the standard U.S. Census employment categories (Infante 2015). These changes also depend on the region, so influences in one may not necessarily be significant in another. Our informal survey with 15 brewery owners tentatively confirms these findings. The owners uniformly stated that neighborhood character was very important or even the primary reason for their location choice. Many referred to themselves explicitly as pioneers and catalysts in neglected historic neighborhoods.

If craft breweries and brewpubs are paths to coveted neighborhood revitalization, planners must keep several things in mind. First, simplifying the permitting process and creating dedicated craft brewery land-use designations can reduce some of the bureaucratic obstacles to the development of breweries. Such cities and neighborhoods thus become more attractive. Second, coordinating revitalization efforts and subsidies with potential breweries can create synergies in the improvement of neighborhood infrastructure. Renovating buildings and improving streets and sidewalks can maximize the effect of surrounding economic development.

Future research may help strengthen some of these conclusions. For example, we expect employment-side factors and planning regulations to influence the locations of new craft breweries; however, there is no nationwide dataset that would allow us to include those factors in our analysis at the census-tract level. For that reason, we investigated only the influence of residential patterns on brewing locations and leave investigations that include these factors at the subregional level for future work. We also suspect that the effect of changes may be different for different brewery types, but we leave this analysis for future work as well. Finally, controlling for metropolitan differences in housing costs might clarify the relationship between housing values and investment and craft brewery locations.

City planners are also agents of neighborhood change and bear a responsibility to current residents to represent their interests. Simply allowing rents to rise as trendy businesses and affluent residents arrive is not a good-faith effort to represent the needs of longtime residents. Rather, diverse and inclusive collaboration among all impacted stakeholders is critical for equitable planning. How can local culture and history be preserved while increasing economic opportunity and amenities for all? Displacement of longtime residents is a key challenge facing economic revitalization of disinvested neighborhoods. If craft beer is a canary in the coal mine for neighborhood change, perhaps it can also be a trigger for proactive planning interventions, harnessing the image of the "local" to ensure people who made the history in the images can remain in their place on the bar stool.

NOTE

1. The third author of this chapter is the cofounder of PubQuest.

REFERENCES

Acitelli, Tom. 2013. *The Audacity of Hops: The History of America's Craft Beer Revolution.* Chicago: Chicago Review Press.

Appleton, R. 2012, June 27. "Council Relaxes Zoning Rules for Alcohol Production." *Dallas Morning News.* http://cityhallblog.dallasnews.com/2012/06/council-relaxes-zoning -rules-for-alcohol-production-fourth-brewery-seeking-city-approval.html.

Associated Press. 2013a, July 4. "A Tale of 6 Cities Craft Brewers Helped Transform." *The Street.* http://www.thestreet.com/story/11969867/1/a-tale-of-6-cities-craft-brewers-helped -transform.html.

———. 2013b, July 4. "How Craft Beer Is Reviving Urban Neighborhoods." *Business Insider.* http://www.businessinsider.com/craft-brews-create-urban-revival-2013-7.

Baginski, James, and Thomas L. Bell. 2011. "Under-Tapped? An Analysis of Craft Brewing in the Southern United States." *Southeastern Geographer* 51 (1): 165–185.

Bartlett, Dan, Steve Allen, Jack Harris, and Larry Cary. 2013. "Revitalization One Pint at a Time: How Breweries and Distilleries Contribute to Main Street." Presented at the Oregon Main Street Conference, Astoria, OR, October 2–4. Accessed May 22, 2015, https:// www.oregon.gov/oprd/HCD/SHPO/docs/2013OMSConf/Revitalization_By_The_Pint .pdf.

Best, Allen. 2015. "Welcome to Beer Country." *Planning,* February, 12–18. https://www .planning.org/planning/open/2015/welcometobeer.htm.

Boddie, K. 2014, March 18. "New Lents Brewers 'Have a Track Record.'" *KOIN News.* http://koin.com/2014/03/18/new-lents-brewers-track-record.

City of San Diego. 2015. "Development Services: Land Development Code Work Program." Accessed May 22, 2015, http://www.sandiego.gov/development-services/industry /landdevcode.

Cortright, Joseph. 2002. "The Economic Importance of Being Different: Regional Variations in Tastes, Increasing Returns, and the Dynamics of Development." *Economic Development Quarterly* 16 (1): 3–16.

Crowell, C. 2013, August 22. "Better Know a Craft Beer Guild: San Francisco Booms Amid Permit Delays." *Craft Brewing Business.* http://www.craftbrewingbusiness.com/business -marketing/better-know-a-craft-beer-guild-san-francisco.

Flack, Wes. 1997. "American Microbreweries and Neolocalism: 'Ale-Ing' for a Sense of Place." *Journal of Cultural Geography* 16 (2): 37–53.

Florida, Richard. 2012, August 20. "The Geography of Craft Beer." *CityLab.* http://www .citylab.com/design/2012/08/geography-craft-beer/2931.

Florida, Richard L. 2002. *The Rise of the Creative Class: And How It's Transforming Work, Leisure, Community and Everyday Life*. New York: Basic Books.

Flynn, Edward, Willard Brooks, Jeff Ware, Mark Woodcock, and Ted Hawley. 2014. "Brewing Economic Development." Presented at the New York Upstate Planning Association Conference, Rochester, NY, September 17–19. http://nyupstateplanning.org/wp-content/uploads/2014/10/6B-Brewing-Economic-Development.pdf.

Freeman, Lance. 2005. "Displacement or Succession? Residential Mobility in Gentrifying Neighborhoods." *Urban Affairs Review* 40 (4): 463–491.

Gohmann, Stephan F. 2016. "Why Are There So Few Breweries in the South?" *Entrepreneurship Theory and Practice* 40 (5): 1071–1092.

Hackworth, Jason, and Neil Smith. 2001. "The Changing State of Gentrification." *Tijdschrift Voor Economische En Sociale Geografie* 92 (4): 464–477.

Hopkins, David. 2014, June. "How Craft Beer (Finally) Came to Dallas." *D Magazine*. http://www.dmagazine.com/publications/d-magazine/2014/june/dallas-first-microbreweries.

Infante, David. 2015, June 9. "The Hipster is Dead, and You Might Not Like Who Comes Next." *Mashable*. http://mashable.com/2015/06/09/post-hipster-yuccie.

Jacobs, Jane. 1961/1992. *The Death and Life of Great American Cities*. New York: Vintage Books.

Lees, Loretta, Tom Slater, and Elvin Wyly. 2008. *Gentrification*. New York: Routledge.

Li, David K. 2014, July 29. "Brooklyn Brewery Plans New Staten Island Plant." *New York Post*. http://nypost.com/2014/07/29/brooklyn-brewery-plans-new-staten-island-plant.

Logan, John R., Zengwang Xu, and Brian Stults. 2014. "Interpolating US Decennial Census Tract Data from as Early as 1970 to 2010: A Longitudinal Tract Database." *Professional Geographer* 66 (3): 412–420.

Mathews, Vanessa, and Roger M. Picton. 2014. "Intoxifying Gentrification: Brew Pubs and the Geography of Post-Industrial Heritage." *Urban Geography* 35 (3): 337–356.

May, Lucy, and Dan Monk. 2015, May 10. "Cincinnati Planners Tap Craft Brewers for Help in Making City More Receptive to Booming Industry." *WPCO*. http://www.wcpo.com/entertainment/local-a-e/beer/cincinnati-planners-tap-craft-brewers-for-help-in-making-city-more-receptive-to-booming-industry.

McLaughlin, Ralph B., Neil Reid, and Michael S. Moore. 2014. "The Ubiquity of Good Taste: A Spatial Analysis of the Craft Brewing Industry in the United States." In *The Geography of Beer*, edited by Mark Patterson and Nancy Hoast-Pullen, 131–154. Dordrecht, the Netherlands: Springer.

Newman, Kathe, and Elvin Wyly. 2006. "The Right to Stay Put, Revisited: Gentrification and Resistance to Displacement in New York City." *Urban Studies* 43 (1): 23–57.

Ogle, Maureen. 2006. *Ambitious Brew: The Story of American Beer*. Orlando, FL: Harcourt.

Perritt, Marcia. 2013, April 5. "Breweries and Economic Development: A Case of Homebrewing." Community and Economic Development program at the UNC School of Government (blog). http://ced.sog.unc.edu/breweries-and-economic-development-a-case-of-home-brew.

Peters, Corbin, and Zach Szczepaniak. 2013, February 6. "Beer: Is It Zoned Out?" Plan Charlotte (blog). http://plancharlotte.org/story/beer-it-zoned-out.

PubQuest. 2015. Accessed April 21, 2015, http://www.pubquest.com.

Schnell, Steven M., and Joseph F. Reese. 2003. "Microbreweries as Tools of Local Identity." *Journal of Cultural Geography* 21 (1): 45–69.

———. 2014. "Microbreweries, Place, and Identity in the United States." In *The Geography of Beer*, edited by Mark Patterson and Nancy Hoast-Pullen, 167–187. Dordrecht, the Netherlands: Springer.

Somerville, H. 2013, July 14. "Oakland: Craft Beer Trend Helps Rebuild Neighborhoods." *San Jose Mercury-News*. http://www.mercurynews.com/ci_23671853/oakland-craft-beer-trend-helps-rebuild-neighborhoods.

Stradling, David, and Richard Stradling. 2008. "Perceptions of the Burning River: Deindustrialization and Cleveland's Cuyahoga River." *Environmental History* 13 (3): 515–535.

Tremblay, Carol Horton, and Victor J. Tremblay. 2011. "Recent Economic Developments in the Import and Craft Segments of the US Brewing Industry." In *The Economics of Beer*, edited by Johan F. M. Swinnen, 141–160. New York: Oxford University Press.

Tremblay, Victor J., and Carol Horton Tremblay. 2005. *The US Brewing Industry: Data and Economic Analysis*. Cambridge, MA: MIT Press.

U.S. Census Bureau. 2000. "Census Regions and Divisions of the United States." Accessed March 1, 2015, http://www2.census.gov/geo/pdfs/maps-data/maps/reference/us_regdiv.pdf.

Watson, Bart. 2014. "The Demographics of Craft Beer Lovers." Presented at the Great American Beer Festival, Denver, CO, October 3. Accessed May 22, 2015, https://www.brewersassociation.org/wp-content/uploads/2014/10/Demographics-of-craft-beer.pdf.

CHAPTER 9

The Spatial Dynamics of Organizational Identity among Craft Brewers

TÜNDE CSERPES AND PAUL-BRIAN MCINERNEY

Introduction

Like many small-scale and artisanal production, craft brewing is predominantly a local and regional phenomenon (Batzli 2014). However, the industry is not evenly distributed across urban centers and regions in the United States. Rather, craft brewers tend to be concentrated in several key cities. Based on data from the *Brewers Almanac* (2013), cities like Portland, San Diego, and Denver have large numbers of craft breweries and brewpubs. Furthermore, craft brewers do not represent a homogeneous organizational identity. As a class, their organizational identity differentiates them from large-scale brewers (Carroll and Swaminathan, 2000). However, field dynamics among craft brewers are predicated upon further identity differentiation. Craft brewers are made up of classes within a class. In other words, the craft brewer class consists of multiple organizational identities, rather than a homogeneous group. Some craft brewers, like Sierra Nevada, Stone, and Lagunitas, are fairly large and tend to brew a stable repertoire of beers for a broad market. In this chapter, we call these members of the established class. Other craft brewers, such as Pipeworks in Chicago, which we call members of the innovator class, experiment with ingredients and techniques. Still others, like Atlas Brew Works in Washington, DC, bring craft brewing to new markets. As members of what we call the up-and-coming class, such brewers take established styles from one market and import them into a new market, like bringing West Coast Ales with strong hop flavors to the

Southeast. At the same time, established, innovators, and up-and-coming craft brewer identities occupy the same geographic space. How might we understand the multiple and dynamic organizational identities that make up the craft brewing industry? How do these identities relate to one another? How are organizational identities a feature of the spatial dynamics of the craft brewing industry?

We begin to answer these questions in this chapter. In doing so, we provide insights into the spatial dynamics of the craft brewing industry, while framing our work within the study of organizations more broadly. Organizational sociologists have often overlooked geographic space in their explanations (Greenwood et al. 2008). Ecological and field theory approaches to organizational sociology implicitly discuss space as analytical rather than geographic (Mohr 2005). For example, resource-partitioning theory in organizational ecology has been used to explain the genesis of craft brewing (Carroll and Swaminathan 2000). Resource-partitioning theory considers resource space as an abstract space in which the study population operates (Boone et al. 2002). As such, a "resource space" is a mathematically formalized concept (Péli and Nooteboom 1999), which refers to the "environmental assets without which a firm cannot operate viably" (Witteloostuijn and Boone 2006, 410). Similarly, field theory emphasizes the relational and social aspects of fields (Fligstein and McAdam 2012; Martin 2003). Organizational fields, according to this theory, are constituted by dynamics of competition and cooperation among field participants (DiMaggio and Powell 1983). Organizations within a field shape one another. However, geographic proximity is rarely considered a factor in field dynamics (Mohr 2005). In contrast, economic geographers study cities, regions, and agglomerations as physical spaces of economic coordination (Storper 1997).

In this chapter, we take a dynamic, relational approach to organizational identities. Organizational identity reflects the answer to the question, "Who are we as an organization?" (Albert and Whetten 1985; Whetten 2006). It is how an organization presents itself to the outside world. Identity is established explicitly through such acts as branding and design and implicitly through internal culture as well as through interactions with other organizations. Within organizational fields, identities operate in relation to one another as firms differentiate themselves from others. Differentiation takes the form of distinct organizational identities that help firms identify and specify market niches (White 1981, 2002). The relationships between identities also have a spatial component (e.g., certain organizational identities will tend to colocate, while others attempt to distance themselves). For example, Whitford and Potter (2007) observe that since the 1980s, economic production systems have become spatially fragmented, leading to regional economies or agglomerations of firms. The scholarship on craft brewing has not examined the spatial relations among producers. This chapter argues that institutional conditions and physical location contribute to craft brewers' field positioning strategies as well as their identity performance.

To account for the missing spatial element in organizational theory, we introduce analytic concepts from economic geography. According to economic geography, spatially clustered production systems act as spatially embedded networks (Storper and Salais 1997). Cities and regions are important because they constitute the spaces where economic coordination happens. Spatial clusters of economic activity are not the outcomes of market economy but rather what makes markets possible (Storper 1997). Spatially clustered economic activity becomes part of an industry's institutional structure and allows for strategic differentiation from other firms. The wider environment in which these firms function, then, affect the kind of identities they are able to create, project, and perform (Glynn 2008). Our approach fits into this tradition as it emphasizes the spatial and institutional embeddedness of organizational identity, and our use of organizational identity focuses on the relationship between the spatial construction of markets and the claims, performances, and actions of organizations.

By bringing spatiality to bear on the relationships among organizational identities in fields and populations rephrases the identity question as, "Who are we as an organization, given that other (competing) firms nearby or farther away are alike or different from us." Such a question better captures organizational identity as a relational concept and better situates it as a feature of organizational fields and populations. This ultimately helps scholars better understand processes how organizational fields and populations are formed and transformed. Furthermore, an organization's institutional environment and physical location enable the formation of identity and facilitate its enactment. Thus, the relationship between identity and spatiality may be recursive: certain organizational identities may seek out and colocate with similar or different identities, which in turn, reinforce the performances of those identities. This would help explain how firms choose potential collaborators, a practice that is widespread among craft brewers.

The Spatial Dynamics of Craft Brewers

The microbrewing industry has been the focus of little sociological research. In one exception, organizational ecologists have used data from the emergence of this industry to refine resource-partitioning theory (Carroll and Swaminathan

2000). Resource-partitioning theory holds that under certain conditions, generalist firms competing for the broadest niche within an industry leave smaller niches to be filled by specialist firms (Carroll 1985). Resource-partitioning theory begins to explain the emergence of craft brewing and several other industries, such as auditing firms (Boone et al. 2000), newspapers (Dobrev 2000), the automobile industry (Dobrev et al. 2001), and microradio (Greve et al. 2006). However, gaps remain, particularly with regard to the dynamics of artisanal industries, such as craft brewing.

In the organizational ecology literature, *generalist* and *specialist* describe organizational strategies. Yet, they can also be seen as crystallizations of organizational identities. Microbrewers identify themselves as authentic producers, as opposed to the large-scale brewers who mass-produce what they call "yellow fizzy water" (Carroll and Swaminathan 2000). Here, authenticity entails organizational practices that reflect traditional production methods as well as judgments about what is appropriate and "real" as opposed to mass produced and commodified (Carroll 2015). Authenticity is a crucial component of organizational identity in artisanal industries. Artisanal industries are small-scale producers who employ traditional methods to manufacture goods for niche markets based on consumer tastes.

According to organizational ecologists, resource partitioning creates an equilibrium in which the two groups do not compete for the same resources. As large producers control larger portions of the market, they create small niches for more nimble firms to fill. In the case of craft brewing, large brewers mass produced lagers for mass consumption; this created niches for small producers to create different, less popular styles of beer. However, more recent work demonstrates the dynamics of resource partitioning, allowing for such actions as departitioning (Sikavica and Pozner 2013). Departitioning occurs when niches are reabsorbed into the mass market. Evidence of departitioning exists in the brewing industry, as large brewers have created or purchased small brands, (e.g., Miller's purchase of Lienenkugel's in 1988 or Anheuser-Busch's purchases of Goose Island, Blue Point, 10 Barrel, and Elysian). Yet, the microbrewery movement has continued to grow, even during the most recent recession.

Prohibition in the United States from 1920 to 1933 banned most forms of alcohol production. The number of breweries in 2013 (2,700) has climbed back to 1873 levels (2,509). The market and the prevalent industry dynamics in which these breweries are situated, however, are vastly different. Prior to Prohibition, breweries in the United States catered exclusively to their immediate surrounding areas, usually not larger than a neighborhood (Baum 2000). Beer was exchanged in a specific physical place—the saloon (Swedberg 2005). Today, microbreweries are integrated into a spatially and organizationally complex system that operates at the city and regional levels while macrobreweries still have a quasi-monopolistic market share on the national level.

In the market for beer, microbreweries carve out a niche from large-scale brewers through differences in product and organizational identity (Tremblay and Tremblay 2011). However, craft brewers are not a homogeneous class. Rather, craft brewing is comprised of multiple organizational identities of different statuses that are linked by geographic proximity. For this chapter, we conduct a latent class analysis to reveal these organizational identities and the spatial dynamics among them.

Data, Measures, and Analytic Methods

We use a dataset collected and maintained by the Brewers Association, a trade association assisting craft brewers. This dataset was published on the *New Yorker*'s website in 2013 as part of a data-visualization project.[1] The dataset provides a rare glimpse into industry conditions that usually remain hidden. We use it to identify classes of organizational identities and explore how they are affected by spatial and institutional conditions. We collected additional data from websites of the Brewers Association and state-level trade associations of the industry.

The Brewers Association data contains a complete list and geographical coordinates of all new craft breweries that opened in the United States in 2011 and 2012, along with names and locations of the 50 biggest and the 50 fastest-growing microbreweries. We exclude from the analysis breweries located in Alaska and Hawaii in order to keep the robustness of spatial analyses. This way we did not consider two new breweries and two from the largest 50. The final sample size is 512, which includes 414 new, 50 fastest-growing, and 48 large breweries. Moreover, this dataset contains indicators of state-level industry performance such as number of craft breweries, craft beer per capita, and number of craft barrels produced in states. As we use these industry-level variables to tap into industry constraints, we do not discuss them separately but use exploratory factor analysis (EFA) as a data-reduction method to create summary indicators.

Measures

We hypothesize that the following six factors are the main drivers of institutionally and spatially embedded organizational identities: ecological, industry strength, license to self-distribute, state guild membership, Brewers Association membership, and spatial clustering.

Ecological. Institutional conditions affect organizational identity. The function of this variable is to account for state-level industry conditions around microbreweries. We used EFA with eleven state-level indicators of industry conditions from the Brewers Association dataset as a data-reduction technique. The results indicate that two factors summarize these variables best. We named these two factors *ecological* and *industry strength*, referring to the fact that the first set of state-level variables taps into ecological conditions while the second measures industry conditions. We include these two factors in further analyses as dichotomous measures of institutional conditions.

Describing industry-level data with two factors is well supported by EFA. The eleven-item scale has a high internal consistency, with a Cronbach alpha of 0.91. After running EFA the first time, we observe that ecological and industry strength are very strong, with eigenvalues of 5.53 and 3.20, respectively. All other measures point in the same direction. Cumulative proportion scores reveal that the first two factors explain 90% of the variation in the data. The Kaiser value, scree plot, and parallel analysis all confirm our decision to keep the first two factors and rerun the factor analysis.

We ran the analysis again using promax rotations, allowing for correlations between the two factors (table 9.1). The low uniqueness scores on factor loadings (with a range of 1 to 35%) indicate that most of the variation in the individual variables is accounted for in the two factors. The Kaiser–Meyer–Olkin measure of sampling adequacy is 0.72, which is above the 0.5 cutoff; this further supports our use of EFA. The loading plot confirms that after rotation, there is little cross-loading of variables between factors. In fact, there is only a weak negative correlation (−0.24) between the two factors.

Overall, we used EFA as a data-reduction technique to create a small number of components that best summarize the 11 industry-level variables. Results show that we can best represent the economic data with two components that tap into state-level ecological and industry conditions surrounding breweries. The original variables that loaded on the ecological factor were number of craft breweries per capita, state rank by the number of craft breweries per capita, number of breweries per capita, and state rank by the number of breweries per capita (table 9.1). We recoded the ecological factor variable as a dichotomous indicator for the latent class analysis. Ecological was coded 1 if the factor variable had positive values and 0 otherwise. Each brewery was assigned this score based on the state where it is located. The variable shows that 35% of the breweries are located in states that are strong in terms of population-level characteristics.

Industry strength. This variable is the second loading factor from the EFA that we described above; it is an indicator of state-level industry conditions.

Table 9.1. Rotated Factor Loadings and Unique Variances (%)[a]

	Industry Strength	Ecology	Uniqueness
No. of craft breweries	0.93		8%
State rank: no. of craft breweries	−0.76		28%
No. of breweries	0.93		8%
Population	0.89	0.45	18%
Craft barrels in 2011	0.93		15%
Craft barrels in 2012	0.94		12%
State rank: craft barrels in 2012	−0.74		36%
State rank: no. of craft breweries per capita		1.00	1%
No. of craft breweries per capita		−0.85	28%
No. of breweries per capita		0.79	33%
State rank: total capita per brewery		0.99	1%

[a]N = 48 (contiguous states).

This factor was created from economic variables such as number of craft breweries in the state, state rank in terms of number of craft breweries, number of breweries, craft barrels produced in 2011 and in 2012, and state rank in terms of craft barrels produced in 2012 (see table 9.1). This variable was coded 1 if the loadings on the second factor in the EFA had positive values and 0 otherwise. Each brewery was assigned this score based on the state where it is located. The variable shows that 75% of the breweries are in states where the industry is considered to be strong.

License to self-distribute. Another measure of industry strength is whether a state allows self-distribution for small-scale breweries. Release from the requirement to go through the three-tier system and use a wholesaler in order to distribute beer to the customer incentivizes microbrewery growth and indicates a strong presence of small-scale breweries in that state. This variable indicates whether breweries belong to states where the law requires breweries to get a license in order to self-distribute. Data were hand collected from the Brewers Association's website; 85% of the breweries were located in such states as of 2012.

State guild membership. Membership in state-level professional associations indicates an orientation toward local industry values. Guild meetings are important venues for information exchange and industry socialization. This variable indicates whether a particular brewery belongs to the professional organization

Table 9.2. Variables Used in Latent Class Analysis

	Definition	**Yes**
Ecological	Factor variable from EFA that indicates that factor variable is positive	35%
Industry strength	Factor variable from EFA that indicates that factor variable is positive	75%
License to self-distribute	State law requires breweries to get a license to self-distribute	85%
Membership in respective state guild	Membership in state guild	66%
Brewers Association membership	Membership in national guild	75%
Spatial clustering	Distance (average nearest neighbor minus actual nearest neighbor) is positive	86%

of the state in which it is located. Data were collected from websites of state guilds. It was found that 66% of breweries were members of state guilds.[2]

Brewers Association membership. Membership in the national-level professional association indicates a general orientation toward the industry and its values. This variable indicates whether a particular brewery belongs to the Brewers Association. Data were collected from the Brewers Association website. A total of 75% of breweries were members of the Brewers Association.

Spatial clustering. Being spatially close to a great number of other industry participants is an indicator of centrality. This variable was created by subtracting actual distance of the nearest neighbor of the brewery from the expected mean distance between two breweries (about 45 miles). A positive number means that the two breweries are closer to each other than would be expected by chance. This was the case for 86% of the breweries. This variable uses geographical coordinates of breweries that were published in the Brewers Association dataset and was created using the average nearest-neighbor functionality in the ArcGIS software.

Table 9.2 provides a summary of the six proposed factors introduced in this section.

Analytical Methods

First, we generated maps using the Brewers Association data to reveal local and regional patterns of firm location. Then we used latent class analysis (LCA) (Collins and Lanza 2010) to interrogate the six outlined factors and delineate a set number of latent classes around which organizational identities can organize. The co-occurrence of different combinations of the six indicators can be explained by an underlying classification of industry dynamics that shape those factors. We conducted the analysis using the Stata LCA plug-in. The result of an LCA is a contingency table, where the observed variables and the latent classes are cross-tabulated (Collins and Lanza 2010, 39). LCA results comprise latent class prevalence (the proportion of data points that are estimated to be in the latent classes) and item-response probabilities (the estimated prevalence of each of the six factors).

Results

Map 9.1 visualizes the three different types of microbreweries: the largest 50 (circles), the fastest-growing 50 (triangles), and the new breweries (rhombi). Based on the density of the brewery locations included in the analysis, the darker circles on this map reveal spatial clusters of breweries. The spatial location of these dark clusters indicates that the market is indeed driven by population density, as these clusters coincide with urban areas. Darker clusters point to well-known brewing cities such as San Diego, Denver, Seattle, and Chicago. Visualizing the urban areas helps researchers to find and analyze relevant industry events in the future.

Although it also uses solely the spatial location of breweries, the kernel density map (Map 9.2) tells a different story. Kernel density is a spatial analytic technique, like point density, but one that produces a more general, smoother surface. The kernel function calculates the surface value for each data point, which has the highest value at the location of the brewery and diminishes until it reaches the search radius distance. Based on the overlaps of surface values of different breweries, we calculate the density of raster cells. In substantive terms, these density circles reveal the regional trends in the industry. There are distinctive clusters of brewery locations in the Pacific Northwest, Rocky Mountain states, the Midwest, and the East Coast. These results could potentially be used to argue why to concentrate on different geographic areas and spatially locate distinctive market dynamics. Also, there are less strong but still distinguishable spatial clusters in Texas and northwest Florida, mainly consisting of newly opened breweries. These areas might constitute the up-and-coming locations within the industry. It is interesting that the Midwest seems to constitute a large area, while California is divided up into two, clearly distinguishable industrial clusters, one in the north and one in the south. California is the only state where there are city- and regional-level industry trade associations, indicating further stratification. They not only have a state-level guild (California Craft Brewers Association) but also several regional trade associations (Northern California

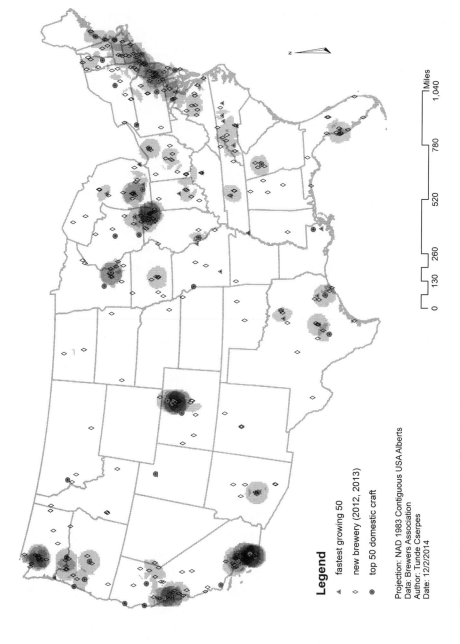

Legend

▲   fastest growing 50

◇   new brewery (2012, 2013)

●   top 50 domestic craft

Projection: NAD 1983 Contiguous USA Alberts
Data: Brewers Association
Author: Tunde Cserpes
Date: 12/2/2014

Map 9.1. Point-Density Analysis Results

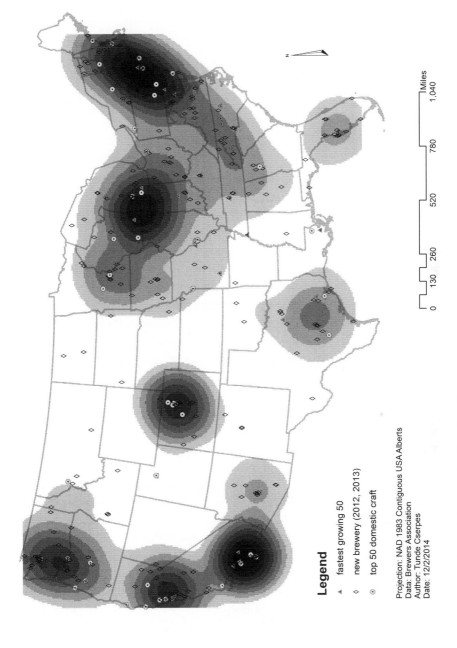

Legend

▲ fastest growing 50

◇ new brewery (2012, 2013)

◉ top 50 domestic craft

Projection: NAD 1983 Contiguous USA Alberts
Data: Brewers Association
Author: Tunde Cserpes
Date: 12/2/2014

Map 9.2. Kernel Density Analysis Results

Table 9.3. Fit of Latent Class Models

No. of Classes (n=512)	df	Log-likelihood	AIC	BIC	CAIC	Adjusted BIC	Entropy R-Squared
4	36	−1573.19	90.14	204.58	231.58	118.88	0.58
3	43	−1577.37	84.52	169.29	189.29	105.80	0.63
2	50	−1610.01	135.78	190.88	203.88	149.62	0.59
1	57	−1643.60	188.98	214.41	220.41	195.37	1.00

AIC=Akaike Information Criterion; BIC=Bayesian Information Criterion; CAIC=Consistent Akaike Information Criterion.

Brewers Guild, San Diego Brewers Guild, and San Francisco Brewers Guild). The proliferation of substate-level trade associations is an indicator of the increasing complexity of interests, which could account for the two distinctive regions in the state.

Beyond descriptive analyses, we ran LCA to determine the optimal number of classes based on the six factors. As discussed above, we included indicators for ecological factors, industry strength, licensing requirements, organizational membership, and spatial clustering. Although obtaining adequate fit between model and data can sometimes be cumbersome in LCA, in our case all the fit measures indicated that the three-class model is the best descriptor of the data, outperforming the two- and four-class options as well. LCA fit indexes for different class solutions (1 to 4) are summarized in table 9.3.

The three-class model generated by LCA supports substantive theorizing about the industry dynamics of craft brewing. By looking at the estimated prevalence of the six indicators in the three classes (table 9.4), we name the classes *established*, *up-and-coming*, and *innovator*.

The established class is the most numerous—57% of the breweries belong to this latent class. Furthermore, these breweries are mainly located in states where the industry itself is strong; high proportions for industry strength (87%) and the state's licensing requirements (91%) indicate that. Another indicator of the established nature of this class is that breweries do use institutionalized ways of resource distribution: the majority of them belong to their respective state guilds (94%) and to the national Brewers Association (83%). This class also features a high item-response loading for spatial clustering (91%) and low item-response loading for ecological factors (22%).

The LCA detected two other, spatially distinct, dynamics that are simultaneously shaping the industry. One is a market dynamic represented by the group

Table 9.4. Latent Class Analysis of U.S. Microbreweries (N=512)

	Established (57%)	Up-and-Coming (24%)	Innovators (19%)
Ecological	0.22	0.67	0.33
Industry strength	0.87	0.46	0.78
License to self-distribute	0.91	0.60	0.99
State guild member	0.94	0.47	0.70
Brewers Association member	0.83	0.91	0.34
Spatial clustering	0.91	0.64	0.98

we call up-and-coming, who comprise 24% of the breweries in our dataset. Breweries belonging to this class are less characterized by spatial clustering (64%). Population ecological arguments seem to matter slightly more (67%). These breweries are located in states with emerging craft brewing industries (thus the name of the class), where the industry is not yet strong (46%) and states do not predominantly require licenses to self-distribute (60%). Representation in state guilds is low (47%) because in some of these emerging states state guilds might not even be present. However, the breweries compensate with membership in the Brewers Association (91%).

The innovator latent class is similar to the established class in many respects. This class comprises 19% of the dataset. Ecological factors matter less for this class (33%). However, LCA reveals high levels of spatial clustering (98%) among the class. While there was a spatial segregation between breweries in the established and up-and-coming classes, breweries in the innovator class are not spatially segregated from the breweries of the established class. They tend to locate in states where the industry is strong (78%) and where the state provides self-distribution licenses (99%). However, unlike breweries in the established class, who seemed to take full membership in brewers' guilds, members of the innovator class seem to have (or possibly require) alternative access to resources. The innovator class has a high participation rate in state guilds (70%) and low enrollment in the national Brewers Association (34%). This suggests that innovators are oriented toward local markets.

Classes and Industry Dynamics

LCA is a probabilistic research method. Probabilities are assigned to breweries indicating the intensity with which they belong to a particular class—0 means full nonmembership and 1 means full membership based on the logic of fuzzy sets (Ragin 2000, 6). In an ideal case, if a probability is high enough, we can assert that a brewery belongs to one latent class and not to the other two. We analyzed the general members and the full-fledged members of each class. We defined general members as those belonging to a certain class with greater than 50% probability. We defined full-fledged members as those belonging to a class with greater than 90% probability (see table 9.4). The total number of breweries that belong to any of the three classes is 488, which means that only 24 breweries cannot be characterized in any of the three classes. Moreover, 273 of these breweries (56%) are full-fledged members of their respective classes. Below, we present three exemplars to illustrate what full-fledged membership in a class means. These exemplars (table 9.5) were chosen from the Brewers Association dataset to highlight organizational identities within classes. All are full-fledged members of each of the three classes as samples (table 9.6).

As our LCA shows, three main types of brewers constitute the craft brewing industry. Each category represents a particular organizational identity. Established brewers represent the stable core of the craft brewing industry. These brewers have developed a recognizable brand name, a few signature styles of beer, and a loyal consumer base. As such, these brewers see themselves as the technical and knowledge base of the industry. New Glarus Brewing exemplifies the established latent class (96.9% probability of being in this class). New Glarus Brewery is often mentioned in the industry press as a reflecting the ideals of craft brewers, which is an anecdotal indication of its centrality to the industry. Dan Carey, the master brewer at New Glarus Brewing, graduated with a degree in Food Science with an emphasis on Malting and Brewing Science from the University of California at Davis, which is a world-renowned program. Furthermore, Carey took his brewing course at the Seibel Institute of Technology, which is the oldest and largest brewing program in the United States, and worked as a production supervisor for Anheuser-Busch. This training and background reflects a "mainstream" within the craft brewery movement, which entails acquiring standard credentials as opposed to being self-taught or starting as a homebrewer. Moreover, 122 other full-fledged breweries had the same indicator pattern on the six factors we outlined. New Glarus Brewing is located in Wisconsin, a state with a strong presence in the craft brewing industry, not to mention a long history in the brewing industry overall. Wisconsin has laws regulating self-distribution. New Glarus Brewing belongs to the Brewers Association as well as to the Wisconsin Brewers Guild. It is one of the largest 50 microbreweries in our dataset. Breweries in the established class are located in

Table 9.5. Brewery Exemplars for the Three Latent Classes

	New Glarus Brewing Co.	SweetWater Brewing Co.	Stumblefoot Brewing
Latent class	Established	Up-and-coming	Innovators
State	Wisconsin	Georgia	California
Type	Top 50	Top 50	New brewery
Factors (1 = present, 0 = not present):			
Ecological	0	1	0
Industry strength	1	0	1
License to self-distribute	1	0	1
State guild member	1	1	0
Brewers Association member	1	1	0
Spatial clustering	1	1	1

Table 9.6. Distribution of Breweries in the Three Latent Classes by Membership Type

	Overall Members		Full-Fledged Members	
	Frequency	Percentage	Frequency	Percentage
Established	288	59	170	62
Up-and-coming	107	22	44	16
Innovator	93	19	59	22
Total	488	100	273	100

states such as California, Colorado, Oregon, Washington, North Carolina, Pennsylvania, Minnesota, and Wisconsin.

Up-and-comers expand the market for craft brewers. They generally export accepted or popular styles of craft beer to markets with few or no craft breweries. In doing so, they introduce craft beer to consumers and attempt to convert them into steady customers. These craft brewers reflect the business side of craft brewing. With their motto, "Don't Float the Mainstream," SweetWater Brewing Co. exemplifies the up-and-coming latent class (90.5% probability of being in this class). This class is diverse in terms of the pattern of the six indicators. However, the spatial distinctiveness is permanent from the established class. Out of the 44 full-fledged members of the up-and-coming class, SweetWater has a reputation outside their state as well. The founders of SweetWater Brewing learned their craft at the American Brewers Guild in California. Their plan was to bring California-style brewing (what they call "hoppy aggressive ales") to Atlanta. In other words, their business strategy was to import an already-successful beer style into a new market. SweetWater Brewing Company is a member of the Brewers Association as well as the Georgia Brewers Guild. It is also one of the largest 50 microbreweries in our dataset. Georgia does not require licenses to self-distribute. However, according to our ecological indicator, the state has potential for market expansion based on its population parameters. Breweries in the up-and-coming class are from states such as Alabama, Georgia, Missouri, Kentucky, and Florida.

Innovators experiment with styles and ingredients. These craft brewers tend to be small organizations, with few employees and small-scale production. Innovators represent the vanguard of the craft brewing industry. With their size and dedication to experimental methods and products, they also reflect the authenticity of craft brewing. Brewers of this type tend to identify as artisans and tastemakers. Exemplifying the innovator latent class is Stumblefoot Brewing, which opened in 2012. It is located in San Marcos, California, a burgeoning craft beer region in one of the strongest craft beer–producing states (93.8% probability of being in this class). Although 59 breweries are full-fledged members of the innovators latent class located in states such California, Illinois, New York, Pennsylvania, Minnesota, and Oregon, Stumblefoot Brewing exemplifies innovation as a commitment to experimentation and the creation of new styles of beer. On their home page, they define Stumblefoot as "The art and science of gaining new knowledge through the happenstance of interesting encounters. Fortune favors the prepared." The founders of Stumblefoot came out of the homebrew scene in San Diego and make no mention on their website of having gained any formal credentials. As innovators, they do not take advantage of institutionalized conduits for resources: they are not members of either the Brewers Association or the California Craft Brewers Association.

These categories also have a spatial dynamic. Innovators tend to locate near established brewers. The clusters of established and innovator breweries make certain cities craft brewing hotspots. For example, Portland, Oregon, has a large number of breweries per capita. It is also home to several established craft brewers and many innovators. Similar dynamics take place in Denver and San Diego. Up-and-comers tend to locate away from both established and innovator brewers. This strategy aligns with the business orientation of these craft brewers. Our data limit our ability to explain these spatial dynamics. We offer some propositions for future research in the discussion below.

In sum (see also table 9.4), our results show that the microbrewery industry is constituted by two spatially separate dynamics: one oriented toward identity maintenance and the other toward market growth. Identity maintenance dynamics are reflected by the spatial closeness of innovators and established craft brewers. The presence of the innovator class may indicate a spatial logic to identity differentiation that can be summarized as, "Be where the winners are, but be yourself." We speculate about the reasons behind these dynamics and suggest areas for future research below. The spatial dynamics of the up-and-comer class (i.e., how they tend to locate away from established and innovator craft brewers) suggests that this organizational identity facilitates market growth. Again, we speculate about the mechanisms driving this dynamic below.

Conclusion

In this chapter, we showed how industry dynamics (classes of organizations within an industry) were also constituted by spatial dynamics (certain classes were more or less likely to be colocated). In the case of craft brewers, members of the innovator class were likely to locate near members of the established class. Established brewers and innovators were more likely to locate in regions with high spatial clustering, meaning they tended to operate in dense markets. We speculate that this may be a case of partitioning within the partition (Negro et al. 2014; Sikavica and Pozner 2013): innovators locate near established brewers in order to serve consumers with sophisticated or adventurous palates who are not being serviced by the more established craft brewers.

Our scheme provides analytical categories for studying microbreweries similar to those for other situated commercial movements. For example, it might be applied to the restaurants studied by Rao et al. (2003). Innovators in our scheme may be seen as authors of institutional change. Up-and-coming restaurants may be those directed toward the business aspects of cuisine, providing a bridge between food as aesthetic good and food as market good. One condition shaping these dynamics is the nature of beer as a consumable. Like haute cuisine, craft beer consumption may increase over time as consumers cultivate a taste for it. Therefore, new entrants may not necessarily take consumers away from existing brewers, but may actually increase the overall size of the market. Therefore, we are unlikely to see spatial dynamics similar to those in zero-sum markets, such as car dealers, sellers of electronics, or bicycle shops.

Based on LCA and with secondary data, the research presented in this chapter is very much exploratory. As such, this research is subject to key limitations.

LCA generates categories from extant data. As such, brewers in our study may not explicitly identify themselves as members of the categories we found. Future research should test the robustness of the categories we present through direct measures. Furthermore, our data limit our ability to make pronouncements about the meanings of these categories or their fixity. Future research should engage in qualitative inquiry to uncover the substantive meanings associated with being within a category. For example, do established brewers see themselves as such? Future research should also examine the fixity of the categories we present in this chapter. We anticipate that brewers move among them with a certain degree of fluidity, especially as particular craft beer styles come in and go out of vogue. A style that is considered innovative at one point in time can become a standard style at another. Correspondingly, the brewer that produces that style could identify as an innovator early in their history and later become an established brewer. Similarly, we suspect that established brewers may have resources that allow them to experiment with and market new styles, effectively reinventing themselves as innovators.

Yet the research we presented in this chapter also suggests important areas for future research. For example, what accounts for the colocation of established and innovator craft brewers? Does the phenomenon reflect the further partitioning of a resource space, as the latter appeal to consumers of craft beer not serviced by the former? Or does it reflect the "spinning off" of apprentices from the former to the latter?

Up-and-coming brewers are oriented toward market expansion. Their aspirations are geared toward developing a successful business and opening new markets. This is evident in their strategies of transposing standardized craft beer styles from more saturated and dense states to those with rapidly growing markets (or none at all). Up-and-coming breweries were likely to be members of the Brewers Association, but not necessarily members of state guilds. This is due in part to the absence of state guilds in some regions. However, this suggests that up-and-comers are paying attention to broader industry trends. How do we explain the location of up-and-comers? Is distance a strategic action as up-and-comers seek out markets to avoid direct competition with established craft brewers?

One of the outcomes of the spatial dynamics described in this chapter is the emergence of craft brewing hotspots—cities in which craft brewers reach a key density, but also play a key role in the local economy. Portland, Oregon; Denver; and San Diego represent such craft brewing hotspots. Future research should examine the local dynamics driving these urban economies. Is this driven by demographic shifts (e.g., a critical mass of young people taking part in discerning taste cultures? Or, are there economic drivers, such as the rise of complementary artisanal industries in these regions)? Finally, what are the cultural factors undergirding the expansion of craft brewing in these areas? Are these artisanal industries concomitant with a rejection of mass culture products and the advancement of niche tastes? This implication is too broad for us to generate specific propositions. However, future research should examine the emergence of the craft brewing industry from a place-based perspective.

The Future of the Craft Brewing Industry

While the market for craft beer continues to expand, we suspect that competition among microbrewers will follow the inverted U-curve found among microradio stations by Greve et al. (2006). They find that diversity among microradio stations with regard to content, leads to increased density. However, over time, competition consumes resources (e.g., listeners), and this reduces subsequent founding rates. Similarly, we may find the same dynamics among microbrewers, as the proliferation of craft brew styles affords opportunities for new entrants.

The industry-life-cycles argument similarly predicts that shakeouts naturally follow periods of mass entry (Horvath et al. 2001). The results indicate that in each cohort, hazard rates to exit are the highest in the first two years after market entry then they drop substantially and level off. The latest entrants are the most vulnerable to such an exit. Horvath et al. (2001) argue that the mechanism through which entry rates increase prior to shakeout is due to information accumulation; the costs of obtaining information about market prospects drop significantly, allowing for firm entry en masse and a shakeout later.

Considerations of economic viability and sustainable growth certainly play a role in the survival of microbreweries (Tremblay and Tremblay 2011). However, the latest accounts show that not all firms opt for following an exaggerated growth model and rather choose to stay small (Hindy 2014). A continuing challenge of craft breweries is to find distribution channels for their products. When the microbrewery sector emerged in the 1980s, interests in the then 50-year-old three-tier system of alcohol distribution had already been solidified, furthering the market advantage of large breweries. Besides wholesalers slowly moving toward representing multiple brands, constructing their own portfolio, and matching it with their own organizational identity, microbrewers also found other ways to distribute their products through self-distribution—in states where laws allow it—or through contracts with wine or spirit wholesalers. Either way, microbreweries operate in a climate in which the number of available distributors has been steadily declining since the 1980s (*Brewers Almanac* 2013).

NOTES

1. We downloaded the data on October 20, 2013, from http://projects.newyorker.com/story /beer. Note that these data are no longer available from this source.

2. Seventeen states did not have an organized state guild (see Appendix).

REFERENCES

Albert Stuart, and David A. Whetten. 1985. "Organizational Identity." *Research in Organizational Behavior* 7: 263–295.

Batzli, S. A. 2014. "Mapping United States Breweries 1612–2011." In *The Geography of Beer Regions, Environment, and Societies*, edited by M. Patterson and N. Hoalst-Pullen, 31–44. New York: Springer.

Baum, Dan. 2000. *Citizen Coors: An American Dynasty*. New York: Morrow.

Boone, Christophe, Vera Brocheler, and Glenn R. Carroll. 2002. "Custom Service: Application and Tests of Resource-Partitioning Theory among Dutch Auditing Firms from 1896 to 1992." *Organization Studies* 21 (2000): 355–381.

Boone, Christophe, Arjen van Witteloostuijn, and Glenn R. Carroll. 2000. "Resource Distributions and Market Partitioning: Dutch Daily Newspapers, 1968 to 1994." *American Sociological Review* 67: 408–431.

Brewers Almanac. 2013. Accessed January 31, 2014, http://www.beerinstitute.org/br/beer -statistics/brewers-almanac.

Carroll, Glenn R. 1985. "Concentration and Specialization: Dynamics of Niche Width in Populations of Organizations." *American Journal of Sociology* 90: 1262–1283.

———. 2015. "Authenticity: Attribution, Value, and Meaning." In *Emerging Trends in the Social and Behavioral Sciences: An Interdisciplinary, Searchable, and Linkable Resource*, edited by Robert Scott and Stephan Kosslyn, 1–13. New York: Wiley.

Carroll, Glenn R., and Anand Swaminathan. 2000. "Why the Microbrewery Movement? Organizational Dynamics of Resource Partitioning in the US Brewing Industry." *American Journal of Sociology* 106: 715–762.

Collins, Linda M., and Stephanie T. Lanza. 2010. *Latent Class and Latent Transition Analysis. With Applications in the Social, Behavioral, and Health Sciences*. Hoboken, NJ: Wiley.

DiMaggio, Paul, and Walter W. Powell. 1983. "The Iron Cage Revisited: Institutional Isomorphism and Collective Rationality in Organizational Fields." *American Sociological Review* 48: 147–160.

Dobrev, Stanislav D. 2000. "Decreasing Concentration and Reversibility of the Resource Partitioning Process: Supply Shortages and Deregulation in the Bulgarian Newspaper Industry, 1987 1992." *Organization Studies* 21: 383–404.

Dobrev, Stanislav D., Tai Young Kim, and Michael T. Hannan. 2001. "Dynamics of Niche Width and Resource Partitioning." *American Journal of Sociology* 106: 1299–1337.

Fligstein, Neil, and Doug McAdam. 2012. *A Theory of Fields*. New York: Oxford University Press.

Glynn, Mary Ann. 2008. "Beyond Constraint: How Institutions Enable Identities." In *The Sage Handbook of Organizational Institutionalism*, edited by Royston Greenwood, Christine Oliver, Kerstin Sahlin, and Roy Suddaby, 413–430. Los Angeles: Sage.

Greenwood, Royston, Christine Oliver, Kerstin Sahlin, and Roy Suddaby. 2008. "Introduction." In *The Sage Handbook of Organizational Institutionalism*, edited by Royston Greenwood, Christine Oliver, Kerstin Sahlin, and Roy Suddaby, 1–46. Los Angeles: Sage.

Greve, Henrich R., Jo-Ellen Pozner, and Hayagreeva Rao. 2006. "Vox Populi: Resource Partitioning, Organizational Proliferation, and the Cultural Impact of the Insurgent Microradio Movement." *American Journal of Sociology* 112: 802–837.

Hindy, Steve. 2014. *The Craft Beer Revolution: How a Band of Microbrewers Is Transforming the World's Favorite Drink*. New York: Palgrave MacMillan.

Horvath, Michael, Fabiano Schivardi, and Michael Woywode. 2001. "On Industry Life-Cycles: Delay, Entry, and Shakeout in Beer Brewing." *International Journal of Industrial Organization* 19:1023–1052.

Martin, John Levi. 2003. "What Is Field Theory?" *American Journal of Sociology* 109: 1–49.

Mohr, John W. 2005. "Implicit Terrains: Meaning, Measurement, and Spatial Metaphors in Organizational Theory." Accessed March 6, 2015, http://www.soc.ucsb.edu/ct/pages/JWM/Papers/ImplictTerrains.pdf.

Negro Giacomo, Fabiana Visentin, and Anand Swaminathan. 2014. "Resource Partitioning and the Organizational Dynamics of 'Fringe Banking.'" *American Sociological Review* 79: 680–704.

Péli, Gábor, and Bart Nooteboom. 1999. "Market Partitioning and the Geometry of the Resource Space." *American Journal of Sociology* 104: 1132–1153.

Ragin, Charles C. 2000. *Fuzzy-Set Social Science*. Chicago: University of Chicago Press.

Rao, Hayagreeva, Philippe Monin, and Rodolphe Durand. 2003. "Institutional Change in Toque Ville: Nouvelle Cuisine as an Identity Movement in French Gastronomy." *American Journal of Sociology* 108: 795–843.

Sikavica, Katarina, and Jo-Ellen Pozner. 2013. "Paradise Sold: Resource Partitioning and the Organic Movement in the US Farming Industry." *Organization Studies* 34: 623–651.

Storper, Michael. 1997. *The Regional World: Territorial Development in a Global Economy*. New York: Guilford.

Storper, Michael, and Robert Salais. 1997. *Worlds of Production: the Action Frameworks of the Economy*. Cambridge, MA: Harvard University Press.

Swedberg, Richard. 2005. "Markets in Society." In *The Handbook of Economic Sociology* (2nd ed.), edited by Neil J. Smelser, and Richard Swedberg, 233–253. Princeton, NJ: Princeton University Press

Tremblay, Carol Horton, and Victor J. Tremblay. 2011. "Recent Economic Developments in the Import and Craft Segments of the US Brewing Industry." In *The Economics of Beer*, edited by Johan Swinnen, 141–160. Oxford: Oxford University Press.

Whetten, David A. 2006. "Albert and Whetten Revisited: Strengthening the Concept of Organizational Identity." *Journal of Management Inquiry* 15: 219–234.

White, Harrison C. 1981. "Where Do Markets Come From?" *American Journal of Sociology* 87: 517–547.

———. 2002. *Markets from Networks: Socioeconomic Models of Production*. Princeton, NJ: Princeton University Press.

Whitford Josh, and Cuz Potter. 2007. "Regional Economies, Open Networks and the Spatial Fragmentation of Production." *Socio-Economic Review* 5: 497–526.

Witteloostuijn, Arjen van, and Christophe Boone. 2006. "A Resource-Based Theory of Market Structure and Organizational Form." *Academy of Management Review* 31: 409–426.

Appendix: Data Sources

Membership data sources and license requirements as provided by the Brewers Association

Brewers Association membership list (updated daily). Accessed October 19, 2013, http://ba .brewersassociation.org/memberlist/members.aspx?memtype=BREW.

"Self Distribution Laws." Accessed March 15, 2014, https://www.brewersassociation.org /government-affairs/laws/self-distribution-laws/.

"Find a State Guild." Accessed October 26, 2013, http://www.brewersassociation.org/pages /government-affairs/guilds/find-a-guild.

Guild Name

Alabama Brewers Guild	http://albeer.org/
Arizona Craft Brewers Guild	https://chooseazbrews.com/
Brewers Association of Maryland	www.marylandbeer.org
Brewers Guild of Alaska	www.brewersguildofalaska.org
Brewers of Indiana Guild (BIG)	https://drinkin.beer/
Brewers of Pennsylvania	www.brewersofpa.org
California Craft Brewers Association	www.californiacraftbeer.com
Colorado Brewers Guild	www.coloradobeer.org
Delaware Brewers Guild	www.delawarebrewersguild.org
Florida Brewers Guild, INC	www.floridabrewersguild.org
Garden State Craft Brewers Guild	www.njbeer.org
Georgia Brewers Guild	www.georgiacraftbrewersguild.org
Illinois Craft Brewers Guild	www.illinoisbeer.com
Iowa Brewers Guild	www.iowabeer.org
Louisiana Craft Brewers Guild	www.labeer.org
Maine Brewers Guild	www.mainebrewersguild.org
Massachusetts Brewers Guild	www.massbrewersguild.org
Michigan Brewers Guild	www.mibeer.com

Minnesota Craft Brewers	www.mncraftbrew.org
Montana Brewers Association	www.montanabrewers.org
Nebraska Craft Brewers Association	www.nebraskabrewers.org
Nevada Craft Brewers Association	www.bigdogsbrews.com/nevadacraftbrewers
New Mexico Brewers Guild	www.nmbeer.org
New York City Brewers Guild	www.newyorkcitybrewersguild.com
New York State Brewers Association	http://newyorkcraftbeer.com/
North Carolina Brewers Guild	www.ncbeer.org
Ohio Craft Brewers Association	www.ohiocraftbeer.org
Oregon Brewers Guild	http://oregoncraftbeer.org/
San Diego Brewers Guild	www.sandiegobrewersguild.org
San Francisco Brewers Guild	www.sfbrewersguild.org
South Carolina Brewers Association	www.southcarolinabeer.org
St. Louis Brewers Guild	www.stlbrewersguild.org
Tennessee Craft Brewers Guild	www.tncraftbrewers.org
Texas Craft Brewers Guild	www.texascraftbrewersguild.org
Vermont Brewers Association	www.vermontbrewers.com
Virginia Craft Brewers Guild	www.virginiacraftbrewers.org
Washington Beer Commission	www.washingtonbeer.com
Washington Brewers Guild	www.washingtonbrewersguild.org
Wisconsin Brewers Guild	www.wibrewersguild.com

The following states do not have a functioning state guild: Arkansas, Idaho, Connecticut, Kansas, Kentucky, Missouri, Oklahoma, Rhode Island, South Dakota, Utah, Mississippi, North Dakota, Nebraska, New Hampshire, South Dakota, Washington, DC, and Wyoming.

PART III

Intersecting Identities

CHAPTER 10

The Cultural Tensions between Taste Refinement and American Middle-Class Masculinity

ANDRE F. MACIEL

Introduction

Taste refinement, which refers to the development of complex systems of aesthetic evaluation, has long presented ambiguous meanings for American middle-class men. In the eighteenth and nineteenth centuries, this social stratum wanted to further distinguish itself from newly arrived immigrants and the working class, but viewed refinement in housing, clothing, and eating as effeminate and elitist (Bushman 1992). In the late twentieth century, Lamont (1992) revealed that taste refinement remained contested even among well-educated, upper-middle-class men, who favor moral and socioeconomic signals over taste in granting someone prestige. Nonetheless, much of the recent market growth for U.S. craft beer relies on taste refinement by middle-class men (Carroll and Swaminathan 2000; Holt and Cameron 2010; Maciel and Wallendorf 2016). This chapter zooms in on the context of craft beer to reveal how this social stratum aligns culturally refined consumption with their class-inflected scripts of gender and morality. Viewing this phenomenon through the theoretical lens of symbolic boundaries (Lamont 1992), I illuminate how these men refine their aesthetic sensibilities while upholding their senses of masculinity and rectitude.

I first identify central notions of masculinity and morality among U.S. middle-class men and briefly explain the concept of symbolic boundaries. I then describe the ethnography conducted with middle-class craft beer aficionados, a cultural stratum committed to pursuing taste refinement. I then follow with the themes that reveal how these men negotiate the cultural tensions that emerge from their pursuit of taste refinement in a particular consumption domain. In the final section, I discuss the broader relevance of the results of this research.

Cultural Scripts of Middle-Class Masculinity

Ideals of democracy, economic self-reliance, and individualism run deep in the American middle-class ethos. In resonance with these ideals, work achievement became a pivotal element in scripts of middle-class masculinity (Kimmel 1995; Lamont 1992). This element prescribes for middle-class men the role of breadwinners, who participate in the marketplace to secure economic resources for themselves and their families, through both hard work and systematic professional challenges (Coontz 2000). The normative strength of the male breadwinner role certainly softened over the second half of the twentieth century, with discourses about gender equality and the increased participation of women in the U.S. labor force. However, these changes have not displaced the ideals of the male breadwinner. The anxieties and stigma faced by contemporary stay-at-home fathers whose wives provide the main source of family income attests to the continuity of these ideals (Coskuner-Balli and Thompson 2013).

The centrality of achievement spills over into middle-class men's ways of consuming. In the public sphere, these men typically engage in sports to win rather than merely to socialize; in the domestic sphere, those involved in do-it-yourself ventures engage in challenging projects, rather than in uncomplicated, relaxing ones (Gelber 1999; Holt and Thompson 2004; Moisio et al. 2013). In parallel, some middle-class men engage in instances of extraordinary consumption to temporarily rebel against what they consider an overly predictable, emasculating urban life. They become "weekend warriors," riding Harley-Davidson motorcycles on their days off, or "mountain men," going to the wilderness as a way of testing their skills to control nature without much technological help (Belk and Costa 1998; Schouten and McAlexander 1995).

Middle-class men who engage in these consumption activities reproduce normative scripts of masculinity, such as achievement, toughness, and escape from civilization (Kimmel 1995). In Bourdieuian terms, these men enact the homology between some gendered consumption practices and their gender habitus (Bourdieu and Wacquant 1992). By contrast, in this chapter I explore a case of heterology. It focuses on how middle-class men engage with taste refinement, a consumption mode that, for connoting femininity and elitism, was foreclosed in their socialization into masculinity (Holt and Thompson 2004; Kimmel 1995; Lamont 1992).

I analyze how middle-class men participate in this heterological route to masculinity through the theoretical lens of symbolic boundaries, which foregrounds the conceptual distinctions made by particular social groups between themselves and those adjacent to them (Lamont 1992). The contents of these boundaries "are determined by available cultural resources and . . . social-structural constraints" (Lamont 1992, 11). Accordingly, my analysis conceptualizes the content of these men's symbolic boundaries as determined by their gender and class positions. These positions determine the socially constrained toolkit of resources, such as cultural scripts and embodied behaviors, from which this social stratum draws to create symbolic boundaries (Swidler 1986, 2003).

Before analyzing these boundaries, I detail the method used to study men involved in the pursuit of taste refinement in the domain of craft beer, the empirical context that opens a theoretical window into the cultural tensions between taste refinement and some prevalent scripts of U.S. middle-class masculinity.

Methodological Procedures

This research relies on an ethnography of craft beer aficionados. Aficionados are people committed to refining their sensory and linguistic competencies in a consumption domain (Strong 2011). They attend courses, interact with other aficionados, and study materials related to their avocations (Benzecry 2011). Often, they also leisurely produce the cultural forms they appreciate. For example, many "foodies" both eat in restaurants known for their great chefs and cook gourmet foods at home (Lupton 1996), and many music aficionados both go to concerts and play musical instruments (Levy 1980/1999). Similarly, craft beer aficionados both drink commercial craft beers and often brew beer at home.

My research design reflects this multifaceted world. I employed multisite participant observation and unstructured interviews to assemble three datasets on craft beer aficionados. Two of these datasets rely on naturalistic observation. This type of data is particularly appropriate to address Lamont's (1992) call for research on the *behavioral* boundaries individuals draw, as a complement to her focus on *discursive* boundaries.

I conducted participant observation at a typical U.S. craft beer and home-brewing club to document aficionados' perspective *in* action (Snow and Anderson 1987). I participated in the activities of this club for almost three years. This club has about eighty members and is located in the southwestern United States. In its monthly meetings, about forty members gather to discuss homebrewing techniques, taste commercial exemplars of craft beer, and share their own home-brews with peers.

Table 10.1. Craft Beer Aficionados Interviewed

Pseudonyms	Sex/Ethnicity	Age Group	Occupation	Degree
Adam	Male/white	20–29	Software developer	Bachelor's
Daniel	Male/white	40–49	Entrepreneur	Bachelor's
Giovanni	Male/white	20–29	Graduate student	Bachelor's
Henry	Male/white	30–39	Nongovernmental organization director	Master's
Jack	Male/white	60–69	Retired	Bachelor's
Jake	Male/white	20–29	Engineer	Bachelor's
Jerry	Male/white	60–69	Homicide detective	Bachelor's
Jordan	Male/white	30–39	Sales associate	Bachelor's
Miguel	Male/Hispanic	40–49	Electric technician	Bachelor's
Marc	Male/white	30–39	Entrepreneur	PhD
Nate	Male/white	40–49	Information technology (IT) analyst	Bachelor's
Oliver	Male/white	30–39	High school teacher	Bachelor's
Peter	Male/white	40–49	Business manager	Master's
Richard	Male/white	40–49	IT manager	Master's
Ryan	Male/white	20–29	Graduate student	Master's
Sean	Male/white	50–59	Entrepreneur	Master's

In addition, I interviewed aficionados to document their perspective *of* action (Snow and Anderson 1987). As table 10.1 indicates, I interviewed 16 men, typically at their homes. To add analytical depth, half of these informants were non–club members (Glaser and Strauss 1967). I began with grand tour questions (McCracken 1988) and then moved to questions about craft beer and homebrewing, exploring specific events to understand these men's actions rather than abstractions. Interviews lasted from 1.5 to 3 hours and were transcribed verbatim. Typically on a different day, I also helped about half of these 16 men to homebrew a batch of beer. In these interactions, I spent an additional 3 to 8 hours with the aficionado, eliciting further information through nondirective probes and observation (Snow and Anderson 1987).

For further data collection, I attended four craft beer festivals and six craft brewery tours in Arizona and California. At these events, I observed the aesthetics and the discourses that institutional actors put forward in the craft beer domain. I also informally interacted with dozens of casual beer drinkers, asking about their trajectories in the craft beer domain and observing their conversations with craft breweries' representatives. I used the field notes on these events to triangulate across sources and sites as a way of crystallizing emergent interpretations (Lincoln and Guba 1985).

All of the aficionados were male, and most were white, married, and heterosexual. These men typically hold four-year college degrees from nonelite universities and work in middle-class jobs, such as midlevel manager and engineer. This sociodemographic homogeneity fits the study of symbolic boundaries, as such boundaries refer to the distinctions that members of a particular social group make between themselves and others (Lamont 1992). Although I interacted with some women during fieldwork, they were usually accompanying their male partners. "I like drinking, but it's mostly his thing" was a common comment these women made when asked about their interest in craft beer. Hence, this chapter focuses on male aficionados to provide a theoretically deeper analysis that parsimoniously reflects the context studied.

Aligning Taste Refinement with American Middle-Class Masculinity

Prevalent scripts of American middle-class masculinity and moralistic notions of democracy have historically associated taste refinement with women and elite groups, thus marginalizing this form of taste as a mode of consumption for American middle-class men (Halle 1993; Lamont 1992). The following analysis reveals how middle-class craft beer aficionados draw symbolic boundaries, both discursive and behavioral, to align this mode of consumption with their class-inflected notions of masculinity and morality.

The first two themes analyze these middle-class men's boundary work to distinguish their pursuit of taste refinement from meanings of femininity and elitism. The third theme analyzes these men's boundary work to assuage the moral ambiguity that involvement with alcohol consumption has historically presented to the American middle class (Gusfield 1987). In particular, this theme shows how these men construct their leisurely, frequent drinking as a respectable middle-class pursuit, in contradistinction to the trivialized drinking associated with the lower classes and youths (Bourdieu 1984).

Gender Boundaries: Eschewing Notions of Femininity

As aficionados pursue taste refinement in craft beer, they learn specific drinking procedures to help them fully appreciate the qualities of this product. These procedures include pouring small amounts of beer into clean, nice glasses, ingesting beer in small sips, and using gracious gestures to swirl and smell the beer to enjoy its sensuousness. These delicate manners, along with reduced drinking portions, form a consumption mode that is legitimate in some cultural fields, such as wine. Outside of specific fields, however, this consumption mode is strongly associated with femininity across various cultures (Bourdieu 2001; Lupton 1996).

As a way of counterbalancing these connotations of conventional femininity, aficionados construct spaces where they express conventional maleness. One of these spaces is beer making. My field notes illustrate the masculinized materiality and physicality involved in *all-grain*, aficionados' preferred homebrewing method:

Oliver uses a manual mill to grind his homebrewing grain. He does so to control for the quality of his beer and for the efficiency of his homebrewing process. He sometimes uses an electric drill to turn the handle of the mill. But when the grain is unusually hard or the drill battery is not fully charged, he has to manually turn the handle of the mill to grind the grain. This was today's case. As the photo below shows, Oliver has to do a bit of contortionism to angle his body in a way that fixes the mill on a bucket and gives him the strength to turn the handle.

After some minutes milling his grain, Oliver was sweating and his face had turned red. He released the handle and asked if I wanted to help. I said yes. After angling my body, I was surprised by the physical strength necessary to turn the handle consistently, as Oliver was doing. After turning the handle about ten times, my arm muscles began to burn. Physical strength also is essential when aficionados lift the heavy, steel pots (10 gallons or more) that contain the hot solutions involved in beer production. For example, to transfer the liquid with the juice of the grains and the hops (*wort*) from the boiling pot (*kettle*) to the fermenter, aficionados often use gravity to pull the wort through a tube. So, they have to place the kettle in a position that is higher than the fermenter (e.g., by putting the kettle on a table and the fermenter on the ground). Oliver grabbed a rag to hold the kettle's hot handles and bent his body to lift this pot from the ground. As Oliver transferred the kettle to the table, the weight of the kettle made his arms tremble (author's field notes, February 2014)

Beer homebrewing is instrumental in aficionados' pursuit of refinement because the physical manipulation of raw materials heightens their sensory competence (Sennett 2008). By touching, smelling, and tasting beer ingredients, aficionados

Figure 10.1. Oliver's Effortful Performance to Mill Grains for his Homebrewing.

sharpen their ability to identify the effect of these ingredients and certain production techniques on the final product (Maciel and Wallendorf 2016).

However, this craft production also performs a symbolic function. Particularly in the U.S. middle class, modernity structured the public and private
spheres as the respective realms of men and women (Coontz 2000). As a corollary
of this structuring, middle-class production was marked primarily as masculine
and middle-class consumption primarily as feminine (Gelber 1999). Hence, by
producing beer, aficionados add a layer of conventional masculinity to their
refined consumption of this product. On a normal all-grain homebrewing day,
they put on production-facilitating apparel, as figure 10.1 shows Oliver wearing
the apron of a local brewery. Further, aficionados spend about seven hours on the
process, almost the same length of the shift for a full-time job. This process,
though located in the conventionally feminine sphere of the home, occurs in
masculinized spaces such as garages and backyards (Gelber 1999; Moisio et al.
2013). In these spaces, aficionados masculinize their paths toward taste refinement by juxtaposing quintessentially masculine elements, such as machinery

and brute physicality, with their evolving sensibilities in beer (Bourdieu 2001; Kimmel 1995). Thus, these middle-class men draw on masculine scripts and embodied behaviors to construct nondiscursive distinctions between their projects of taste refinement and conventional notions of femininity.

Aficionados construct other ways of aligning their refined consumption with their class-inflected notions of masculinity. As compared to mass-produced beers, craft beers present a wide range of color, bitterness, and alcohol levels. Aficionados eagerly explore this range as part of their refinement pursuit, rather than settling on only one brand or beer style as their favorite. As with other omnivorous consumers (Peterson and Kern 1996; Warde 2011), aficionados embrace variety in taste experiences, but they do so systematically, in a single consumption domain, with a clear goal in mind: taste refinement. For example, when aficionados identify gaps in their aesthetic competence, such as limited knowledge of a certain beer style, they are likely to engage with this style. However, they will do so by studying materials and tasting exemplars of that style for extended periods until they close that knowledge gap. Then they move on. Their systematic eagerness for novel aesthetic experiences as a way of building their trajectories in this consumption space echoes the American script of the self-made man. In the nineteenth century, men aspiring to social mobility flocked to the Wild West to make their living, forging a cultural legacy that valorizes men who build character by purposefully exploring the unknown (Kimmel 1995). Aficionados draw on this gender script to construct taste refinement as an adventurous project, thus further masculinizing the path toward their elaborate sensibilities.

Aficionados seek and valorize breadth of knowledge within a consumption domain. Their primary goal is not to legitimate their own tastes as superior, but rather to develop enduring skills to confidently appreciate a wide range of beers (Maciel and Wallendorf 2016). Yet aficionados do have subjective preferences, which tend to gravitate toward darker and bitter beers that often feature alcohol levels near 10%. These preferences are symbolically instrumental. Beverages that are low in alcohol, fruity in taste, and light in color tend to connote fragility; conversely, the ability to drink beverages that are high in alcohol, bitter in taste, and dark in color connotes the drinker's toughness (Levy 1986/1999; Lupton 1996). Aficionados thus further eschew the feminine connotation of their refined consumption by favoring beer styles that feature elements culturally linked to masculinity, while they continue appreciating well-executed exemplars of other styles.

Aficionados rarely draw gender boundaries discursively. When they do so, these boundaries are simplistic and non-judgmental. At a festival, an aficionado gave me a grand tour of the main craft breweries and explained: "This brewery here made a fruity beer for the festival. It's a watermelon IPA, I guess. I think they're trying to appeal to the female public." Overall, the dominant discourse is gender-inclusive. Aficionados often tell one another their specific efforts to help their wives appreciate craft beer, such as brewing beer that pleases these women's palates, but not their own. At the club where I conducted field work, event announcements always encouraged members to bring their wives to these activities. The gender-inclusiveness in aficionados' discourses differs sharply from the discourses of working-class males, who often try verbally to keep women away from their preserves (Epstein 1992).

To further align taste refinement with class-inflected notions of masculinity, aficionados also rely on institutionally provided resources in the craft beer world. Craft breweries often choose highly masculine names for their beers such as "Panty Peeler" and "Arrogant Bastard," and employ in their iconography aggressive symbols such as dragons and demons. Further, institutional actors in the craft beer domain often promote competitions, a type of sociality that co-constitutes American masculinity (Kimmel 1995). In a common competition type, craft beer clubs and craft breweries jointly organize homebrew contests, in which aficionados submit their homebrewed beers to the evaluation of a panel of beer judges. The winners of these contests often earn the right to have their recipes commercially brewed by the partnering craft breweries. In participating in these competitions, aficionados bring their refined tastes nearer the realm of work and infuse them with the possibility of public achievement. They thus further masculinize their refined engagement with the aesthetic dimensions of a consumption domain.

In many social strata, discursive boundaries that draw on attributes typically viewed as ascribed (e.g., gender) have lost prevalence; people have come to see such boundary making as politically incorrect (Lamont and Fournier 1992). However, this loss does not prevent the operation of nondiscursive boundaries among the same strata. This section shows how embodied scripts, along with discourses provided by some market institutions, serve as a primary resource for middle-class aficionados to make symbolic distinctions that eschew their projects of taste refinement from meanings of femininity.

I now turn to analyzing aficionados' symbolic boundaries based on morality, an attribute that people tend to see as achieved rather than ascribed; hence, they more often verbalize it in their boundary work.

Moral Boundaries: Eschewing Notions of Elitism

As aficionados refine their sensibilities for beer, they increasingly socialize with people who share similar beer tastes. However, reflecting the still limited market share of craft beer, aficionados' social ties continue to include people who prefer mass-produced lagers (e.g., Budweiser). Echoing notions of omnivorousness (Peterson and Kern 1996), aficionados adopt discourses of aesthetic tolerance to judge these people's tastes. Nate (40–49, IT analyst) describes how he and a group of aficionados accommodated a friend's preference for this mass-produced beer style, "This friend knew we're all craft beer enthusiasts and homebrewers. So, he brought his Coors Light and he was waiting for us to give him grief. I'm like 'No, dude! Drink what you like!' He likes it, so I have no problem with it. I don't look down on him."

At first, Nate illustrates middle-class Americans' loose cultural boundaries, as he discursively resists determining someone's worth based on taste (Lamont 1992). But when probed further, Nate discloses the behavioral boundaries of this aesthetic tolerance:

RESEARCHER: How about when your preference for craft beer is the exception?
NATE: I had gone to someone's house that only had Coors Light or Bud Light. I was like "I'm going to go to the store to grab some beer." And he said, "No, I have some beer here." I said, "No it's cool. I just want to try something that's near here." I was kind of lying. . . . I did feel kind of bad because the people were like "We got this beer. We thought you wanted this!"
RESEARCHER: Tell me about coming back with craft beer to this house.
NATE: So I came back with a Sierra Nevada pale ale. I was like, "I kind of like hoppier beers." Of course, they all tried it and hated it. They were like, "How can you drink this?!" So I'm like, "It's just a different palate." I guess that's along the same line of, if somebody cooks something bad, would you be forced to eat it? I don't know. It was bad.

Aficionados acknowledge cultural norms that demean picky guests. Yet, they perform their refined consumption in contexts out of the craft beer domain by respecting other people's choices, while trying to graciously uphold their own preferences. They do so by silencing their beliefs about the taste superiority of craft beer and, instead, frame their tastes simply as idiosyncratic in order to normalize others' preferences. Rather than proclaiming their refinement to elevate their status in social settings out of the craft beer domain, they hold back their tastes to avoid a feared label: the beer snob.

Aficionados discursively shun the term *beer snob*, even though they perform practices that conventionally convey elitism, such as using specialized vocabulary to discuss their perceptions and restricting their beer drinking to non-mainstream brands:

> It's a fine line between being specific, knowledgeable and pretentious. . . . [But] beer has less of an elitist attitude. You can get beer at a baseball game. So, it's not really a culture of elitism and exclusiveness like wine. Some wine will be hundreds of dollars and $15 just for a glass. . . . Not all vineyards are guilty of this, I must say. Some do a very good job to be approachable. But, anyway, you can't use your knowledge as a weapon to make someone feel stupid. That's the defining characteristic of a snob I think. So it's kind of snobby in a way when I refuse to go to certain places because they don't have good beer or at someone's house not drinking a beer. Other than that, it's my own—I don't know if I should call it snobbery, it's just education, knowing what you drink, what is good beer. It's a *geek* hobby. You need to know a bit of chemistry, biology, and physics to understand beer taste. Like I said, my beer journey—as you learn more and more you get more sophisticated with it. I think people it like better to be called beer geeks. (Marc, 30–39, PhD)

Aficionados are much more verbal about drawing moral boundaries than about drawing gender boundaries. In the eighteenth and nineteenth centuries, middle-class men framed their refined consumption of housing, clothing, and eating as a pursuit of comfort; they did so to assuage the elitist meaning from the gentrified lifestyle they had incorporated from the British aristocracy (Bushman 1992). In a contemporary enactment of this strategy, aficionados assuage elitism by verbally framing their taste refinement as a pursuit of knowledge. Instead of beer snob, they put forward the knowledge-related label *beer geek*. They subjectively negotiate the meaning of their refined tastes not as a practice that excludes others, but rather as a tool that helps them make informed decisions about beer, a product that permeates most middle-class men's social trajectories (Barr 1999). They thus reorient the meaning of their refined consumption away from elitist connotations to two legitimate virtues among middle-class men: practical knowledge and the ability to be a self-defining consumer (Holt and Thompson 2004; Lamont 1992).

The previous passage, when referring to wine prices, also foreshadows the role of craft beer institutions in providing resources for aficionados to align taste refinement with their class-inflected, moralistic notions of a democratic, inclusive marketplace. Craft breweries price most of their bottles below $10, including their award-winning products. Their prices are certainly higher than those of mass-produced American lagers, but that beer style is not aficionados' price touchstone. Aficionados compare the price of craft beers against that of wines, a beverage often associated with snobbery in the United States (Lehrer 2009). Their framing of craft beer prices as reasonable serves to maintain the historic link between beer drinking and the myth of an American society constituted through weak social hierarchies (Barr 1999).

Another boundary resource provided by craft beer institutions is brand. In addition to the masculinized names mentioned in the previous section, U.S. craft breweries often adopt witty names for their beers, such as "Modus Hope-randi" (a pun combining a Latin expression and hops, a vital beer ingredient) and "Genealogy of Morals" (an allusion to Nietzsche's book). This branding style is the same as that adopted by many American wineries since the 1970s. To enhance the resonance of wine with U.S. middle class's long-held ideals of democracy, these wineries excluded from their labels aristocracy-alluding terms that prestigious wines often carry, such as the French word for castle, "chateau" (Lehrer 2009). Instead, these U.S. wineries, just like U.S. craft beer breweries, market casual brands to resonate with prevalent notions of anti-elitism among the American middle class.

A third institutionally provided resource is commercial setting. Craft breweries often are located in industrial areas. They choose these locations mostly to respect zoning restrictions and to benefit from lower land prices. However, they do not offset the semiotic meanings of their somewhat remote, ordinary locations with sumptuous facilities to attract customers and enhance the status of their products, as some shopping malls and casinos do (Gottdiener 1998; Sallaz 2012). Rather, they proudly extend these semiotic meanings into one of their key touchpoints with consumers: taprooms. Taprooms typically feature unpretentious, industrial vintage décor including cement floors, recycled wooden tables, unpainted walls, and ceilings with visible steel beams. The vintage industrial décor eschews aficionados' tastes from potential meanings of elitism, as it wraps their refined consumption with symbols of work and casualness rather than leisure and extravagance (Creighton 1998).

Moral Boundaries: Eschewing Trivialization

Aficionados' focus on knowledge indicates that their participation in the craft beer domain is serious leisure (Stebbins 2007). In the previous quote, Marc used *journey* to describe his pursuit of taste refinement. Like Marc, other aficionados construct their systematic beer drinking as a consumption career (Becker 1953):

Take sour beer. It's horrible! It goes against everything you read about our physiological disposition to like sweet and salty. People say that someone is sour-faced for a reason [laugher]. It says 'danger' to your body, you know [laughs]? But sour beers are the darling of many aficionados these days. And it really is an acquired taste. I didn't like it when I first tried, maybe two years ago. Now, I'm obsessed with sours. It's the current step in my beer journey. Every bar I go to, I look for them and ask about them. And I've chosen to take some brewery tours mainly because the brewery makes sours. (Richard, 40–49, IT manager)

Beer has historically been an outlet for working class's and young men's socially shaped dispositions toward abundant, facile consumption (Barr 1999; Bourdieu 1984; Holt 1998). In contrast to the stereotyped consumption mode of these two groups, aficionados' quest for taste refinement often involves making small sacrifices (e.g., tasting unpleasant beer) for a delayed reward they consider valuable: refined aesthetic knowledge. They decouple immediate bodily pleasures from enduring, sensory–intellectual achievements, thus enacting conventional middle-class morality (Holt 1998; Levy 1966/1999). Through this morality, they construct their systematic engagement with craft beer as educational, thereby distinguishing their frequent beer drinking from the trivialized consumption that typifies social groups from which they want to keep some symbolic distance.

This morally infused engagement with craft beer provides aficionados with the impetus to sometimes try to "elevate" (Adam, 20–29, software developer) other people's tastes. For instance, Jake (20–29, engineer) has co-founded a university-based craft beer club that includes underage students. One of his main motives in starting this club was educational:

We usually don't drink there. Not all of them are necessarily twenty-one and stuff like that, plus we do it on campus . . . [but] one of my major goals is to educate kids on what real beer is. . . . I like to talk about the different styles and descriptions, and then the people that are twenty-one can go and try those beers and think about it for themselves. That's what I really want, is for people to not just sit there and drink beer, but to actually think about it—think about what you're consuming. . . . Like I said, I'm a big advocate of quality over quantity, and just educating them that, "Sure, you're going to party and stuff, that's what kids do, but to actually understand and appreciate the beverage that you're consuming."

Although the scale of Jake's educational initiative occurs sparsely among aficionados, it offers an entry point to discussing the morality that aficionados assign to their taste refinement. As indicated above, aficionados fear the label *beer snob*; as such, they avoid proselytizing people about the superior taste of craft beer. However, this self-restraint coexists with a sense of mission to enlighten unreflexive beer drinkers. This sense is flagrant in how Jake employs the term *kids*, although he is just a few years older than they are. Aficionados not only drink moderately and reflectively, but they also seek to develop this consuming mode in others by teaching them to appreciate craft beer as cultivated, sensible consumers. Their sense of mission reflects a long-standing morality in the American middle class that regards alcoholic beverages as dangerous, even if pervasive (Gusfield 1987). Aficionados thus seek to align beer consumption with their class-inflected morality by detrivializing beer, casting it as something that "is good to think" rather than only good to drink (Lévi-Strauss 1962).

Discussion

Many middle-class markets such as coffee, bourbon, and olive oil have been recently refined in the United States (Holt and Cameron 2010; Risen 2014). Research suggests that men are particularly drawn to these middle-class areas of recently refined taste (Lehrer 2009; Lupton 1996). As a substantive contribution, this chapter studies one of these refined areas—craft beer—to analyze the symbolic boundaries that middle-class men draw to construct taste refinement as a legitimate route to masculinity. As a theoretical contribution, this chapter articulates a specific relationship among taste, gender, and morality, which I unpack below.

Aficionados' relationship with taste refinement involves *masculinization*. Aficionados juxtapose their developing sensory and linguistic sensibilities with conventionally masculine elements, including systematic pursuit of knowledge, brute physicality, and machinery. Further, by literally working to refine their tastes as homebrewers, they develop competence in a way that resonates with U.S. middle-class men's emphasis on work achievement. These middle-class men thus draw on their socially conditioned toolkits (Swidler 1986) to construct an exploratory, masculinized, labor-based path toward forms of taste that might otherwise connote femininity and elitism.

Aficionados' relationship with taste refinement also involves *intellectualization*. Their focus on knowledge further keeps at bay notions of elitism by allowing middle-class men to construct refined consumption as a way of becoming enlightened, self-defining consumers. They regard their refinement as a pragmatic project that allows them to see behind the advertisement-induced veil created by large corporate breweries to disguise the impoverished taste of mass-produced lagers (Maciel and Wallendorf 2016). Further, their focus on knowledge helps them eschew meanings of trivialization. They regard their knowledge as the painstaking achievement of a consumption career, a middle-class value that assuages the moral ambiguity of their frequent, hedonic engagement with alcohol consumption (Levy 1966/1999; Stebbins 2007).

These results both confirm and extend Lamont's (1992) theoretical scheme, which discusses three types of symbolic boundaries. Socioeconomic boundaries refer to subjective and interpersonal distinctions made on the basis of someone's wealth and professional achievements; cultural boundaries refer to these distinctions made on the basis of someone's manners, tastes, and education; and moral boundaries refer to these distinctions made on the basis of someone's honesty, work ethic, and personal integrity.

In line with Lamont's scheme, the analysis of middle-class men's pursuit of taste refinement ratifies the importance of moral boundaries in the United States. As these men acquire forms of taste that they perceive as potentially exclusionary, they perform a good deal of moral work to align this taste with the notions of democracy and aesthetic tolerance that constitute the American middle class (Lamont 1992; Peterson and Kern 1996).

As an extension of Lamont's scheme, this study reveals the analytical autonomy of *gender boundaries*. As middle-class men acquire forms of taste that might otherwise connote femininity, they use their socially conditioned toolkits to instead align this taste with class-inflected scripts of masculinity. This alignment does not serve to simply distinguish their social identities from people with different levels of wealth, as socioeconomic boundaries mainly do. Moreover, this alignment does not serve to simply distinguish their social identities from people endowed with different notions of personal integrity, as moral boundaries mainly do. Finally, this alignment does not serve merely to distinguish their social identities from people with different education levels and tastes, as cultural boundaries mainly do. Rather, aficionados' alignment of their pursuit of refined taste with conventional scripts of masculinity serves to distinguish their social identities from other gender positions that are more strongly associated with this pursuit in the larger society, such as middle-class women and gay men (Rinallo 2007).

Gender boundaries thus refer to the subjective and interpersonal distinctions individuals make on the basis of someone's gender identity in the social space. As my analysis indicates, these boundaries may be at odds with the discourses of social inclusiveness that characterize U.S. middle-class relationships with taste. On the one hand, heterosexual, middle-class, male aficionados verbally encourage and praise the growing presence of other gender identities in the consumption domain in which they are culturally invested. On the other, they pursue taste by enacting embodied, gender-inflected mannerisms and mental schemas that dissuade the effective participation of other gender positions in the practices of taste learning. In doing so, they discursively democratize an object of consumption, while they construct ways of learning as a potential mechanism of social exclusion in consumption domains that valorize the systematic development and expression of taste.

Conclusion

Taste, morality, and gender are intersecting axes of social life (Bourdieu 1984), but their trajectories are distinct. These distinct trajectories shape how individuals use taste, morality, and gender for the construction of symbolic boundaries (Beisel 1992).

Taste has historically been contested among the U.S. middle class because it contradicts the democratic and work ethic ideals that forged this social stratum; this contested trajectory shaped taste into a relatively *loose* resource for members of this social stratum to express and define group affiliations (Halle 1993; Lamont 1992; Peterson and Kern 1996). Conversely, middle-class Americans use morality as a relatively *strict* resource to determine group affiliations and other people's prestige; this resource is aligned with the Puritan legacy that also forged this social stratum (Lamont 1992).

In light of the trajectory of gender in the United States, how should we conceptualize this axis of social life as a resource for the construction of symbolic boundaries? The metaphor of "waves" has been used to characterize the dramatic back and forth between the women's movement and conservative backlashes that have shaped gender scripts in the United States (Faludi 1991). This sinuous trajectory suggests a different metaphor to conceptualize gender as a resource for symbolic boundaries. Rather than loose or strict, gender constitutes a *resilient* resource on which people iteratively work to express and define group affiliations in and through the marketplace.

This resilience does not appear primarily in discursive gender boundaries; the women's movement marked such boundary making as politically incorrect in middle-class ideology. Nonetheless, gender boundaries spring back in embodied ways of thinking and doing. Gender remains a primary axis of socialization in families and schools (Fausto-Sterling 2000; Martin 1998), patterning particular mental schemas and behaviors in ways that are often inarticulate.

Gender exclusion in middle-class consumption domains can thus take subtle tones, displacing the focus from *what* people visibly consume to *how* they learn to consume in ways that are valued in these domains. The divergence that this chapter reveals between discursive and behavioral practices in gender boundary making suggests the need for further study of this divergence in the making of socioeconomic, moral, and cultural boundaries in other realms of social life. What people say in boundary making may be at odds with what they do.

REFERENCES

Barr, Andrew. 1999. *Drink: A Social History of America*. New York: Carroll & Graf.

Becker, Howard S. 1953. "Becoming a Marihuana User." *American Journal of Sociology* 59 (3): 235–242.

Beisel, Nicola. 1992. "Constructing a Shifting Moral Boundary: Literature and Obscenity in Nineteenth-Century America." In *Cultivating Differences: Symbolic Boundaries and the Making of Inequality*, edited by Michèle Lamont and Marcel Fournier, 104–128. Chicago: University of Chicago Press.

Belk, Russell W., and Janeen A. Costa. 1998. "The Mountain Man Myth: A Contemporary Consuming Fantasy." *Journal of Consumer Research*, 25 (3): 218–140.

Benzecry, Claudio E. 2011. *The Opera Fanatic: Ethnography of an Obsession*. Chicago: University of Chicago Press.

Bourdieu, Pierre. 1984. *Distinction: A Social Critique of the Judgment of Taste*. Cambridge, MA: Harvard University Press.

———. 2001. *Masculine Domination*. Stanford, CA: Stanford University Press.

Bourdieu, Pierre, and Loïc J. D. Wacquant. 1992. *An Invitation to Reflexive Sociology*. Chicago: University of Chicago Press.

Bushman, Richard L. 1992. *The Refinement of America: Persons, Houses, Cities*. New York: Knopf.

Carroll, Glenn R., and Anand Swaminathan. 2000. "Why the Microbrewery Movement? Organizational Dynamics of Resource Partitioning in the US Brewing Industry." *American Journal of Sociology* 106 (3): 715–762.

Coontz, Stephanie. 2000. *The Way We Never Were: American Families and the Nostalgia Trap*. New York: Basic Books.

Coskuner-Balli, Gokcen, and Craig J. Thompson. 2013. "The Status Costs of Subordinate Cultural Capital: At-Home Fathers' Collective Pursuit of Cultural Legitimacy through Capitalizing Consumption Practices." *Journal of Consumer Research* 40 (1): 19–41.

Creighton, Millie. 1998. "The Seed of Creative Lifestyle Shopping." In *Servicescapes: The Concept of Place in Contemporary Markets*, edited by John F. Sherry Jr., 199–227. Chicago: American Marketing Association.

Epstein, Cynthia F. 1992. "Tinkerbells and Pinups: The Construction and Reconstruction of Gender Boundaries at Work." In *Cultivating Differences: Symbolic Boundaries and the*

Making of Inequality, edited by Michèle Lamont and Marcel Fournier, 232–256. Chicago: University of Chicago Press.

Faludi, Susan. 1991. *Backlash: The Undeclared War against American Women*. New York: Crown.

Fausto-Sterling, Anne. 2000. *Sexing the Body: Gender Politics and the Construction of Sexuality*. New York: Basic Books.

Gelber, Steven M. 1999. *Hobbies: Leisure and the Culture of Work in America*. New York: Columbia University Press.

Glaser, Barney, and Anselm Strauss. 1967. *The Discovery Grounded Theory: Strategies for Qualitative Inquiry*. New York: Aldine Transaction.

Gottdiener, M. 1998. "The Semiotics of Consumer Spaces: The Growing Importance of Themed Environments." In *Servicescapes: The Concept of Place in Contemporary Markets*, edited by John F. Sherry Jr., 81–108. Chicago: American Marketing Association.

Gusfield, Joseph. 1987. "Passage to Play: Rituals of Drinking Time in American Society." In *Constructive Drinking*, edited by Mary Douglas, 73–90. New York: Cambridge University Press.

Halle, David. 1993. *Inside Culture: Art and Class in the American Home*. Chicago: University of Chicago Press.

Holt, Douglas B. 1998. "Does Cultural Capital Structure American Consumption?" *Journal of Consumer Research* 25 (1): 1–25.

Holt, Douglas B., and Douglas Cameron. 2010. *Cultural Strategy: Using Innovative Ideologies to Build Breakthrough Brands*. New York: Oxford University Press.

Holt, Douglas B., and Craig J. Thompson. 2004. "Man-of-Action Heroes: The Pursuit of Heroic Masculinity in Everyday Consumption." *Journal of Consumer Research* 31 (2): 425–440.

Kimmel, Michael. 1995. *Manhood in America: A Cultural History*. New York: Free Press.

Lamont, Michèle. 1992. *Money, Morals and Manners: The Culture of the French and American Upper-Middle Class*. Chicago: University of Chicago Press.

Lamont, Michèle, and Marcel Fournier. 1992. *Cultivating Differences: Symbolic Boundaries and the Making of Inequality*. Chicago: University of Chicago Press.

Lehrer, Adrienne. 2009. *Wine and Conversation* (2nd ed.).Oxford: Oxford University Press.

Lévi-Strauss, Claude. 1962. *La Pensée Sauvage*. Paris: Plon.

Levy, Sidney J. 1966/1999. "Social Class and Consumer Behavior." In *Brands, Consumers, Symbols, and Research*, edited by Dennis Rook, 297–308. Thousand Oaks, CA: Sage.

———. 1980/1999. "Arts Consumers and Aesthetic Attributes." In *Brands, Consumers, Symbols, and Research*, edited by Dennis Rook, 343–358. Thousand Oaks, CA: Sage.

———. 1986/1999. "Meanings in Advertising Stimuli." In *Brands, Consumers, Symbols, and Research*, edited by Dennis Rook, 251–260. Thousand Oaks, CA: Sage.

Lincoln, Y. S., and E. G. Guba. 1985. "Establishing Trustworthiness." In *Naturalistic Inquiry*, edited by Y. S. Lincoln and E. G. Guba, 289–331. London: Sage.

Lupton, Deborah. 1996. *Food, the Body and the Self.* London: Sage.

Maciel, Andre F., and Melanie Wallendorf. 2016. "Taste Engineering: An Extended Consumer Model of Cultural Competence Constitution." *Journal of Consumer Research*, September 11, 2016, http://jcr.oxfordjournals.org/content/early/2016/10/23/jcr.ucw054.

Martin, Karin A. 1998. "Becoming a Gendered Body: Practices of Preschools." *American Sociological Review* 63 (4): 494–511.

McCracken, Grant. 1988. *The Long Interview.* Newbury Park, CA: Sage.

Moisio, Risto, Eric J. Arnould, and James W. Gentry. 2013. "Productive Consumption in the Class-Mediated Construction of Domestic Masculinity: Do-it-Yourself (DIY) Home Improvement in Men's Identity Work." *Journal of Consumer Research* 40 (2): 298–316.

Peterson, Richard A., and Roger M. Kern. 1996. "Changing Highbrow Taste: From Snob to Omnivore." *American Sociological Review* 61 (5): 900–907.

Rinallo, Diego. 2007. "Metro/Fashion/Tribes of Men: Negotiating the Boundaries of Men's Legitimate Consumption." In *Consumer Tribes*, edited by Bernard Cova, Robert V. Kozinets, and Avi Shankar, 76–92. Oxford: Butterworth-Heinneman.

Risen, Clay. 2014. "The Billion-Dollar Bourbon Boom." *Fortune* 169 (3): 58–65.

Sallaz, Jeffrey J. 2012. "Politics of Organizational Adornment: Lessons from Las Vegas and Beyond." *American Sociological Review* 77 (1): 99–119.

Schouten, John W., and James H. McAlexander. 1995. "Subcultures of Consumption: An Ethnography of the New Bikers." *Journal of Consumer Research* 22 (1): 43–61.

Sennett, Richard. 2008. *The Craftsman.* New Haven, CT: Yale University Press.

Snow, David A., and Leon Anderson. 1987. "Identity Work among the Homeless: The Verbal Construction and Avowal of Personal Identities." *American Journal of Sociology* 92 (6): 1336–1371.

Stebbins, Robert A. 2007. *Serious Leisure: A Perspective for our Time.* New Brunswick, NJ: Transaction.

Strong, Jeremy. 2011. *Educated Tastes: Food, Drink, and Connoisseur Culture.* Lincoln: University of Nebraska Press.

Swidler, Ann. 1986. "Culture in Action: Symbols and Strategies." *American Sociological Review* 51 (2): 273–286.

———. 2003. *Talk of Love: When Culture Matters.* Chicago: University of Chicago Press.

Warde, Alan. 2011. "Cultural Hostility Re-Considered." *Cultural Sociology* 5 (3): 341–366.

CHAPTER 11

———————

You Are What You Drink

*Gender Stereotypes and Craft Beer Preferences within
the Craft Beer Scene of New York City*

HELANA DARWIN

Introduction

"To lemon or not to lemon. . . . I will say that if you're a male beer geek seeking
the respect of your equally geeky friends, you had best leave it off," warns Randy
Mosher (2009) in *Tasting Beer*, a guide to craft beer that the beer sommelier
program Cicerone (n.d.) endorses as authoritative. Mosher's (2009) casual reference to the misogyny undergirding craft beer culture deemphasizes the struggles that women have reported in their attempts to assert cultural legitimacy
within the inarguably masculinized scene. The 2014 Great American Beer Festival's official data suggest that women consume 32% of craft beer within the
United States; yet, women continue to report marginalization on every level,
from consumers to brewers (Brewers Association 2014). The purpose of this investigation is to determine whether beers that are considered feminine are also
considered less legitimate.

Mosher is not the only craft beer writer who observes gender anxiety about
ordering fruity "feminine beers"; similar references proliferate throughout the
craft beer blogosphere. In this chapter, I test the external validity of these anecdotal references to a conflation between fruit, femininity, and illegitimacy, by
asking 93 craft beer bar patrons in four locations across New York City to provide me with operational definitions of "masculine beer" and "feminine beer,"
along with their assumptions about gender-transgressive drinkers. Informed by
cultural sociology, symbolic interactionism, and the craft beer communities in

cyberspace, I hypothesize that cultural capital increases in conjunction with a preference for "masculine beers."

Originally, beer was brewed domestically by women, as a safe and nourishing alternative to water. However, once beer production became a lucrative industry, the location of its production shifted from the home to the factory; contingently, control over the product shifted from women to men. Following the Prohibition era, the product itself became masculinized, contrasted against the feminized cocktail. This masculinization of beer further intensified during World War II, when soldiers developed a taste for cheap lager, returning home with a thirst that inspired the mass production of the adjunct lager that comprises mainstream beer culture today. After Jimmy Carter passed the Home Brewing Act in 1978, the homebrewing culture and commercial craft breweries that emerged were dominated by men. When craft beer connoisseurship became more established, women exponentially entered the previously homosocial cultural scene (Mosher 2009). As is typical when women enter formerly homosocial spaces, a marginalizing stereotype emerged about women's capabilities and preferences, a stereotype that reinforces male dominance: women do not like the "taste of beer," and thus gravitate toward fruity beers. As this chapter explores in closer detail, this stereotype reinforces women's cultural marginalization as both brewers and consumers.

It is important to clarify that there is no "taste of beer." Between ales and lagers, the taste spectrum for beer encompasses sweet, sour, salty, bitter, and umami; yet, when people refer to the "beer taste," they generally refer to beers that taste bitter. Moreover, it is these bitter beers to which women and new drinkers are supposed to be averse. This conflation leads to the legitimization of bitter beers as "real beer" and the contingent myth that women prefer beer that is not bitter, that does not "taste like beer." This myth inspires such products as "Chick Beer," which appeals to female consumers through references to the product's appearance instead of its taste:

> Chick Beer finally gives women a beer choice that suits their tastes and their style. The bottle is designed to reflect the beautiful shape of a woman in a little black dress. The six-pack looks like you are carrying your beer in a hip stylish purse. Chick's unique reflective bottle blings you up! It's fun, fabulous, and female! (Anonymous 2011)

In response, beer writer Lorna Juett (2012) protests that, "Dumbing women drinkers down to the lowest common beer denominator does not legitimize our presence in the marketplace." Chick Beer, and other comparable products that target female beer drinkers, delegitimizes female connoisseurs through rhetoric that casts female beer drinkers as uninformed and uninterested and even incapable of enjoying the range of beer flavors.

Beers "for women" that do not "taste like beer" are generally sweet and fruity. This reflects the conflation between fruit, femininity, and illegitimacy that simultaneously delegitimizes female beer geeks while rendering male connoisseurs of fruit beer vulnerable to homophobic and misogynistic taunting. For example, beer blogger Troy Patterson warns his readers:

> Treating this matter with the seriousness it deserves, I'd like briefly to address any social insecure bros who happen to be grazing these pixels: You need to know that, if you publicly drink a fruit beer—if you are drawn to the not-bad taffyish tug of Wells Banana Bread Beer or to the raspberry creamy-crispness and after-dinner dulcitude of Founders Rübæus— there's a 20 to 30 percent chance that your fellow bros will tease you about it, possibly by way of strained ovary jokes. (2014)

Tired of this relentless gender-policing, male connoisseurs of fruit beer advocate for fruit beer's rise in cultural legitimacy, conditioned upon its disassociation from femininity. For example, beer blogger Colin Joliat rebuffs:

> Fruit ≠ girly. In what world is fruit for chicks? The saying doesn't go, "apple a day keeps the yeast infection away." Our ancestors were picking berries long before Bear Grylls stuck his head in a dead zebra. Plus, those 100+IBU Double IPAs you love so much? That's right, not only do they taste like grapefruit (holy shit, a fruit!), they're flavored with hops—a flower. Who's girly now? (2014)

Others advocate for fruit beer's legitimization by invoking the subcultural value of experimentation and food pairing:

> Fruit-flavored beers have been much maligned by men the world over for being, well, of questionable masculinity. But these weeks between the brutal summer and much-awaited fall are the perfect time to try beers that are as flavorful as they are refreshing. Below are four carefully researched fruit beers that have real body, color, and flavor and will prime your palate for autumn's heavier fare. You may not be toting them to Monday

Night Football, but they're worth your time at any cookout or dinner party as this summer winds down. (Guest writer 2010)

This author reports an awareness of fruit beer's feminized stigma by warning fellow men to be smart about the context within which they drink fruit beer; evidently, when participating in masculinity rituals such as football, fruit beer consumption is risky.

In opposition to the sweet and feminized fruit beer, the bitter taste profile of India pale ale is a masculinized "real" beer. Dan Conley (2013) from Community Beer Works testifies to the cultural superiority of this initially off-putting beer type within his blog post "The IPA Hegemony:"

Innately, we like the taste of sweet things as children, but perhaps do not take to sour or bitter flavors right away. But as we grow up and try new things, our brain figures out that not all sour and bitter flavors are bad, such is the case with IPAs.

Problematically, Conley (2013) ignores the socializing forces that steer women away from hoppy beers, further infantilizing those who prefer sweet beers. Conley also suggests that those who do not cultivate a taste for IPAs are illegitimate as craft "beer geeks" when he declares that, "professing your love of them [IPAs] can show you're really 'one of us.'" He follows this with the qualifier, "This is more subconscious than overt, and I may have pulled it out of thin air, because nobody has ever asked me for the secret code word before letting me into a tasting." Almost as an afterthought, Conley admits that there are other routes toward cultural legitimacy besides becoming a "hop-head," but this admission is half-hearted.

According to Conley's (2013) logic, one must be prepared to take taste risks in order to cultivate a status of cultural legitimacy. Unfortunately, risk-taking is culturally associated with masculinity more so than femininity and as a result, men are more likely to take such risks and thereby accrue cultural capital (West and Zimmerman 1987). For instance, a multinational study into gendered wine consumption found that men are more likely than women to purchase wine in the highest price range (categorized as above $25) (Atkin and Sutanonpaiboon 2007). Yet another study noted that men were significantly more likely than women to favor foods that pose a health risk, such as items high in fat and calories (Allen-O'Donnell et al. 2010). In contrast, female "foodies" report that when they indulge in high-fat foods they are stigmatized as "piggish" (Cairns et al. 2010). Finally, another study found that women were four times less likely to consider eating a hot pepper than were men, "even if they were starving" (Alley and Burroughs 1991). Unlike Conley (2013), these researchers are all careful to avoid attributing these gender differences to biological disposition, citing gender socialization as the more likely explanation for taste divergence.

Thus discouraged from taking masculinized risks that lead to palate cultivation, women become constructed as uninformed drinkers. Pierre Bourdieu famously expounded upon the meanings behind such a paradox:

> The paradox of the imposition of legitimacy is that it makes it impossible ever to determine whether the dominant feature appears as distinguished or noble because it is dominant—i.e., because it has the privilege of defining, by its very existence, what is noble or distinguished as being exactly what itself is, a privilege which is expressed precisely in its self-assurance—or whether it is only because it is dominant that it appears as endowed with these qualities and uniquely entitled to define them. (1984, 92).

In other words, "illegitimate beer" is feminine precisely because those with the power to designate legitimacy are men. Furthermore, the taste profile that is deemed legitimate is that which the palate must conquer in a masculinized quest of man versus nature. As Bourdieu further explained, "Rejecting the 'human' clearly means rejecting what is generic, i.e., common, 'easy' and immediately accessible, starting with everything that reduces the aesthetic animal to pure and simple animality, to palpable pleasure of sensual desire (1984, 32)." Flavors that are easy to appreciate, such as fruit, become constructed as culturally inferior while those that require cultivation and practice, such as IPA, become constructed as superior. The stereotype that women prefer the beers that are considered easier and less legitimate leads to a self-fulfilling prophecy that reinforces men's status as culturally superior connoisseurs.

Methods

I interviewed 93 patrons of the New York City craft beer scene in order to test the extent to which beer preference is gendered and whether the masculine is afforded greater cultural legitimacy than the feminine. The total sample included 63 self-identified men, ranging in age from 21 to 58 (mean, 33.64) and 30 self-identified women, ranging in age from 22 to 50 (mean, 30.06). I employed nonrandom sampling techniques in order to purposively sample the minority demographics of women and older patrons while convenience sampling the dominant demographic of young men, often based upon their physical proximity to the female survey respondents.

The bars that I selected market themselves explicitly as craft beer venues, attracting patrons who desire craft beer highly enough to seek it out and pay the premium price associated with the luxury product (average price for a 12-oz pour is typically $8 to $10, as opposed to a $6 draft of Industrial American Lager or Guinness). In order to eliminate the possible demographic confounding of a bar's location, I selected a diverse range of craft beer bars, including one in the Bronx, another in Washington Heights, one in Greenwich Village, and another on the North Fork of Long Island. My intention was to counterbalance any effect of the bar's location on the clientele's political beliefs about gender. Despite this counterbalancing, it must be noted that New York City is famously liberal, a political leaning that tends to correlate with more egalitarian gender ideology; as such, findings about the gendered stereotypes within the New York City craft beer scene do not represent the attitudes in other regions of the United States. For example, fruit beer in New York City may be less gender-stigmatized than elsewhere.

Each interview lasted from 5 to 15 minutes. I approached respondents as they waited to place beer orders at the bar and introduced myself before asking whether they would consent to answer four quick questions about gender and beer preference. It is impossible to know whether respondents had consumed alcohol prior to answering the questions, but I did not survey those with slurred speech or impaired motor functions. Upon receiving verbal consent, I asked, "When I say 'feminine beer,' what descriptors come to mind?" As the respondent listed adjectives and brand names, I recorded notes until they were finished. Next I asked, "When I say 'masculine beer,' what descriptors come to mind?" Once again, I recorded the respondents' associations until they stopped. I then asked, "What assumptions, if any, would you have of a man who ordered what you just defined as a 'feminine beer,'" followed by "What assumptions, if any, would you have of a woman who ordered what you just defined as a 'masculine beer'?"

Because few patrons were alone, this survey process was often administered to a couple or a group of three or four people, which possibly compromised the internal validity of the responses. However, this group effect proved to be enlightening, since I was able to record the interplay between associates as they adjusted their opinions to account for the possible judgments of their companion(s). Group feedback during the debriefing also helpfully highlighted the difference between the gendered stereotypes that patrons espoused and their beliefs in those stereotypes.

In order to process the data, I collated the key adjectives patrons associated with feminine beer and masculine beer, along with keywords associated with their assumptions about transgressive drinkers. I analyzed these findings with regard to impression management, cultural capital, and gender equality within the craft beer scene.

Results

Defining Masculine Beer *and* Feminine Beer

Male respondents and female respondents generally report the same definitions for *feminine beer* and *masculine beer*, with concordance rates of 83.75% and 88.73%, respectively. Although men and women both report that *feminine beer* is a bit of a misnomer, since women stereotypically do not like beer at all, the descriptions that respondents gave unanimously defines *feminine beer* as light, fruity, and sweet, including flavored lagers and hefeweizens/wheat beers/white ales; masculine beers are defined as hoppy/bitter/strong/high-alcohol IPAs, and dark/heavy/strong/high-alcohol stouts.

Although men and women alike typically agreed on definitions of *feminine beer* and *masculine beer*, minor discrepancies occasionally arose. Certain terms and types of beer seem to be more contentious than others, such as malt and barley wine, which are claimed by both men and women without corroboration. Similarly, "pumpkin" appears as a descriptor of feminine beer according to both men and women, yet here it appears again under masculine beer, reported by men without female corroboration.

Curiously, even Belgian ale appears in the terrain of both genders, despite references to it as a typical gateway beer. For example, Maggie Hoffman's (2010) article subtitled, "The 3 Best Crossover Beers for Wine-Loving Women," lists only Belgian beers, prefaced by the introduction "Does your lady drink more chardonnay than IPA? Try converting her—gently—with these crossover brews: They're smooth Belgian-style ales with hardly any bitterness but a ton of luscious flavor." In light of the high cultural capital afforded to the long-standing tradition of Belgian ale, it may be significant that men do not acknowledge the category as a feminine beer, but rather think of it as masculine when they think of it at all.

Notably, women use technical terminology much more than do men to describe feminine beer, connoting their cultural legitimacy as educated connoisseurs. When prompted to describe feminine beer, women report such beers as barley wine, frambois, saison, sour, and triple. They also use technical terminology associated with tasting culture, such as *aromatic, crisp*, and *malty*. These results reflect the respondents' intellectual involvement with tasting culture and informed validation of such feminine beer. In contrast, male respondents typically report simple descriptors such as *sugary, perfumed*, and *frothy*, in addition to trivializing and condemnatory terms such as *crappy* and *bad*. It is unclear whether this terminology reflects men's best efforts at describing feminine beers or whether it reflects their opinions of those who would hypothetically prefer such beers; if it is the latter, then the women in men's imaginations are not nearly as educated as the female craft beer bar patrons in this study. Perhaps men are not as familiar with beers that women stereotypically drink and thus remain uninitiated with regard to the knowledge that female respondents possess about the technical terminology and taste profiles. It is further possible that female and male respondents are not describing the same beers at all, as some men think that women drink beer that women do not mention, including lambic, pilsner, cherry-wheat, coffee-flavored, and nonalcoholic.

While describing the beer type that is stereotypically assigned to their own gender, men and women tend to use adjectives descriptive of hegemonic (idealized) masculinity and femininity (Connell 1987). For instance, while describing masculine beer, men describe the drink as *rich, powerful*, and *bold*. Similarly, women describe feminine beer as *pretty, aromatic, expensive*, and *flowery*. Both genders agree that feminine beer is *light, sweet*, and *refreshing*, all of which describe idealized femininity. Similarly, both genders illustrate masculinity as *stout, heavy, strong, bitter, full*, and *rough*. This distinctly gendered lexicon suggests that the public consumption of beer is a gendered performance of identity construction that can either affirm or dispel mainstream gender stereotypes.

Lager proves to be a unique case, assigned to both genders, depending on whether the lager is flavored; flavored lagers are associated with femininity, presumably because of the stereotype that women require a sweet flavor to mask the beer taste. Unflavored lager, on the other hand, is associated with traditional hegemonic masculinity. The deep entrenchment of this cultural trope was recently made explicit by the Super Bowl Budweiser advertisement, wherein Budweiser drinkers were labeled "hard," as compared with men who drink "peach pumpkin ale." This ad constructed male craft beer drinkers as "soft" by portraying a group of fleshy, pale, bespectacled men sniffing their beer, specified as "pumpkin peach ale." Without further elaboration, these representatives of craft beer culture are implied to be "not real men," because of their concern with the quality of their beverage and their appreciation for sweet-flavored beer, which respondents in my study identify as stereotypically feminine. This rhetoric reflects Michael Kimmel's (1995) observation that men's gendered performances are much more influenced by the fear of judgment by other men than by the fear of judgment by women. Indeed, the advertisement's narrating voice is unmistakably masculine; this ad is about men sizing one another up based on alcohol preferences.

Perhaps reflecting this fear of not measuring up to ideals of hegemonic masculinity, men in this study report more appearance-based concerns than women when imagining the difference between masculine and feminine beer. For example, men mention citrus garnish (á la Randy Mosher 2009), tulip glassware, and packaging. This trend reflects Bourdieu's observation that working-class masculinity favors function over form, encouraging men to opt for quantity over quality:

> And the principal philosophy of the male body as a sort of power, big and strong, with enormous, imperative, brutal needs, which is asserted in every male posture, especially when eating, is also the principle of the division of foods between the sexes, a division which both sexes recognize in their practices and language. It behooves a man to drink and eat more, and to eat and drink stronger things. (1984, 192)

Bourdieu's reasoning would corroborate my finding that "frills" such as citrus garnish potentially compromises the impression management of a man who wishes to assert a hegemonic masculine identity. Whether or not the connoisseurs hail from working-class backgrounds, these findings suggest that a working-class aesthetic is a component of the public performance of masculinity within the craft beer culture (Kimmel 1995).

Cultural Capital Fluctuations for Gender-Transgressive Drinkers

In summary, female transgressive drinkers are rewarded through higher cultural capital, while male transgressive drinkers' cultural capital either remains the same or decreases slightly; this confirms my hypothesis that beers deemed masculine are associated with higher cultural capital than beers deemed feminine. I expected men's cultural capital to markedly decline in conjunction with gender-transgressive drinking; however, nearly two-thirds of my respondents replied with "no comment" when I asked for their assumptions about men who preferred what they just defined as feminine beer. In contrast, these same respondents freely reported positive evaluations of female transgressive drinkers.

In general, respondents' assumptions about transgressive drinkers fall into three dominant categories: reason for transgression, implications of the drinker's gender/sexuality, and implications about the drinker's personality. Female respondents typically assume that men's beer orders are influenced by their expertise, regardless of which type of beer they order. Men do not similarly assume that fellow men select feminine beer because of expert knowledge; rather, men are more inclined to excuse the transgression as a matter of taste or novice status within the craft beer scene. Both men and women attribute male transgressive drinking to taste, season, and calories, and men also consider factors such as the male transgressive drinker's mood, situational circumstances, and reluctance to becoming inebriated.

Only one woman uses the word *lesbian* in a possibly derogatory manner; the other instance of its usage is by a self-identified lesbian who asked her friend, "Is she a lesbian? Can you give me her number?" The female respondents do not reference gender or sexuality aside from these two references to lesbianism, suggesting that the hypothetical woman's gender-transgressive drinking is generally irrelevant to her gendered and sexual status.

In contrast, approximately one-third of the male respondents refer to the female transgressive drinker's sexuality. Examples of positively encoded sexualized rhetoric include: "Does she have plans on Friday night," "She likes to be on top," "She's very hot," and tellingly, "Kinda hot. It's always hot when a woman does something a man does like when she drinks whiskey or a Manhattan." Ambiguous sexualized rhetoric includes "Marry her unless she has testicles, then no," and "That's cool, but she can't be a dude, growing a beard and brewing at home. I like feminine girls. If you want to try it though, that's cool." Despite the presence of this sexualizing rhetoric, male respondents typically cite the hypothetical woman's personality and knowledge as predominant reasons for awarding her higher cultural capital.

Despite Goffman's observation that teammates police one another's gendered fronts, gender-policing within each gender is much less conspicuous than heteronormative aspersions concerning the opposite sex (1959, 44–66). Only two of thirty female respondents had anything negative to say about a woman who preferred masculine beer. Moreover, the positive evaluations respondents report do not suggest jealousy or competition, just praise. Similarly, male respondents are extremely reluctant to say anything negative about a man who prefers feminine beer, excusing the behavior with a wide range of hypothetical considerations.

Heterosexism and homophobia are prevalent throughout the responses, but generally such judgments are made about the opposite gender and not the same gender. For instance, men are more likely than women to cast female transgressive drinkers as gender-inverse, saying: "Where's her beard, did she shave this morning," "You don't want to wrestle with her, she might mess you up," and

"She'd probably be a little intimidating." Similarly, women are more likely than men to cast a male transgressive drinker as gender-inverse. When asked about their assumptions, if any, of a man who preferred a feminine beer, 23.33% referred to him as gay, fag, pussy, or bitch, and two admitted that they would make fun of him if he was a friend or a relative. In contrast to women, only 6.35% of men referred to the hypothetical transgressive male drinker as gay, bitch, or homosexual, and only 3.17% (compared to 6.66%) supposed that they would make fun of him if he was a friend. Female respondents were harsher than their male counterparts when it came to reflecting on the personality of a male transgressive drinker, though neither gender voiced such condemnatory opinions as often as they demurred entirely by saying "No comment."

Both genders consider a female transgressive drinker to be "cool" and "awesome," but they elaborate upon this evaluation differently. Women explain the transgressive drinker's positive evaluation in terms of words indicative of her power, expressing an interest in being friends with her. Women primarily think more highly of other women who prefer masculine beer (56.66%), followed closely by no/ambiguous opinion (43.33%). Men also predominantly think more highly of the hypothetical female transgressive drinker (60.32%) followed by no/ambiguous opinion (30.16%), and six report an explicitly lower opinion (9.52%). Women's positive evaluations tend to focus on the woman's personality, such as: "She's a badass bitch who knows what she's doing," "She's a stud, she rocks, probably drives a pickup truck, independent," and "She's an experienced beer drinker."

Conclusion

The results from my investigation confirm the existence of gendered stereotypes that denigrate women's palates and ability to appreciate "complex" beers, while simultaneously feminizing men who prefer simple or fruity beers. Evidently, there exists a gendered hierarchy within craft beer culture that assigns masculinity to the beer types that are regarded as more culturally legitimate and assigns femininity to the beers that are widely regarded as inferior. The conflation between hierarchies, patriarchy, and beer typology is difficult, if not impossible, to disentangle. However, it is clear that the semantic conflation between femininity and cultural illegitimacy is problematic for women who are joining the ranks of craft beer enthusiasts in progressive numbers only to find themselves defending their palates against gendered stereotypes or alternatively find themselves eroticized as accessories to the men's scene.

It is important to recognize that the most frequent assumption about a transgressive drinker was "No comment." As one respondent specifies, "No comment.

The craft beer scene is open-minded." Male respondents were generally reluctant to say anything condemnatory about men who prefer feminine beer, but they were equally withholding of explicit support. Given the recent rise in fruit beer's popularity, I suspect that I observed a transitional moment within Bourdieu's (1984) paradox, as a critical mass of men became advocates of fruit beer.

I was surprised by the lack of homophobic responses in my findings, but several methodological limitations and confounders might have influenced my results. For one, my sex and gender might have made men reluctant to report homophobic and misogynistic assumptions about male transgressive drinkers. It is also possible that New York City craft beer patrons are more politically correct than patrons in other U.S. regions. They might even be less homophobic and misogynistic and thus less complicit within gender policing. Finally, the focus-group style of these interviews might have influenced positive reporting bias. Future investigations into patrons' cognitive associations should eliminate the confounding variable of audience feedback, to obtain a clearer impression of the extent to which these stereotypes exist in patrons' minds when alone versus while interacting with others.

This investigation confirms an ideological current within craft beer culture that conflates fruit, femininity, and illegitimacy. The craft beer scene constructs itself as an alternative to the mainstream beer scene, which is notoriously rife with gender inequality; yet, it appears that gender inequality is reproduced within the craft beer scene, though less overtly. For instance, in 2013 the beverage director at Howells and Hood began a Women's Forum by saying "Ladies, I know beer can be confusing. . . ." This statement created an uproar across Twitter as a prime example of beer culture's implicit misogyny. Metropolitan Brewing's Tracy Hurst responded:

> Dear Media: Please do stop trying to identify what a person will drink based on their genitals. Unless a drinking vessel requires the *actual use* of a woman's delicate flower or a man's joystick, please just stop. Just. Stop.—Signed, the broad who owns a brewery and drinks whatever the hell she wants. (Karl 2013)

This assumption that women do not and cannot appreciate beer the same way that men can reinforces male dominance and women's marginalization and subordination.

In an attempt to embolden female beer geeks to take risks with their palate cultivation and thereby establish cultural legitimacy, craft breweries across the country have begun to offer women-only beer-tasting opportunities. Simultaneously, male advocates of fruit beer have encouraged men to experiment with these. As more men publicly consume fruit beers and more women publicly embrace stouts and IPAs, the binary beer typology will progressively be eliminated, deviants will become less conspicuous, and beer orders will come to reflect the drinker's true taste preference; however, in the meantime, drinkers should consider beer a political medium for challenging gender stereotypes, one drink at a time.

REFERENCES

Allen-O'Donnell, Molly, et al. 2011. "Impact of Group Settings and Gender on Meals Purchased by College Students." *Journal of Applied Social Psychology* 41 (9): 2268–2283.

Alley, Thomas R., and W. Jeffrey Burroughs. 1991. "Do Men Have Stronger Preferences for Hot, Unusual, and Unfamiliar Foods?" *Journal of General Psychology* 118 (3): 201–214.

Anonymous. 2011. "Chick Beer, Yet Another Beer Targeted at Women." *Huffington Post*, September 7, http://www.huffingtonpost.com/2011/09/07/chick-beer_n_952249.html.

Atkin, Thomas, and Janejira Sutanonpaiboon. 2007, August. "A Multinational Study of Gender Wine Preferences." Proceedings of the International Decision Sciences Conference. https://www.researchgate.net/profile/Thomas_Atkin/publication/228755508_A _Multinational_Study_of_Gender_Wine_Preferences/links/00b7d5245cd1b5e2d7000000 .pdf.

Bourdieu, Pierre. 1984. *Distinction: A Social Critique of the Judgment of Taste*. Cambridge, MA: Harvard University Press.

Brewers Association. 2014, December 9. "The Year in Beer: 2014 Craft Beer in Review from the Brewers Association." https://www.brewersassociation.org/press-releases/year -beer-2014-craft-beer-review-brewers-association/.

Cairns, Kate, Josée Johnston, and Shyon Baumann. 2010. "Caring about Food: Doing Gender in the Foodie Kitchen." *Gender & Society* 24 (5): 591–615.

Cicerone. n.d. Cicerone Certification Program. Accessed October 13, 2016, http:// cicerone.org.

Conley, Dan. June 7, 2013. "The IPA Hegemony." *Community Beerworks*. http://www .communitybeerworks.com/2013/07/the-ipa-hegemony.

Connell, R. W. 1987. *Gender and Power*. Palo Alto, CA: Stanford University Press.

Goffman, Erving. 1959. *The Presentation of Self in Everyday Life*. New York: Doubleday.

Guest writer. 2010, September 14. "Four Fruit-Flavored Beers that Won't Cost You Your Man-Card: More Fruit. Less Fruit."' *Gearpatrol*. http://gearpatrol.com/2010/09/14/four -fruit-flavored-beers-that-wont-cost-you-your-man-card.

Hoffman, Maggie. 2010, July 22. "Eat Like a Man: The 3 Best Crossover Beers for Wine-Loving Women." *Esquire*. http://www.esquire.com/blogs/food-for-men/beer-for-women -072210.

Joliat, Colin. 2014, May 28. "In Defense of Fruit Beers: 5 Reasons You Should Drink Them." *Brobible*. http://www.brobible.com/lifestyle/alcohol/article/defense-fruit-beers-5-reasons -drink.

Juett, Lorna. 2012, October 3. '"Chick Beer': A Lady Beer Nerd's Rant." *Chicagoist*. http:// chicagoist.com/2012/10/03/the_chicago_beer_festival_and_chick.php.

Karl. 2013, July 3. "A Few Thoughts about Beer, Gender, and What Women 'Should' Drink." Beer News, http://www.guysdrinkingbeer.com/a-few-thoughts-about-beer-and -gender.

Kimmel, Michael. 1995. *Manhood in America: A Cultural History*. New York: Free Press.

Mosher, Randy. 2009. *Tasting Beer: An Insider's Guide to the World's Greatest Drink*. North Adams, MA: Storey.

Patterson, Troy. 2014, July 29. "Is Fruity Beer Girly? Examining the Taste Profile and Gender Politics of Cherry Lambic, Watermelon Wheat Beer, and Blueberry Ale." *Slate*. http:// www.slate.com/articles/life/better_summer/2014/07/fruit_beers_girly_lambic _watermelon_wheat_and_blueberry_ale_reviewed_and.html.

West, Candace, and Don H. Zimmerman. 1987. "Doing Gender." *Gender & Society* 1 (2): 125–151.

CHAPTER 12

Brewing Boundaries of White Middle-Class Maleness

Reflections from within the Craft Beer Industry

ERIK T. WITHERS

Introduction

Summer 2004

I was standing in front of the beer cooler after my shift at the specialty foods market, trying to decide which beer to take home with me for the evening. Just as I started to hone in on my choice, I heard a voice from behind me. "Hey my friend, can I help you with something?" said a man from behind the cheese counter. The man (who appeared to be Caucasian) wore a chef's coat, a beret-style hat, and sported a well-groomed beard. I recognized him as the manager of the specialty foods section of the market. "No," I replied "I'm just checking out what you all have here." "Sure thing," he replied, "just let me know if you have any questions." Just as the man started to turn away and return to his work, a question came to my mind. "Hey, you know I do have a question," I said, "Where are all the normal beers like Budweiser, Miller, and Coors?"

After I asked the question, he looked up and grinned at me, as if to say, "Are you really asking me that?" He put down whatever he was working on and walked around the cheese preparation counter to face me. He looked straight at me, still grinning, crossed his arms and replied, "My friend, the kind of people who buy Budweiser are not the kind of people we want to shop here."

This vignette is an account of an interaction that I had while working as an associate in a large-scale specialty foods store. It was one of the first times I had experienced the exclusive nature of specialty foods, and more specifically, the craft beer industry. To many craft beer drinkers, the product offers a sense of style, identity, community, and, to some, a way of life (Acitelli 2013). Craft beer is a cultural form used to establish certain types of people. In this instance, my co-worker was implying that people who drink "macrobeers" (Miller, Coors, and Budweiser), which are considered to be cheap and less sophisticated beers, were undesirable in the culture and industry. My co-worker's judgment was being passed on both the beers themselves and the kind of people who are assumed to consume them.

From my more than 10 years of observations of the craft beer industry, I have found that these types of judgments are common. "Good People Drink Good Beer" (Maryland-based craft brewer Flying Dog Brewery's slogan) and "Bad People Drink Bad Beer" is a common mantra that is ground into the fibers of the craft beer culture, and the sentiment surfaces in many forms. If one takes into account the demographics of craft beer consumers—around 80% are white non-Hispanic and most are middle-class males with a higher-education degree and above average annual family income (Murray and O'Neill 2012)—what can be quickly concluded is that those "good people" who drink the "good beer" are white, middle-class men. In short, I argue that despite some minority involvement, the craft beer culture is informed and defined by whiteness. Whiteness can be understood as "the defining principle of social organization by which white values, ideas, aesthetics, preferences, and privileges are made to appear as the normalized, taken-for-granted basis of interacting and engaging social reality" (Hancock 2013). This normalized basis for social interaction also encompasses gender and class relations.

In this chapter, I explore some of the elements that uphold this culture's white middle-class masculine dominance. Scholarship that investigates the link between consumer practices and racial relations is lacking (Reskin 2012). This piece will serve as an addition to this much-needed line of research. It is believed that there are themes in any given cultural arena (e.g., food, fashion, and music); this belief upholds racialized cultural spaces (Hartigan 2010). I will use the craft beer culture as an example of one of these cultural spaces. The question that I will investigate is: What are some of the racializing cultural elements at play in the craft beer arena that construct and maintain it as a predominantly middle-class/white-male cultural form?

During my analysis and observations from within the culture, three elements emerged that are used as mechanisms within the craft beer industry to establish and uphold it as a white-male cultural form: marketing, distinctions, and space and place. These will be referred to as "elements of cultural construction and maintenance," and they are thought to be implicit mechanisms, which uphold this mainly male-dominated, white-racialized culture. I also provide insight into how white masculinity is defined and redefined through consumption. The larger goal is to further the understanding of how white cultures and spaces are actively constructed and maintained.

I employ a multimethod approach in this project. I utilized craft beer packaging, websites, slogans, and other marketing material to highlight the latent discourses of white-maleness from within the industry. I also draw on my first-hand experience as a 10-year observer and participant within the craft beer and fine beverage industry. From 2004 through 2014, I served as retail associate, retail buyer, and distributor representative of craft beer and fine beverages in multiple, large-scale companies. My position as both a participant and a researcher within the industry offer me a unique insider status. Moreover, my social position as a white heterosexual male allowed me to blend into the culture. During my time in the industry, I experienced the use of craft beer to brighten the boundaries of whiteness in white cultural spaces such as country clubs, affluent-neighborhood craft beer bars, and craft beer festivals. The craft beer culture is ripe for this type of analysis because it is a trending cultural form that has grown exponentially in popularity during the past couple of decades (Acitelli 2013) and spans all the regions of the nation, all while remaining defined by whiteness.

Cultural Forms and Racialized Spaces

Races are not biologically but socially determined categories of identity and group association (Bonilla-Silva 1997). Omi and Winant (2015, 55) argue that these racial categories are "created, inhabited, transformed and destroyed." In this view, race is seen in an anti-essentialist manner and is considered as an organizing principle of society that shapes the identities at the microlevel and frames all spheres of social life at the macrolevel (Bonilla-Silva 1997). Whites will be the racial group of focus in this chapter, but more specifically whiteness will be explored. Whiteness can be understood as the defining principle of social organization (Hancock 2013). In a society built to benefit whites, such as American society, white values, ideas, aesthetics, preferences, and privileges are made to appear as normal, a taken-for-granted basis of interacting and engaging in social life (Hancock 2013). Whiteness as a social organization is deeply institutionalized and naturalized, so much so that it is invisible even to whites themselves. To expand on this idea, according to Hancock (2013, 18): "Whiteness is not just an unseen system of norms, but also a sense of entitlement and privilege that emerges out of this social organization of resources and opportunities." The mechanisms used in the maintenance of whiteness must be uncovered and deeply explored.

Races are the outcome of the process of racialization in which they are constructed and identified (Omi and Winant 2015). Racialization is "the extension of racial meaning to a previously racially unclassified relationship, social practice or group" (Omi and Winant 2015, 64). It is believed that through the process of creating the category of the "other," the creation of the category of the "same" is achieved. In other words, as Blumer (1958, 4) suggested, "to characterize another racial group is, by opposition, to define one's own group." The focus of this analysis is to examine the ways in which sameness is created through everyday cultural practices. Furthermore, much scholarship has been directed toward examining how the process of racialization has focused on the racialization of minorities. However, whites are not free from the process of racialization (Omi and Winant 2015); yet little research has been directed toward the racialization process for whites (Bonilla-Silva et al. 2006). Cultural forms and racialized spaces are two mechanisms that are involved in the continual construction and maintenance of whiteness.

My analysis also draws from scholarship on maleness and masculinities. Gender, just like race, is understood as a social construction. It has been shown that different cultures during different sociohistorical periods construct and treat gender differently. Connell (1998, 57) states that masculinities "are sustained and enacted not only by individuals but also by groups and institutions." Gender and masculinities, in this case, are constructed and perpetuated through group and structural activities, not only individually. In this sense, masculinities come into being as people act. Moreover, Connell posits that masculinities are not homogeneous states of being. Gender is under constant flux, structuring and restructuring, and takes on different meanings in different social groups. Scholarship on gender and masculinities forms this chapter because white-maleness will be specifically looked at, which must be understood as a different gendered identity than any other cultural forms of gender.

Constructing Whiteness through Cultural Forms

Consumption has, throughout history, served as a significant site for the reproduction of social boundaries (Holt 1998). Cultural consumption is a process involved in the construction of racial/ethnic collective identities (Lamont and

Molnár 2001; Zukin and Maguire 2004). The construction of racialized knowledge has also been linked to capitalist practices, such as consumption (Cole 2008). Cultural consumption is a group practice surrounding a cultural form, such as music, fashion, or food (Pitcher 2014). Aside from being a cultural process that is involved in the construction and maintenance of racial boundaries, consumption is an element of the formation of class-based boundaries as well. Bourdieu (1984) has documented how cultural capital is carried out in fields of consumption such as the arts, food, interior decorating, fashion, popular culture, leisure hobbies, and sports. To Bourdieu, cultural capital is a set of socially rare and distinctive tastes, skills, knowledge, and practices (Holt 1998). Bourdieu (1984) argues that the social field of consumption is stratified and that there are different lifestyles that are organized through the consumer practices of social classes. The idea that consumption practices structure class boundaries can also be extended to racial boundaries. Racial meaning is made through the act of consumption (Pitcher 2014). In this sense, race is not something that precedes the act of consumption, but is something that is assigned meaning through the practice. In short, consuming practices are related to the construction, maintenance, and perpetuation of gendered, racial, and class-based boundaries and ideologies.

For example, the cultural form of dance has been linked to the maintenance of racial inequalities. In his empirical work on the 1920s historically African-American Lindy Hop dance, Hancock (2008) has shown how cultural forms can be unconsciously stripped of their racial meaning by hegemonic white culture. Hancock uses the discourses of the Lindy Hop revival to provide a window into understanding how the dominant racial logic of white American society exists even in the most apparently harmless of cultural practices.

Leisure travel is another cultural practice that has been associated with racial construction. The scholarship of Perry Carter (2008), for instance, locates differences in travel behaviors between African-American and white leisure travelers. Carter finds that the sociohistorical construction of the place of travel affects the views and behaviors of different racialized groups. Food and its consumer practices is also the site for much scholarship involving the intersection of culture and race. Research on food consumption (Adams and Raisborough 2010; Johnston et al. 2011) and high-end dining (Johnston and Baumann 2014) illustrates that the consumption practices surrounding different genres of food are key components in racial, ethnic, and class-based collective identities. Consumption is a process that is deeply embedded in the cultural landscape of our social world and is an important element in the formation of racial, class, and gendered symbolic boundaries. The connection between consumption of cultural forms and racial group identities has been made in many facets of social research.

Racialized Spaces

Racialized space is an area of growing scholarship pertaining to the maintenance of social boundaries. There is now a vast literature on how space is racialized (Goldberg 1993; Hill 1998; Mohanram 1999; Razack 1999, 2004; Reitman 2006). Hargrove (2009) uses the cityscape as a vehicle of spatial analysis. He demonstrates how particular strategies of urban development serve as "security checkpoints" in the maintenance of race-based inequality across the broader "social field of whiteness." Another example of scholarship that looks at how space is racialized can be found in the work of Diane Harris (2013), who uses the domestic space of the home to analyze racial segregation. Harris examines how media after World War II used representation to associate the ordinary single-family home with middle class whites. She posits that this association is a key element in segregation based on race and class, which still continues to resonate today.

This growing body of scholarship focuses on the key idea that racialized groups must operate within and among racialized spaces. Racialized spaces are a key component in the understanding of how racial formations, identities, and privileges are maintained and perpetuated. These spaces are also afforded greater or lesser social status depending on whether they are racialized as middle-class white or minority spaces.

Whites tend to live in social isolation from other racial groups (particularly blacks), but, at the same time, do not interpret this phenomenon as having any racial implications. Bonilla-Silva et al. (2006, 247) argue that "whites live in a white habitus that creates and conditions their views, cognitions, and even sense of beauty." The authors suggest that this "white habitus" creates a sense of racial solidarity and leads to the idea that white is a collective identity. This white collective identity leads to the belief among whites that whiteness is normal and the correct way of being and doing things. Whites are conditioned into this collective mentality, and racialized attitudes and prejudices toward minority groups are continuously legitimated and recycled.

When faced with the facts of racial exclusivity, such as contact rates, neighborhood demographics, and interracial marriage statistics, whites tend to use color-blind terminology in their explanations. For example, in explaining these phenomena, whites tend to posit: "that's just the way it is" or deny involvement in the exclusionary practice (Bonilla-Silva et al. 2006). The white habitus creates a space where racial isolation is normalized; therefore, the questioning of this circumstance is avoided and denied. Whites, therefore, tend to lack reflexivity. Bonilla-Silva et al. suggest that more research must be directed toward the active process involved in the production and maintenance of white spaces, identities, and cultures. This is in part because of the tendency of past studies to ignore the topic of white racialization.

In a last example of scholarship that investigates the connection between race and space Anderson (2015, 10) states, "while white people usually avoid black space, black people are required to navigate the white space as a condition of their existence." Anderson finds that the black space, which is commonly avoided by whites, is constructed and ideologically maintained through the mediated repetitive imagery of the "black urban ghetto." Anderson goes on to say that "the wider society is still replete with overwhelmingly white neighborhoods, restaurants, schools, universities, workplaces, churches, and other associations, courthouses, and cemeteries, a situation that reinforces normative sensibility in settings in which black people are typically absent, not expected, or marginalized when present" (Anderson 2015, 11). These white spaces are areas for the perpetuation and maintenance of cultural capital, and if racial minorities are systematically excluded from these spaces, they are not included in this process. Anderson's work backs this analysis because it highlights the importance and social consequences that racialized space has on social life.

The fields of study that investigate cultural forms and racialized spaces would benefit from more examination that combines the two ideas. For example, Anthony Harrison (2013) advances the concept of *racial spatiality* to illustrate how processes of everyday racism work to secure social spaces as a predominantly white cultural form. According to Harrison, racist practices restrict the participation and representation of blacks from the cultural practice of skiing. He suggests that examining the racialized underpinnings of cultural forms, such as skiing, illuminates the less formal, less direct, and less obvious ways in which discourses surrounding race shape society. This analysis serves as a working example of how the leisure options available to African Americans and other racially marginalized groups are restricted. This work is an example of blending racial–cultural practice with racialized spaces.

Up to this point we are faced with the ideas that race is a social construct and is an organizing factor of social existence and that racialization is the process in which racial meaning is constructed and attached, cultural forms are used in the construction and perpetuation of class/racial meanings, and space is racialized and the use of it is involved in the perpetuation of racial formations and meanings. Craft beer will be explored as an example of how cultural forms are used to maintain and create white-male spaces.

In this chapter, I will build on the aforementioned pieces in two ways. First, I will explore racialized space as not only something that is preexisting but that also has an exclusionary framework that must be used as boundaries; but I will add that racialized cultural space is something that is actively maintained by racial and gendered groups. Second, my analysis will illustrate that racialized cultural space is not maintained only through actions on the individual level, but also through collective cultural and institutional practices. The main idea is that the cultural practices of racial construction in any given industry (e.g., sport, food, fashion, music, and dance) are used to maintain and create racialized spaces. The aim of this analysis is to explore the active process involved in the production and maintenance of white-male social space and the cultural underpinnings of whiteness.

An Observation from Within

The data for this analysis come from craft brewery websites, product packaging, marketing slogans, and other promotional materials. In addition, I draw upon my observational field notes, which I compiled during different stages of my career within the industry. Together, these data illustrate some of the ways that whiteness operates through seemingly innocuous cultural ways. I am not setting out to present rates, frequencies, and totals. Rather, my aim is to illustrate the recurring cultural narratives of white/middle-class/maleness from within craft beer culture. It is important to note that not all of the interactions and observations I made during this project made blatant reference to race, class, or gender. Whiteness (and race/racism more broadly) is embedded in the structure and ideology of American society (Bonilla-Silva 1997) and is "the invisible, underlying, unspoken, normalized operation of the racial organization of society" (Garner and Hancock 2014). However, not all craft beer production materials and the interactions throughout the culture overtly refer to race, class, or gender. Furthermore, it is not my claim that the data and analysis of this essay encompasses every aspect of the craft beer culture, but it does locate a prominent narrative theme that runs strongly throughout it.

I used the Brewer's Association's "Top 50 U.S. Craft Brewing Companies of 2014" as a starting point in which to find production materials for analysis. I visited the websites (if available) of each of the breweries on the list, focusing on the brand slogans, images, and product packaging. I used open coding to organize the data and focused on materials that made reference to three categories:

race, class, and gender. To expand the scope of the analysis, I also included data from outside the top 50 that I came upon during my experiences within the culture. These outside examples provide useful insight into the culture. These data did—in one instance—include examples from a cider company (Original Sin). However, as I will explain briefly, cider is usually an invited and included product within the culture. To many, ciders are considered a part of the craft beer culture and industry.

As far as the participant observation goes, I draw upon firsthand experiences from my career within the craft beer and fine beverage industry. I collected the observational data between 2004 and 2014, during which time I filled the positions of specialty beverage team member, beer buyer, and wine buyer at a large-scale specialty grocery chain. Toward the end of my career, I spent time as a wine/specialty beverage sales representative at a national beverage distribution company.

Some of the duties I was responsible for in my roles in the craft beverage industry included making retail- and sales-related decisions with regard to craft beer, conducting and attending craft beer trade shows and tastings, coordinating and conducting craft beer and wine training classes for customers and co-workers, and visiting craft breweries. These industry events and job-related duties often took place in white-male spaces that included high-end craft beer bars, upscale restaurants, and—in a few instances—country clubs. During these events, I consistently saw and experienced craft beer being used as a cultural form to produce and maintain white cultures, spaces, and identities.

During my time in the industry, I recorded my observations while I navigated the corporate culture. I took detailed notes on each observation shortly after it happened, recording the context and manner in which it occurred. During the days following, I would draw from those notes to form detailed narratives of the observations. For the current project, I am focusing on the observations that I believe highlight these themes. I was treated as an insider because of my occupational position and social location. Being a person who presents as a white, heterosexual, middle-class male benefited me during my data collection because the industry is largely comprised of white straight males. Because I was treated as an insider, I was able to have interactions in which I was seamlessly absorbed into the culture of the industry.

Elements of Cultural Construction and Maintenance

Craft beer is a white, male, middle-class–dominated cultural form and industry. Studies show that 80% of craft beer consumers are white and non-Hispanic

(Clark 2012). As far as gender goes, statistics show that women are the minority consumers of craft beer—only 35% (Mosbaugh 2014). Young women in particular (ages 21–34) make up 15% of craft beer consumers (Vorel 2014). Class-wise, craft beer drinkers tend to be from the middle- and upper-middle-class levels. Nearly 80% of craft beer enthusiasts have reported higher family incomes than the national mean (Murray and O'Neill 2012). In addition, the craft beer consumer is more likely than the national average to have a college degree and to have a management-level position (Murray and O'Neill 2012). This culture is ripe for analysis directed toward the active process involved in the production and maintenance of middle-class white-male cultures. The craft beer culture, in this case, is merely an example of a white-male–dominated culture. Analysis of how it is constructed and maintained as such provides further insight into how white dominance maintains itself on a larger scale.

What follows is a discussion of the cultural elements I observed throughout my career in the beverage industry that I find to account for the construction and maintenance of the culture. These elements are *marketing, distinctions,* and *space and place.* I will refer to these elements moving forward as "cultural elements of construction and maintenance of the craft beer culture." It is important to note that I am not suggesting that these elements are the only ones at play in the process of construction and maintenance, but they are the ones that were most apparent in my observations.

Marketing

One element that is used to construct and maintain craft beer as a white middle-class male cultural form is marketing. After all, it is situated in a consumer-based market, so of course the presence of marketing strategies are abundant. Marketing strategies are used by breweries in part to inform potential customers about the brewery's identity. Besides identity construction, another function that marketing provides is separation. Breweries commonly rely on themes of exclusion and separation in the identification and framing of their brands. What follows are some examples of craft brewery slogans that promote a consumer divide and that have implications of exclusion between social groups.

A theme among craft beer marketing slogans is that "normal" is an undesirable quality. For example, Dogfish Head Brewery has a slogan that states: "Off-centered ales for off-centered people." The message here is one of separation. This brewery is telling the consumer that there are people who are in and people who are not. It is also implying that their beers are not for the normal consumer, they are for those who are unique or "off-centered." Another example comes from Three Floyds Brewing, which tells its customers (via brand slogan) that its beers are "Not Normal." Here the message is clear: their beers are not for the normal, the average, or the boring; they are for the special few who can appreciate them. Left Hand Brewing prints on their six-packs: "Sometimes you're just not in the mood for what everyone else is having." Once again, slogans such as these suggest that normal or that "everyone else" is an undesirable quality and that folks who imbibe craft beer are the more desirable or unique people.

These marketing phrases bring up questions such as: What is the "normal" that is being referred to? And who are these normal people? A feasible answer is that "normal" is associated with the macrolager (Bud, Miller, Coors) and the people who consume them. This being the case, one can see strong class implications within these slogans. The rejection of the concept *normal* within craft beer slogans is an attempt by the breweries to establish a consumer divide between craft (unique) and noncraft beer drinkers (normal). However, when the demographics of the craft and noncraft consumer are taken into account, one can see racial and class-based inferences. As already established, the majority of craft beer drinkers are white and middle-class or above. According to 2014–2015 reporting in the *Restaurant, Food & Beverage Market Research Handbook* (Miller 2014), macrobeer drinkers, or average beer consumers, have an annual household income that is less than that of the craft drinker (55% of them below $49,000 a year), and have a racial/ethnic makeup that more closely reflects that of the overall U.S. population. When this comparison is taken into account, messages from within craft brewery slogans facilitate a divide between white middle-class consumers (the unique) and the less affluent (the normal).

Other brand slogans within the craft beer industry link craft beer drinkers to desirable personality qualities and suggest that the craft consumer is essentially of higher social standing. Take for instance Victory Brewing's catchphrase "A Victory for Your Taste." Victory is conveying the idea that their product is for those with good taste or with high taste expectations. Brooklyn Beer Company references a John Ciardi quote when telling the public, "Fermentation and civilization are inseparable." At first take, this phrase may come off as suggesting that beer and the formation of civilizations are connected, which some argue is true. However, when civilization is defined as "sophistication" or "advanced culture," the message that comes across is that fermentation and elite culture are inseparable. Great Divide Brewery tells you that "Great Minds Drink Alike," and Flying Dog Brewery of Maryland advertises its beers as, "Good Beer for Good People."

If you take a look at who is consuming craft beer (80% white non-Hispanics, middle class, and predominantly male) then the message is clear: the "good people," ones with "great minds," people who are "civilized," and those who have good "taste" are white middle-class males. The brand slogans of the craft beer industry are a colorful example of where the language of whiteness is being spoken. These marketing slogans are a main element in the process of ideologically separating the craft beer consumer from all other types of beer consumers. The racial implications are hidden in the implicit meanings of the slogans. Simply put, the people who are considered insiders, who are not normal or boring, and who are good (if you take into account the racial statistics of the culture) are white people.

Imagery is another aspect of craft beer marketing that operates within a frame of whiteness and promotes a divide among social groups. Many of the images used by craft beer companies to promote their products are void of people and mostly picture places or things. These images will be discussed later in this chapter in relation to space and place. However, when people are pictured, they are often pictured through a lens of whiteness. This lens promotes white values, beliefs, and aesthetics as normative and desirable. For instance, when white males are pictured, they are often pictured in positions of masculine dominance or fun-loving humor. In contrast, when females are pictured they are often depicted in positions where their bodies are the focus. Finally, when minorities appear within the images of craft beer marketing (which they rarely do), they are often shown in a manner that identifies them as the "ethnic other," an element of oppressive whiteness (hooks 2000).

Up to this point my goal has been to illustrate some of the marketing elements that construct and maintain the craft beer culture as white, male, and middle class. The aforementioned images and slogans operate and participate within a discourse that values the preferences and privileges of whiteness, which encompasses class and gender. This discourse of whiteness views different ethnicities as "others," objectifies female bodies, glorifies masculinity, and promotes a social group–based consumer divide.

The marketing of craft beer operates within whiteness in ways other than slogans and imagery. A common practice among craft beer producers is to release beers that pay tribute to events and holidays that have strong connections to white normativity. Take, for example, Brooklyn Beer Company's "Pennant Ale," which pays tribute to the Major League Baseball World Series (a sporting event with a dominantly white fan base), or Blue Grass Brewing Company's "Dark Star Porter," which is named after the 25–1 longshot winner of the Kentucky Derby. Producers also release beers that correlate with white-centric holidays such as Sam Adams OctoberFest and Harpoon Brewery's Celtic Red (which is released in conjunction with St. Patrick's Day). This trend carries over into the retail sector as well. In my position as beer buyer at a large-scale specialty grocery retailer, I was expected, and instructed by my store leadership and industry representatives, to build large displays of craft beer at the stores during the aforementioned holidays. These examples shed insight into how craft beer is racialized as a culture of whiteness. Evidence can be seen on both the producer side and the retail side.

In contrast, holidays or events with a strong minority connection receive little to no attention within the craft beer culture. The one example that arose from my observations was the Latin American holiday Cinco de Mayo. It was routine—during my career as a retail beer buyer—that every year during the week leading up to May 5th, I was expected to build a mountainous display of Corona (a macrobeer brewed in Mexico and Texas) at the front of the store in order to promote the upcoming festivities. Corona is considered a premium imported beer, but it is typically not embraced by the craft beer audience. Instead, Corona is looked at—within the industry and by craft beer fans—as a beer for the "common drinker," or at best, a "no-brainer" beer that is "OK" to consume when you don't want to have to think too much about what you are drinking. For instance, it would be deemed OK by the craft beer audience to consume Corona at the beach, on a boat, or at a picnic. In this instance, simple beer for the masses was—not so latently—associated with a minority holiday by the beer industry at large. The promotion of craft beer during normative white holidays and events and the promotion of macrobeer during Cinco de Mayo (for example) illustrates how craft beer operates within the frame of whiteness, which excludes, reduces, or eliminates minority cultures.

I also experienced craft beer being marketed to upper-class whites during my career in fine-wine sales. In my field notes, I refer to an instance when I went on a seasonal sales call to a high-end country club in Florida. The goal of that day was to get the club to start offering some of my company's wines for the upcoming golf season. In my field notes I summarized the country club.

Summer 2012

It is not long after entering into the confined and guarded land of the country club that you realize the area is a very high-end area. The winding, tree-lined streets give way to mansions with long driveways and perfectly groomed yards. This confirms the notion that the members and residents of this club are rich and live a luxurious lifestyle. These are the kind of people who spend lots of money on wine, the best wine, which would confirm the reason why I am here.

The floors were made of dark wood and covered with large area rugs, and the hallways were lined with pictures of hunting dogs and ducks.

The rooms of the country club were very aesthetically pleasing. As the young lady led us through the main dining room, where a large chandelier hung from the ceiling in the center of the room, we could see through to the back window of the club that looked out over the rolling hills of the empty golf course.

The country club was an upper-class establishment that catered to whites. After a long day of tasting wines, I was informed by the club manager that the club was going to actually be reducing the size of its wine list. Upon my asking why, the manager told me it was because the country club was expanding the amount of craft beer it was going to be offering to members. The manager told me that the demand was high for craft beer and the management thought it would capitalize on this new trend. This trend of marketing craft beer to the elite allows the consumers (privileged whites) to maintain their high status but also to embrace "rugged" masculinity by consuming beer (a masculine performance); all this could be done while maintaining a distinction from the working-class or "normal" beer consumer. This instance made me realize that craft beer was now being marketed toward a rich, white-male demographic.

Craft beer is marketed through the lens of whiteness. This is one way that craft beer is maintained as a white culture. In this section, four areas of craft beer marketing were explored. First, craft breweries use marketing slogans to establish an identity separation between who drinks the product (according to Flying Dog Brewery the consumers of craft beer are the "Good" people) and who drinks macrobeers (statistically, largely nonwhites). If the messages employed by these marketing strategies are interpreted using a racial and gendered lens, one can see that the "good, sophisticated, and nonboring" people are white males. Second, craft beer producers turn to marketing images that glorify masculinity, objectify the female body, and reduce races and ethnicities to sexualized otherness. Third, craft beer is marketed in accordance to white-centric events and holidays such as the Kentucky Derby, the World Series, Oktoberfest, and St. Patrick's Day. Whereas macrobeer (beer with lesser cultural capital) is marketed during ethnic holidays such as Cinco de Mayo. Lastly, high-end establishments such as country clubs and restaurants serve as sites where craft beer is marketed toward patrons. These places are systematically white. These normalized marketing practices are one element in which craft beer is established and maintained as a white culture.

Distinctions

Pierre Bourdieu (1984) explored the ways in which cultural forms, such as music, art, and food are used in the creation of social space between social groups. According to Bourdieu, tastes are affirmations of an inevitable difference between social groups. In short, groups use tastes, and more specifically distastes, to shape and maintain group boundaries. This social process runs rampant throughout the craft beer industry. Distinctions around what products are desirable, and what products are undesirable are common practice and a vital cultural tool for the navigation of the scene.

Distinctions operate literally within the language of the craft beer culture and industry and are spoken by both the consumer and the producer. As has been established, the craft beer culture operates through the lens of whiteness. The values, norms, and beliefs of white-normative America are the taken-for-granted basis for interaction and communication within the culture. This lens of whiteness is exclusionary because it celebrates masculinity, objectifies female bodies, views different ethnicities as others, and promotes a consumer divide among classes. Distinctions operate within the written and spoken language of producers and consumers as a means of symbolic boundary maintenance between whiteness and nonwhiteness.

Examples of the commonly used element of distinction can be found within promotional materials. For example, Stone Brewery's description of its beer, Arrogant Bastard, from the company's website, says:

> This is an aggressive ale. You probably won't like it. It is quite doubtful that you have the taste or sophistication to be able to appreciate an ale of this quality and depth. We would suggest that you stick to safer and more familiar territory—maybe something with a multimillion dollar ad campaign aimed at convincing you it's made in a little brewery, or one that implies that their tasteless, fizzy, yellow beverage will give you more sex appeal.

In this statement it is first insinuated that the people who can enjoy this beer are the desirable or sophisticated consumers and the people who can't should resort to drinking a "tasteless, fizzy, yellow beverage" (in other words, a macrolager). When the class demographics of the craft and macrobeer drinker are taken into account, once again it is suggested that the lower-class consumer is undesirable and cannot "appreciate" this cultural form. Second, this description offers an example of the masculine characteristic of the written and spoken language of the culture. The aggressive tone of this description taunts the consumer. This aggressive and masculine style runs throughout the culture. Another example of where this is happening in the language of the culture is in the names of craft beers. For example, popular beers from well-known breweries such as: Ruination Ale (Stone Brewery), Torpedo Ale (Sierra Nevada), Demolition Ale (Goose Island), Judgment Day (Lost Abbey), and Hop Slam (Bells) make reference to war and aggression. This masculine language glorifies masculinity (or instrumentalism) and in turn devalues femininity (or expression). This is the language of whiteness.

Examples like this are common throughout the culture and perpetuate the idea that to be part of the "real" culture of craft beer you have to be able to identify, understand, and enjoy the "real" craft beers. These distinctive practices are mechanisms for formation of a group boundary. That is, in order to navigate this culture, you must know and be able to differentiate between the desirable tastes of the culture and the undesirable tastes of the culture. You must be able to speak the language. To do this, you have to first and foremost have access to and be exposed to this culture. Furthermore, craft beer must hold some symbolic capital in a person's social world in order for it to act as a beneficial cultural form. Exposure and access to the culture happens to mainly white middle-class males in part because of the marketing strategies of the industry and the written and spoken language of the culture. Both the marketing strategies and language operate within the lens of whiteness, which includes whites and excludes nonwhites.

Another example of distinction as a cultural element of construction and maintenance came from my observations. In this instance, I had met with a few of my co-workers after one of our shifts at the large-scale specialty grocery retailer. All of the co-workers that I met that night were white males, and they were involved in the craft beer industry as well. We met at a well-renowned craft beer bar in Chicago. The bar was located in a hip, gentrified area, known for its white yuppie-hipster demographic. What struck me most during our night at the bar was the manner in which one of my co-workers talked about a customer interaction that he had during his shift that day.

Winter 2008

My coworker was deeply disturbed because a male customer approached him earlier that day during his shift and asked where he could find the Sierra Nevada Pale Ale. Then, the customer claimed that Sierra Nevada was the best pale ale on the market. My coworker was so disturbed that he carried on by venting to us about the guy, saying things like: The customer was just plain wrong! His breath stunk! The customer's child was annoying! The customer's child stunk like shit! And that he wanted to drown out the smell of the child's shit with the customer's favorite beer (Sierra Nevada Pale Ale). Which my co-worker thought to be "shit beer."

This is an example of how distinctions are used in the culture of craft beer to establish products and people as superior and inferior to one another. Here my coworker was actively maintaining the exclusiveness of the culture by illustrating to the rest of us his ability to know who the undesirable people and products were. In this instance, we were a group of white males, together in a white male–dominated bar, in a hip white area of town, consuming a white cultural form, all while passing judgments about other craft beer consumers' authentic knowledge of the product. This common practice is one of group boundary maintenance and is implicitly racialized. Odds are that if you have access to this authentic knowledge in which to pass judgment on others within the culture, if you are in a bar in a "hip" white area of town, and if you are consuming craft beer in the first place, then more than likely you are white yourself. After all, it has been shown that whites, despite what they might think or say, tend to stick together (Bonilla-Silva et al. 2006; Sallaz 2010).

Another place where this commonly happens is at industry tastings. One example of this came from my observations of a 2011 Big Beer industry tasting that I attended as a participant. Every year, a massive Chicago-land specialty beer, wine, and spirits distributor, which I will refer to as "Big Beer," hosts an event at which it showcases a large majority of the craft beer brands that it distributes. This tasting event is one of the biggest trade events of its kind in the nation; therefore, it is known throughout the Chicago craft beer scene as the most extensive beer expo. That year at the expo, I ran into my sales representative, who I will call Don from Big Beer. Don and I had a good business relationship, and he was the guy who gave me the tickets to the event in the first place. The following is an account of the event from my field notes.

Winter 2011

The room was huge, giant even, with fluorescent lighting and outdated ballroom style carpeting. There was a loud cavernous roar of crowd and bassy music. Each brewery present at the event had its own tasting station; the stations were lined up in rows and somewhat arranged by geographical region of where the brewery is located. The rows seem to go on forever, giving off the feeling that there was no way one man could possibly visit every station in one night, probably not even in a week. There were, literally, hundreds of breweries present at the event, and thousands of beers to sample.

The place wasn't very well organized. I wandered through each aisle trying to find the microbrew section. Some breweries had hired female models to pour at their stations, where some had strobe lights and smoke machines to draw in tasters. The deeper I got, the more apparent it became that the place was a mob scene. It was about an hour into the event when I had arrived, and drunkenness was rampant. Stumbling patrons who had lost all awareness of their surroundings, due to a beer-induced stupor, bumped into me as I walked through the event. Trash and half-eaten cocktail weenies were all over the floor, and I witnessed people grabbing food from the catering tables with their bare hands, taking bites, and then throwing the remainders of the half-eaten appetizers on the ground only to go in for another helping. Every station had a mass of men at least five deep surrounding it and yelling at the attendants for a sample of their offerings.

During our short conversation that day, Don went on to tell me which beers to check out and which ones to avoid. I remember him telling me to stay away from the mass-produced "fake" craft beers and told me to make sure to check out the high-end craft offerings. Furthermore, it was a running joke that day among the patrons of the event that a large-scale beer manufacturer was there and had a booth set up. Don said things like: "Why are they even here?" and "That's such shit beer."

Ron's distaste toward macro-producer products is an example of distinctions being used within the spoken language of the culture to maintain symbolic boundaries. By rejecting this type of beer (which is thought of as an inferior beer in the craft beer culture and industry), Don was positioning the tastes of white males with authentic knowledge of craft beer as the superior taste. These judgments of taste or "manifested preferences" (Bourdieu 1984) are mechanisms of exclusion and separation among the consumers of craft beer.

The racial implications of these distinctive judgments are a little complicated. It has been established that this cultural space is a white middle-class male cultural space, meaning that it is occupied primarily by white middle-class and above males. In addition, these distinctive judgments are needed to navigate the culture. In order to be considered a true craft beer consumer, one must know the good craft beers from the bad, which is a prime example of Bourdieu's (1984) notion of cultural capital. And in order to adapt and learn this language, one has to be involved in the craft beer scene. Most likely, if you are involved, you are white, male, and above working class. These distinctive judgments can be seen in the written and spoken language as mechanisms in the reinforcement and maintenance of the racial, gendered, and class-based status quo of the craft beer culture. This language operates within whiteness, which systematically excludes and devalues nonwhites. This is an example of how white-male cultural forms are used in the creation of symbolic boundaries between groups.

Space and Place

At one point in my career as a beer buyer, I was invited to a local Chicago brewery for a tour. During the tour, I got a chance to converse with one of the brewers. The brewer happened to be female, which was rare in the industry. She instantly identified herself as the wife of the man who was CEO, owner, and master brewer. This positioned her as a female present as the companion of a male. The brewer told me that their beers were unique because of their commitment to old-fashioned German brewing techniques. She also went into detail about how they use local ingredients to make their beers. The conversation seemed similar to one I would be having in the wine world, because the brewer was putting a large emphasis on where the company got the products used to make the beer. The brewer then told me that at the brewery they like to say, "Drink beer from here," which suggests that the beer that tastes the best is made with local ingredients, brewed locally, and best enjoyed close to where it is made. This brewery is located in a middle- to upper-class neighborhood in Chicago.

Many craft breweries abide by the German Beer Purity Law, which relates to the brewer's claim that the brewery adheres strictly to historical German brewing practices. This law (it's more of an ethical practice) places restrictions on what ingredients can and cannot be used in the brewing process. In addition, many American craft breweries are influenced by traditional Belgian, German, and English styles. This practice is evidence of a connection between the craft beer culture and Old Country European roots, which have deep histories of Anglo rule. This connection is another way of affirming a white European legitimacy, and it is a way that space and place is used as a mechanism to construct and maintain a white culture. After all, white hierarchy persists in large part because of sociolegal history (Haney-Lopez 2006).

This focus on space and place is a very strong theme throughout the craft beer culture, much like the wine industry's focus on place, land, and terroir (a French term that means "of the land"). Focusing on how space and place are used within the craft beer arena shows how whiteness operates on the structure of the culture. It is common practice for breweries to highlight and focus on their connections to certain cities and places (Flack 1997; Schnell and Reese

2003). This connection offers a sense of identity for the brand, and it offers the consumer a means of identity construction. It is also a means of constructing and maintaining a racialized space. This method of using space and place serves the latent function of solidifying the culture as white.

For instance, take the use of maps by breweries. A strategy by craft beer breweries is to build the brand's identity by including images of maps on their product packaging. These maps place the breweries in culturally white areas of the country and the world. Kalamazoo, Michigan; Portland, Oregon; and Fort Collins, Colorado, for instance, are cities where some of the most popular craft breweries are located. These places are known for their strong, white, hipster cultures. These cultures are strongly associated with the craft beer culture.

You will find that much of the imagery used by craft breweries on their websites and promotional materials has strong connections to white sociohistorical times and spaces. For example, breweries whose beer names and packaging are within white-historical contexts, such as Great Lakes Brewing Company's Commodore Perry IPA or Conway's Irish Ale. Other breweries, such as Bells and New Belgium, use imagery to suggest a white, all-American culture, showing Norman Rockwell–ish images such as vintage bikes, old-looking cameras, and old-fashioned country landscapes. These images refer to iconic "American dream-like" times in space and history. These historical spaces have deep roots in white ideology and aesthetics. In short, the maps and images of the craft beer culture refer to places and spaces associated with whites and whiteness. They are mechanisms of identification and provide reference to the white racial frame from which one can locate the product.

Lastly, during my experiences, I found the craft beer culture taking place, time and time again, in white social spaces. For instance, high-end grocery stores host craft beer tasting nights, exclusive and expensive restaurants carry an assortment of craft beers on tap, beer festivals take place in predominantly white neighborhoods, where white bands play white music. Craft beer is given to those who finish marathons (yes, running marathons is a white thing), country clubs host private craft beer tastings for their members, white hipsters with vintage-style mustaches get together to listen to Sigur Rós music and drink craft beer in their trendy, gentrified-area apartments, and at major league baseball games across the country, beer concessions guys walk up and down the aisles yelling "Bud, Bud Light, SIERRA NEVADA!" The craft beer culture may span certain social groups, but one thing remains clear, it happens in white spaces and it operates through the frame of whiteness. Furthermore, the majority of the participants in the culture are white, male, and middle class or above. The use of space and place by the craft beer industry is a structural element in the maintenance and construction of the culture as a white, male, middle-class culture. Craft beer companies make reference to white space and place through maps and images on their packaging, and the culture takes place mostly in white spaces. Whiteness resides in the structure of the culture, so much so that craft beer is "white" even before white people imbibe.

Discussion and Conclusion

In this chapter, I have illustrated some of the elements that construct the craft beer culture as a white middle-class male–dominated culture. Statistics show that white males are the main consumers of craft beer (80% white non-Hispanic, 65% male, and largely middle-class or above). When women are present in the culture, they are typically present as companions to men. The question is then asked: What are some of the cultural elements at play in the craft beer cultural arena that perpetuate its demographics and ideologies? Three themes were presented that do this: marketing, distinctions, and space and place. Collectively, these frames construct and maintain the culture as predominantly white, middle class, and male by promoting separation and exclusion, marketing the product in a white-normative manner, and offering reference to and operating within white space and place. These elements work in tandem and collectively operate through the lens of whiteness. This lens promotes white norms, values, and esthetics, which are presented as the normalized basis for social reality and interaction.

It is important to note that these cultural themes are not overt tactics of racial, class, and/or gender-based exclusion. Rather, they are normalized ways of latent boundary construction. The craft beer culture is not overtly excluding women and minorities from participating in and enjoying the product. The participants of this culture actually suggest that they are doing the opposite; that is, they say that they are promoting the idea of a multicultural arena (O'Brien 2006). The craft beer culture and industry often present an inclusive and democratic identity. It is common practice for craft beer producers to support beneficial causes such as social movements and community-building organizations. The craft beer culture is also generally committed to ethical business and environmentally friendly practices. This provides an interesting conclusion to my analysis. Oppressive whiteness can still be found woven into the fibers of cultural arenas that overtly promote good causes and represent social justice.

The elements of construction and maintenance presented in this chapter work both culturally and structurally to perpetuate an exclusionary divide between social groups. This analysis is—in part—an answer to a call for more research involving both the link between consumer practices and racial relations (Reskin 2012) and the active process involved in the production and maintenance of white identities and white cultures (Bonilla-Silva et al. 2006). The aim of this research was to provide insight into how white middle-class masculinities are defined and redefined through consumption. The overall goal was to add to the scholarship dedicated to investigating the implicit ways in which white cultures are actively constructed and maintained.

It is important for me to address that this chapter did not focus specifically on race, class, or gender as separate social phenomena. Instead, the concept of "whiteness" was employed to refer to the oppressive frame in which race, class, and gender exist in American society. These socially constructed categories operate within and are perceived through the lens of whiteness. Therefore, every social category is racialized. Whiteness can often be misrecognized as class. Frankenburg (2001, 75) notes that whiteness, "annoying for those who are trying to name it," often gets confused with class or ethnicity. It is also important to note that throughout my observations, the racial element within the craft beer industry was the most evident but also the least recognized by participants and producers.

The craft beer industry and culture remains a fertile ground for further analysis of race and consumer cultures. This being said, it is important to recognize that as a white, straight, working/middle-class, male, my observations were both situated within and came from a standpoint of whiteness. Although the geographical locations of my analyses were diverse, the specific places where I experienced the craft beer culture taking place were white spaces. I hold that these white spaces are the "hubs" of this culture. They are where decisions are being made and where cultural capital is being gained. The fact that my observations occurred in white spaces does not take away from my findings that the culture and industry operate within a frame of oppressive whiteness, which perpetuates the culture as white. Further analyses are needed that explore the presence of craft beer in minority spaces and how it is used in the construction of racial meanings within those spaces.

Another suggestion for future research is to conduct in-depth interviews with industry representatives to further uncover the discursive framework of exclusion within the culture. This field also could be used to dig deeper into how whiteness is not simply one homogeneous thing, but rather a racial identity that takes on multiple forms. A further suggestion is to use craft beer, or other "craft" cultural products, as a site to investigate how cultural forms are used not only in separating ideological whiteness from nonwhiteness, but also how the form is used in the process of boundary formation among above-average whites. Race- and gender-driven analyses may also be expanded to other "craft" cultural genres such as farmers markets, food trucks, cheese consumption, and the wine industry. Analyses that lend insight into how whiteness and masculinities are culturally constructed and maintained may collectively contribute to a greater understanding of how racial and gendered inequalities perpetuate our social world.

REFERENCES

Acitelli, Tom. 2013. *The Audacity of Hops*. Chicago: Chicago Review Press.

Adams, Matthew, and Jayne Raisborough. 2010. "Making a Difference: Ethical Consumption and the Everyday." *British Journal of Sociology* 61 (2): 256–274.

Anderson, Elijah. 2015. "The White Space." *Sociology of Race and Ethnicity* 1 (1): 10–21.

Blumer, Herbert. 1958. "Race Prejudice as a Sense of Group Position." *Pacific Sociological Review* 1 (1): 3–7.

Bonilla-Silva, Eduardo. 1997. "Rethinking Racism: Toward a Structural Interpretation." *American Sociological Review* 62 (3): 465–480.

Bonilla-Silva, Eduardo, Carla Goar, and David G. Embrick. 2006. "When Whites Flock Together: The Social Psychology of White Habitus." *Critical Sociology* 32 (2–3): 229–253.

Bourdieu, Pierre. 1984. *Distinction: A Social Critique of the Judgment of Taste*. Cambridge, MA: Harvard University Press.

Carter, Perry L. 2008. "Coloured Places and Pigmented Holidays: Racialized Leisure Travel." *Tourism Geographies* 10 (3): 265–84.

Clark, Jim. 2012, May 1. "Who Is the New Beer Consumer?" *Beverage Media Group*. http://www.beveragemedia.com/index.php/2012/05/who-is-the-new-beer-consumer-brewers-ready-to-say-ihola-and-more-to-expand-reach.

Cole, Nikki Lisa. 2008. "Global Capitalism Organizing Knowledge of Race, Gender and Class: The Case of Socially Responsible Coffee." *Race, Gender & Class* 15 (1–2): 170–187.

Connell, R. W. 1998. "Masculinities and Globalization." *Men and Masculinities* 1 (1): 3–23.

Flack, Wes. 1997. "American Microbreweries and Neolocalism: 'Ale-ing' for a Sense of Place." *Journal of Cultural Geography* 16 (2): 37–53.

Frankenberg, Ruth. 2001. "The Mirage of an Unmarked Whiteness." In *The Making and Unmaking of Whiteness*, edited by Bridget Brander Rasmussen, Eric Klinenberg, Irene J. Nexica, and Matt Wray, 72–96. Durham, NC: Duke University Press.

Garner, Roberta, and Black Hawk Hancock. 2014. *Social Theory: Continuity and Confrontation*. Toronto: University of Toronto Press.

Goldberg, David Theo. 1993. *Racist Culture*. Cambridge: Blackwell.

Hancock, Black Hawk. 2008. "Put a Little Color on That!" *Sociological Perspectives* 51 (4): 783–802.

———. 2013. *American Allegory: Lindy Hop and the Racial Imagination*. Chicago: University of Chicago Press.

Haney-Lopez, Ian. 2006. *White by Law: The Legal Construction of Race*. New York: New York University Press.

Hargrove, Melissa. D. 2009. "Mapping the 'Social Field of Whiteness': White Racism as Habitus in the City Where History Lives." *Transforming Anthropology* 17 (2): 93–104.

Harris, Dianne Suzette. 2013. *Little White Houses: How the Postwar Home Constructed Race in America*. Minneapolis: University of Minnesota Press.

Harrison, Anthony Kwame. 2013. "Black Skiing, Everyday Racism, and the Racial Spatiality of Whiteness." *Journal of Sport & Social Issues* 37 (4): 1–25.

Hartigan, John. 2010. *Race in the 21st Century: Ethnographic Approaches*. Oxford, UK: Oxford University Press.

Hill, Jane H. 1998. "Language, Race, and White Public Space." *American Anthropologist* 100 (3): 680–689.

Holt, Douglas B. 1998. "Does Cultural Capital Structure American Consumption?" *Journal of Consumer Research* 25 (1): 1–25.

hooks, bell. 2000. "Eating the Other: Desire and Resistance." In *The Consumer Society Reader*, edited by Juliet B. Schor and Douglas Holt, 343–359. New York: New Press.

Johnston, Josee, and Shyon Baumann. 2014. *Foodies: Democracy and Distinction in the Gourmet Foodscape*. London: Routledge.

Johnston, Josee, Michelle Szabo, and Alexander Rodney. 2011. "Good Food, Good People: Understanding the Cultural Repertoire of Ethical Eating." *Journal of Consumer Culture* 11 (3): 293–318.

Lamont, Michele, and Virag Molnár. 2001. "How Blacks Use Consumption to Shape Their Collective Identity Evidence from Marketing Specialists." *Journal of Consumer Culture* 1 (1): 31–45.

Miller, Richard K., and Associates. 2014. *Restaurant, Food & Beverage Market Research Handbook, 2014–2015*. Loganville, GA: Richard K. Miller and Associates.

Mohanram, Radika. 1999. *Black Body: Women, Colonialism, and Space* (vol. 6). Minneapolis: University of Minnesota Press.

Mosbaugh, Erin. 2014, November 20. "How Craft Beer Fails Its Female Fan Base." *First We Feast*. http://firstwefeast.com/drink/how-craft-beer-fails-its-female-fan-base.

Murray, Douglas W., and Martin A. O'Neill. 2012. "Craft Beer: Penetrating a Niche Market." *British Food Journal* 114 (7): 899–909.

O'Brien, Christopher Mark. 2006. *Fermenting Revolution: How to Drink Beer and Save the World*. Gabriola Island, BC: New Society.

Omi, Michael, and Howard Winant. 2015. *Racial Formation in the United States*. London: Routledge.

Pitcher, Ben. 2014. *Consuming Race*. London: Routledge.

Razack, Sherene H. 1999. "Making Canada White: Law and the Policing of Bodies of Colour in the 1990s." *Canadian Journal of Law and Society* 14: 159.

———. 2004. *Dark Threats and White Knights: The Somalia Affair, Peacekeeping, and the New Imperialism*. Toronto: University of Toronto Press.

Reitman, Meredith. 2006. "Uncovering the White Place: Whitewashing at Work." *Social & Cultural Geography* 7 (2): 267–282.

Reskin, Barbara. 2012. "The Race Discrimination System." *Annual Review of Sociology* 38: 17–35.

Sallaz, Jeffery J. 2010. "Talking Race, Marketing Culture: The Racial Habitus in and out of Apartheid." *Social Problems* 57 (2): 294–314.

Schnell, Steven M., and Joseph F. Reese. 2003. "Microbreweries as Tools of Local Identity." *Journal of Cultural Geography* 21 (1): 45–69.

Vorel, Jim. 2014, October 4. "The Expanding Demographic of Craft Beer." *Paste.* http://www.pastemagazine.com/articles/2014/10/the-expanding-demographics-of-craft-beer.html.

Zukin, Sharon, and Jennifer Smith Maguire. 2004. "Consumers and Consumption." *Annual Review of Sociology* 30: 173–197.

GLOSSARY

A

ADJUNCT   Any unmalted grain or other fermentable ingredient used in the brewing process. Adjuncts used are typically either rice or corn; they can also include honey, syrups, and numerous other sources of fermentable carbohydrates. They are common in mass-produced light American lager-style beers.

ALCOHOL   A synonym for ethyl alcohol or ethanol, the colorless primary alcohol constituent of beer. Alcohol ranges for beer vary from less than 3.2% to greater than 14% ABV. However, the majority of craft beer styles average around 5.9% ABV.

ALCOHOL BY VOLUME (ABV)   A measurement of the alcohol content of a solution in terms of the percentage volume of alcohol per 100 milliliters of the total volume of beer at 20°C. This measurement is always higher than alcohol by weight (ABW). To calculate the approximate volumetric alcohol content, subtract the final gravity from the original gravity and divide by 0.0075. For example: 1.050–1.012=0.038/0.0075=5% ABV.

ALE   Beers fermented with top-fermenting yeast. Ales typically are fermented at warmer temperatures than lagers and are often served warmer. The term *ale* is sometimes incorrectly associated with alcoholic strength.

AMERICAN HOMEBREWERS ASSOCIATION (AHA)   The American Homebrewers Association was founded in 1978 and is dedicated to promoting the community of home brewers and advocating for home brewers' rights in the United States. The AHA hosts the annual National Homebrew Competition, which is the largest beer competition in the world.

AMERICAN SOCIETY OF BREWING CHEMISTS (ASBC)   The American Society of Brewing Chemists was founded in 1934 to improve and bring uniformity to the brewing industry on a technical level. Specifically, the ASBC provides analytical, scientific process control methods to ensure high quality and safety standards, science-based approaches and solutions to industry-wide issues, and scientific support to evaluate raw materials for optimum performance.

B

BARREL   (1) A standard measure in the U.S. that is 31.5 gallons. (2) A wooden vessel that is used to age/condition/ferment beer. Some brewer's barrels are brand new and others have been used previously to store wine or spirits.

BEER JUDGE CERTIFICATION PROGRAM (BJCP)   The Beer Judge Certification Program certifies and ranks beer judges through an examination and monitoring process, sanctions competitions, and provides educational resources for judges. Founded in 1985, the BJCP has administered the Beer Judge Examination to over 9,000 individuals worldwide.

Bittering units (*see* International bittering units)

BITTERNESS   In beer, the bitterness is caused by the tannins and isohumulones of hops. The bitterness of hops is perceived in the taste. The amount of bitterness in a beer is one of the defining characteristics of a beer style.

BOTTLE-CONDITIONED   A process by which beer is naturally carbonated in the bottle as a result of fermentation of additional wort or sugar intentionally added during packaging.

BOTTOM FERMENTATION   One of the two basic fermentation methods characterized by the tendency of yeast cells to sink to the bottom of the fermentation vessel. Lager yeast is considered to be bottom-fermenting as opposed to ale yeast, which is top-fermenting. Beers brewed in this fashion are commonly called lagers or bottom-fermented beers.

BREWER'S ASSOCIATION   The Brewers Association is an organization dedicated to promoting and protecting American craft brewers and their beers. More than 2,800 U.S. brewery members and 45,000 members of the American Homebrewers Association are joined by members of the allied trade, beer wholesalers, retailers, individuals, other associate members, and the Brewers Association staff to make up the Brewers Association.

BREWPUB   A restaurant-brewery that sells 25% or more of its beer on site. The beer is brewed primarily for sale in the restaurant and bar. The beer is often dispensed directly from the brewery's storage tanks. Where allowed by law, brewpubs often sell beer "to go" and/or distribute to off-site accounts.

C

CONTRACT BREWING COMPANY   A business that hires another brewery to produce some or all of its beer. The contract brewing company handles marketing, sales and distribution of its beer, while generally leaving the brewing and packaging to its producer-brewery.

CRAFT BREWERY   According to the Brewers Association, an American craft brewer is small, independent and traditional. (1) Small: Annual production of 6 million barrels of beer or less (approximately 3% of U.S. annual sales). Beer production is attributed to the rules of alternating proprietorships. (2) Independent: Less than 25% of the craft brewery is owned or controlled (or equivalent economic interest) by a beverage alcohol industry member that is not itself a craft brewer. (3) Traditional: A brewer that has a majority of its total beverage alcohol volume in beers whose flavor derives from traditional or innovative brewing ingredients and their fermentation. Flavored malt beverages (FMBs) are not considered beers.

D

DEGREES PLATO   An empirically derived hydrometer scale to measure density of beer wort in terms of percentage of extract by weight.

DRAUGHT/DRAFT BEER   Beer drawn from kegs, casks or serving tanks rather than from cans, bottles, or other packages. Beer consumed from a growler relatively soon after filling is also sometimes considered draught beer.

E

EIGHTEENTH AMENDMENT   The Eighteenth Amendment of the U.S. Constitution (January 18, 1920) effectively established the prohibition of alcoholic beverages in the country by declaring the production, transport, and sale of alcohol (though not the consumption or private possession) illegal.

F

FERMENTATION   The chemical conversion of fermentable sugars into approximately equal parts of ethyl alcohol and carbon dioxide gas, through the action of yeast. The two basic methods of fermentation in brewing are top-fermentation, which produces ales, and bottom-fermentation, which produces lagers.

FINAL GRAVITY   The specific gravity of a beer as measured when fermentation is complete (when all desired fermentable sugars have been converted to alcohol and carbon dioxide gas). Synonym: Final specific gravity; final SG; finishing gravity; terminal gravity.

H

HOMEBREWING   The art of making beer at home. In the United States, homebrewing was legalized by President Carter on October 14, 1978, through a bill introduced by California Senator Alan Cranston. The Cranston Bill allows a single person to brew up to 100 gallons of beer annually for personal enjoyment and up to 200 gallons in a household of two persons or more of legal drinking age.

HOPS   A perennial climbing vine, also known by the Latin botanical name *Humulus lupulus*. The female plant yields flowers of soft-leaved pine-like cones (strobile) measuring about an inch in length. Only the female ripened flower is used for flavoring beer. Because hops reproduce through cuttings, the male plants are not cultivated and are even rooted out to prevent them from fertilizing the female plants, as the cones would become weighed-down with seeds. Seedless hops have a much higher bittering power than seeded. There are at present over 100 varieties of hops cultivated around the world. Some of the best known are Brewer's Gold, Bullion, Cascade, Centennial, Chinook, Cluster, Comet, Eroica, Fuggles, Galena, Goldings, Hallertau, Nugget, Northern Brewer, Perle, Saaz, Syrian Goldings, Tettnang, and Willamettes. Apart from contributing bitterness, hops impart aroma and flavor and inhibit the growth of bacteria in wort and beer. Hops are added at the beginning (bittering hops), middle (flavoring hops), and end (aroma hops) of the boiling stage, or even later in the brewing process (dry hops). The addition of hops to beer dates from 7000–1000 B.C.; however, hops were used to flavor beer in pharaonic Egypt around 600 B.C. They were cultivated in Germany as early as A.D. 300 and were used extensively in French and German monasteries in medieval times and gradually superseded other herbs and spices around the fourteenth and fifteenth centuries. Prior to the use of hops, beer was flavored with herbs and spices such as juniper, coriander, cumin, nutmeg, oak leaves, lime blossoms, cloves, rosemary, gentian, gaussia, chamomile, and other herbs or spices.

HYDROMETER   A glass instrument used to measure the specific gravity of liquids as compared with water; the device consists of a graduated stem resting on a weighted float.

I

INTERNATIONAL BITTERING UNITS (IBUS)   The measure of the bittering substances in beer (analytically assessed as milligrams of isomerized alpha acid per liter of beer, in ppm). When hops are boiled in the making of beer, alpha acids are released from the hop glands and isomerized from the heat. It is these iso-alpha acids that are the main source of bitterness in beer. The IBU measurement depends on the style of beer. Light lagers typically have an IBU rating between 5 and 10 while big, bitter India Pale Ales can often have an IBU rating between 50 and 70.

K

KEG   A cylindrical container, usually constructed of steel or sometimes aluminum, commonly used to store, transport, and serve beer under pressure. In the United States, kegs are referred to by the portion of a barrel they represent, for example, a 1/2 barrel keg = 15.5 gal, a 1/4 barrel keg = 7.75 gal, a 1/6 barrel keg = 5.23 gal. Other standard keg sizes will be found in other countries.

L

LAGER   Any beer that is fermented with bottom-fermenting yeast at colder temperatures. Lagers are most often associated with crisp, clean flavors and are traditionally fermented and served at colder temperatures than ales.

LARGE BREWERY   A brewery with an annual beer production of over 6,000,000 barrels.

M

MALT   Processed barley that has been steeped in water, germinated on malting floors or in germination boxes or drums, and later dried in kilns for the purpose of stopping the germination and converting the insoluble starch in barley to the soluble substances and sugars in malt.

MASH   A mixture of ground malt (and possibly other grains or adjuncts) and hot water that forms the sweet wort after straining.

MASH TUN   The vessel in which grist is soaked in water and heated in order to convert the starch to sugar and to extract the sugars, colors, flavors and other solubles from the grist.

MASTER BREWER'S ASSOCIATION OF THE AMERICAS (MBAA)   The Master Brewer's Association of the Americas was founded in 1887 to promote, advance, and improve the professional interest of brew and malt house production and technical personnel. With over 3,000 members in more than 55 countries, the MBAA strives to the globally recognized authority in brewing science, technology, education, and operations.

MICROBREWERY   A brewery that produces fewer than 15,000 barrels of beer per year with 75% or more of its beer sold off site.

O

ORIGINAL GRAVITY   The specific gravity of wort before fermentation. A measure of the total amount of solids that are dissolved in the wort as compared to the density of water, which is conventionally given as 1.000 and higher. Synonyms: starting gravity; starting specific gravity; original wort gravity.

P

PACKAGE   A general term for the containers used to market beverages. Packaged beer is generally sold in bottles and cans. Beer sold in kegs is usually called draught beer.

PROHIBITION   A law instituted by the Eighteenth Amendment to the U.S. Constitution (stemming from the Volstead Act) on January 18, 1920, forbidding the sale, production, importation, and transportation of alcoholic beverages in the United States. It was repealed by the Twenty-first Amendment to the U.S. Constitution on December 5, 1933. The Prohibition Era is sometimes referred to as The Noble Experiment.

R

REGIONAL CRAFT BREWERY   An independent regional brewery having either an all malt flagship or has at least 50% of its volume in either all malt beers or in beers that use adjuncts to enhance rather than lighten flavor.

REINHEITSGEBOT   The German beer purity law passed in 1516, stating that beer may contain only water, barley, and hops. Yeast was later considered an acceptable ingredient after its role in fermentation was discovered by Louis Pasteur.

S

SESSION BEER   A beer of lighter body and alcohol that one might expect to drink more than one serving of in a sitting.

SPECIFIC GRAVITY   The ratio of the density of a substance to the density of water. This method is used to determine how much dissolved sugars are present in the wort or beer. Specific gravity has no units because it is expressed as a ratio. See also, *Original gravity* and *Final gravity*

T

TWENTY-FIRST AMENDMENT   The Twenty-First Amendment to the U.S. Constitution repealed the Eighteenth Amendment, which had mandated a nationwide prohibition on alcohol on January 17, 1920.

V

VOLSTEAD ACT   This national prohibition act was enacted to carry out the intent of the Eighteenth Amendment, which established prohibition in the United States.

W

WORT   The bittersweet sugar solution obtained by mashing the malt and boiling in the hops, which becomes beer through fermentation.

Y

YEAST   During the fermentation process, yeast converts the natural malt sugars into alcohol and carbon dioxide gas. Yeast was first viewed under a microscope in 1680 by the Dutch scientist Antonie van Leeuwenhoek; in 1867, Louis Pasteur discovered that yeast cells lack chlorophyll and that they could develop only in an environment containing both nitrogen and carbon.

REFERENCES

Brewer's Association of America. 2015. Accessed August 1, 2015, https://www.brewersassociation.org/.

Oliver, Garret, ed. 2012. *The Oxford Companion to Beer*. Oxford: Oxford University Press.

Papazian, Charlie. 2003. *The Complete Joy of Homebrewing* (3rd ed.). New York: HarperCollins.

CONTRIBUTORS

EDITORS

Nathaniel G. Chapman is an assistant professor of sociology in the Department of Behavioral Sciences at Arkansas Tech University. His research focuses on craft beer and the production of culture in the United States. He has also researched racial dynamics at electronic dance music (EDM) festivals and EDM more broadly. Currently, he is conducting research on gender and consumption in the craft beer industry, and the construction of authenticity in craft brewing.

J. Slade Lellock is a PhD student in the Department of Sociology at Virginia Tech. His research interests include culture, digital sociology, consumption, taste, and qualitative methodologies. His work generally focuses on the symbolic and expressive realms of culture such as music, art, film, and dress as well as social and symbolic boundaries. His interest in many cultural dimensions of digital social life has led him to conduct ethnographic fieldwork in multiple online communities.

Cameron D. Lippard is an associate professor of sociology at Appalachian State University in Boone, North Carolina. His teaching and research interests are in social inequality, focusing on the social problems and racialization Latino immigrants face while living in the American South. Recent publications include two books: *Building Inequality: Race, Ethnicity, and Immigration in the Atlanta Construction Industry* and *Being Brown in Dixie: Race, Ethnicity, and Latino Immigration in the New South*. He also has researched the connections between immigrant labor and growing industries in the American South, including the construction, meatpacking, and Christmas tree industries.

CONTRIBUTORS

Jessica Bain is a lecturer in the Department of Media and Communication, University of Leicester, United Kingdom. Her research has focused on the construction and framing of social and political identities through both mainstream news media and social media, focusing in particular on the international identity of the European Union. Her current research explores the online communities that have emerged around domestic cultures. She has published in such journals as *Journal of International Communication, Journal of Common Market Studies*, and *Communication, Politics and Culture*.

Jesus M. Barajas is a PhD candidate in city and regional planning at the University of California, Berkeley. His primary research activities explore questions of travel behavior for marginalized populations. His research interests in craft beer arise from wanting to understand the connection of brewing to places and neighborhoods, an enthusiasm for the history of the industry and product, and occasional home brewing. He holds a master's degree in urban and regional planning from California State Polytechnic University, Pomona and a bachelor of science degree in computer science from Pennsylvania State University.

J. Nikol Beckham is an assistant professor of communication studies at Randolph College in Lynchburg, Virginia. Her scholarship examines how power and inequality manifest in food systems and in forms of sociality that are rooted in the production, distribution, preparation, and consumption of food. She is particularly interested in bringing culturally attentive theories of valuation to the exploration of what might be called an everyday politics of food and drink.

Geoff Boeing is a PhD student studying city and regional planning at the University of California, Berkeley. His research revolves around urban form and complexity theory. He is the graduate student instructor for a course on urban informatics and visualization and a researcher in the UC Berkeley Urban Analytics Lab; he also teaches seminars and workshops on data-intensive social science methods at the UC Berkeley D-Lab (Social Sciences Data Laboratory). He previously spent several years as a consultant and project manager with Accenture in New York, London, and California. His work on information discovery tools has received U.S. and European patents.

Ignazio Cabras is professor of entrepreneurship and regional economic development at Newcastle Business School, Northumbria University, United Kingdom. He is also an associate fellow of the York Centre for Complex Systems Analysis at the University of York, United Kingdom. During his career, Ignazio researched and analyzed many issues related to the beer and brewing industry and led several research projects to investigate the significant role pubs play in rural areas, contributing to measuring and unveiling the positive impact of these businesses on local communities, economies, and supply chains. He is an active member of the Beeronomics Society and chaired the third Beeronomics Conference in 2013, the first organized and hosted by a British institution.

Tünde Cserpes is a PhD candidate at the Center on Organizational Dynamics in the Department of Sociology at the University of Illinois–Chicago. Her research investigates the spatial and relational aspects of markets. She uses spatial and network techniques embedded in both qualitative and quantitative research traditions to uncover mechanisms that lead to field-level outcomes such as inequality or institutional change.

Helana Darwin holds a bachelor's degree in psychology from Lewis and Clark College and a master's degree in Jewish studies with a concentration in women and gender from the Jewish Theological Seminary of America. She is currently pursuing her doctorate in sociology at State University of New York, Stony Brook, under the advisement of Michael Kimmel. Her research focuses include the body, gender, culture, and collective behavior/social movements.

Andrea Davies is a senior lecturer in the School of Management, University of Leicester, United Kingdom. Contemporary and historical aspects of consumption and consumer research methodologies are her research focus, with current topics including ideology and neoliberalism, technology and retail, family and motherhood, consumer ambivalence/empowerment, posthumanism, and oral history. She is co-editor of *Consumer Research Methods* (Volumes I–IV) SAGE Major Works Series (2013), was joint editor of *Journal of Consumer Behaviour* (2006–2009), and has published in *Marketing Theory, Journal of Macromarketing, Consumption Markets and Culture, European Journal of Marketing, Journal of Marketing Management,* and *Journal of Consumer Behaviour.*

Michael A. Elliott is associate professor of sociology at Towson University, Maryland, where he teaches courses on globalization, political sociology, and sociological theory. In addition to his work on the rationalization of beer, he has also conducted research on the global expansion of human rights and world heritage and is planning a study of the religious dimensions of fan communities in the realm of popular culture.

Daina Cheyenne Harvey is an assistant professor of sociology at the College of the Holy Cross. His work pays particular attention to the urban and environmental conditions that result in both acute and chronic suffering. He is currently working on a book about ecological citizenship.

Ellis Jones is an assistant professor of sociology at the College of the Holy Cross. His work focuses specifically on the relationship between ethical consumers and corporate social responsibility. The publicly relevant results of his research are available in the fifth edition of his book, *The Better World Shopping Guide*.

Andre F. Maciel holds a PhD in marketing from the University of Arizona. He recently joined the department of marketing at the University of Nebraska, Lincoln, as an assistant professor. His research examines the interplay between market institutions and formations of social class and gender. On this topic, Andre has a forthcoming article at the *Journal of Consumer Research*, a premier research outlet for marketing academics. He has also published a book on the links between marketing and interpersonal relationships based on his master's thesis. Andre speaks English, French, Portuguese, and conversational Spanish.

Jennifer Smith Maguire is a senior lecturer on cultural production and consumption in the School of Management, University of Leicester, United Kingdom. Her research examines the construction of markets, tastes, and value, with special focus on wine and beer markets and the valuation of provenance and authenticity. She has published in such journals as *International Journal of Cultural Studies, Consumption, Markets and Culture, Marketing Theory, Journal of Macromarketing*, and is the co-editor of *The Cultural Intermediaries Reader* (Sage, 2014).

Paul-Brian McInerney is Associate Professor in Sociology at the University of Illinois–Chicago. Broadly, his research focuses on economic and organizational sociology, social studies of technology, social movements and collective behavior, and sociological theory. McInerney is the author of *From Social Movement to Moral Market: How the Circuit Riders Sparked an IT Revolution and Created a Technology Market* (Stanford University Press, 2014). He is also the author of numerous articles and book chapters on various topics, including the open source software movement, technology use among activists, collaboration between nonprofit and for-profit organizations, and the hybrid organizational forms of social enterprise. Most recently, McInerney is studying the network dynamics of innovation in the craft brewing industry.

Krista E. Paulsen received her PhD from the University of California, Santa Barbara, and is currently associate professor of sociology and chair of the Department of Sociology, Anthropology, and Social Work at the University of North Florida. Her research examines how places—whether regions, cities, or neighborhoods—develop and maintain distinct cultures and practices. She is most recently the author of *Introduction to Cities: How Place and Space Shape Human Experience* (Wiley-Blackwell, 2012, with Xiangming Chen and Anthony Orum) and co-editor of *Home: International Perspectives on Culture, Identity and Belonging* (Peter Lang Publishers, 2013, with Margarethe Kusenbach).

Thomas Thurnell-Read is senior lecturer in cultural sociology in the Department of Social Sciences at Loughborough University, United Kingdom. His research uses contemporary leisure and consumption practices, and drinking and drunkenness in particular, to explore a range of sociological issues relating to sociality, identity, and diversity. His research on British stag party tourism in Poland has been published in a range of international journals, including *Sociology* and *Men and Masculinities*, and focuses on the social construction of masculinity through transgressive drinking practices. He is the editor (with Dr. Mark Casey, Newcastle, United Kingdom) of *Men, Masculinities, Travel and Tourism*, published by Palgrave Macmillan in 2014. He is a founder member of the British Sociological Association Alcohol Study group and co-convenor of the group since July 2012.

Maria Touri is a lecturer in the Department of Media and Communication, University of Leicester, United Kingdom). Her research focuses on the construction of media frames and discourses that connect actors and communities in social and cultural contexts. She is currently researching the role of participatory communication in sustainable food production and global governance. Her published works include *Alcohol Advertising and Young People's Drinking: Representation, Reception and Regulation* (Palgrave, 2010)

Hayley E. Tuller is an undergraduate student at the University of North Florida majoring in sociology with a minor in economics. Her primary interests lie in how social and economic inequality are perpetuated through place-based social institutions and processes. She is also a retired Senior Chief Petty Officer of the U.S. Navy, where she served as an Arabic linguist and cryptologist.

Julie Wartell is an independent advisor on public safety issues. Previous positions include crime analyst and project director for multiple law enforcement agencies, researcher for nonprofit criminal justice organizations, and a National Institute of Justice fellow. Julie has performed a range of research on and analysis of crime problems and police-related issues, worked on strategic planning efforts, and assessed technologies. She conducts training for officers and analysts internationally on topics relating to crime analysis and policing, has edited or authored numerous publications, and currently teaches at the University of California, San Diego, and Michigan State University. Wartell has an MPA with an emphasis in criminal justice administration from San Diego State University and a postgraduate diploma in applied criminology from University of Cambridge, United Kingdom.

Erik T. Withers is a PhD student and graduate associate instructor at the University of South Florida. His research interests focus on racial and ethnic inequalities and consumer culture. Currently, Erik's research investigates the role of cultural consumption in maintaining and perpetuating an unequal racial and ethnic order.

Index

Note: Information in figures and tables is indicated by *f* and *t*.